Economics and Culture

In an increasingly globalised world, economic and cultural imperatives can be seen as two of the most powerful forces shaping human behaviour. This book considers the relationship between economics and culture both as areas of intellectual discourse and as systems of societal organisation. Adopting a broad definition of 'culture', the book explores the economic dimensions of culture and the cultural context of economics. The book is built on a foundation of value theory, developing the twin notions of economic and cultural value as underlying principles for integrating the two fields. Ideas of cultural capital and sustainability are discussed, especially as means of analysing the particular problems of cultural heritage, drawing parallels with the treatment of natural capital in ecological economics. The book goes on to discuss the economics of creativity in the production of artistic goods and services; culture in economic development; the cultural industries; and cultural policy.

'What a pleasure to read an economic analysis of culture and a cultural critique of economics by a well trained, thoroughly cultured economist! This is a book we all ought to read.'
Mark Blaug
University of Amsterdam

'David Throsby has long been known as a leading contributor in cultural economics. His book marks a major step forward: far from a mindless application of orthodox economics to the arts, he does full justice to its special characteristics, without giving up good economic reasoning. His treatment of the value of the arts, of cultural capital and heritage are of special note.'
Bruno S. Frey
University of Zürich

DAVID THROSBY is Professor of Economics at Macquarie University. He has published extensively in leading economic journals, including *Journal of Economic Literature*, *Economic Record*, *Oxford Bulletin of Economics and Statistics*, *Journal of Public Economics*, *Journal of Cultural Economics* and *International Journal of Cultural Policy*, and is co-author of a standard text on the economics of the performing arts. He is a past president of the Association for Cultural Economics International, an elected Fellow of the Academy of Social Sciences in Australia and has been a member of the Scientific Committee for UNESCO's *World Culture Reports*.

Economics and Culture

David Throsby

CAMBRIDGE
UNIVERSITY PRESS

PUBLISHED BY THE PRESS SYNDICATE OF THE UNIVERSITY OF CAMBRIDGE
The Pitt Building, Trumpington Street, Cambridge, United Kingdom

CAMBRIDGE UNIVERSITY PRESS
The Edinburgh Building, Cambridge CB2 2RU, UK
40 West 20th Street, New York, NY 10011–4211, USA
477 Williamstown Road, Port Melbourne, VIC 3207 Australia
Ruiz de Alarcón 13, 28014 Madrid, Spain
Dock House, The Waterfront, Cape Town 8001, SouthAfrica

http://www.cambridge.org

First published 2001
Reprinted 2002, 2003

Typeface Times Roman 10/12pt   *System* 3b2   [CE]

A catalogue record for this book is available from the British Library

Library of Congress cataloguing in publication data

Throsby, C. D.
Economics and culture / David Throsby.
    p.   cm.
Includes bibliographical references.
ISBN 0 521 58406 X (hardback)   0 521 58639 9 (paperback)
1. Economics – Sociological aspects. 2. Culture – Economic aspects. I. Title.
HM548.T48 2000
306.3–dc21   01-063072

ISBN 0 521 58406 X hardback
ISBN 0 521 58639 9 paperback

Transferred to digital printing 2004

To Robin, Edwina and Corin

Contents

Contents

Preface

About ten years ago I gave a lecture under the title 'Art and the Economy' at a symposium on cultural policy held in Canberra. In introducing the topic for a generalist audience, I speculated on what the twin subjects of the lecture might look like if they took on human form. Being an economist myself, I was licensed to poke some gentle fun at my own profession, so I suggested that the economy as a real person would certainly be male, somewhat overweight, prone to hypochondria, garrulous and inclined to neglect his personal freshness – in short not the sort of individual you would relish sitting next to on a long aeroplane flight. In the same vein, I went on, art would just as certainly be female, smart, unpredictable and somewhat intriguing. The metaphor seemed to strike a chord with the listeners; perhaps it is that everyone enjoys a joke at economists' expense, or perhaps it is more that the idea of art as mystery, a riddle whose secrets are not easily unlocked, has a wider appeal than we might think. I proceeded in the lecture to ponder the following question: suppose these two individuals ran into each other at a party, would they have the slightest interest in each other and, if they did, would they perhaps get together? If so, I asked, what sort of relationship might develop between them?

In one sense this frivolous allegory provided the origins of the present volume. It is apparent that the economy and art – or, on a wider canvas, economics and culture – exist as separate spheres of human interest, both as scholarly disciplines and in the more prosaic context of daily human life. Both economic and cultural concerns are of manifest importance to most if not all people at some time in their lives – few if any of us are touched only by one and not the other. Therefore an attempt to consider them both together would seem to present an interesting project. Not that such an enterprise is a novel one. Cultural scholars have for generations addressed economic questions of one sort or another in their efforts to understand the role of culture and cultural practices in society.

More particularly, a number of economists have tried, explicitly or implicitly, to comprehend what could be termed the 'cultural context' of economic activity ever since Adam Smith laid the foundations for modern economic science in the late eighteenth century.

But in the late twentieth century, with increasing refinement and specialisation of the tools of neoclassical economics, and a deepening understanding of culture in a variety of discourses from sociology to linguistics, a widening gap between the two areas seems to have developed. When I began working on the economics of the arts in the mid-1970s, few colleagues saw 'cultural economics' as any more than a dilettante interest, doomed forever to lie beyond the scope of serious economic analysis. They were apparently not persuaded by the fact that, even at that early stage, a number of respected economists had written eloquently about various matters linking economics, art and culture, including John Maynard Keynes, Lionel Robbins, Alan Peacock and Mark Blaug on one side of the Atlantic, John Kenneth Galbraith, William Baumol, Tibor Scitovsky, Kenneth Boulding and Thorstein Veblen on the other.

In the intervening years the economics of the arts and culture has consolidated into a recognisable and respectable area of specialisation within economics, and now attracts the attention of a much wider range of practitioners within the profession than it did twenty or even ten years ago. Even so, it cannot be said that thoughts of culture have fired the imaginations of contemporary economists more generally, or that the economics of the arts and culture is yet regarded as an especially important element in the great tapestry of modern political economy. Even the acknowledgement by the profession of the legitimacy of cultural economics as a subdiscipline seems somewhat grudging; the classification granted to cultural economics in the *Journal of Economic Literature*'s taxonomy of the subject is category Z1, as far away down the alphabet from the rest of economics as it is possible to be. And as yet the volume of research and scholarship that finds its way into that classification in the *JEL* is still relatively small.

Yet even if a recognition of culture within economics itself is gaining ground only slowly, there is evidence that a wider interest in the relationships between economic and cultural phenomena is developing in the world at large. As I argue in the final chapter in this volume, the emergence of powerful forces in the global marketplace set the stage for a much sharper confrontation between the economic and cultural concerns of contemporary society. Two recent meetings would seem to confirm the fact of a heightened political and institutional interest in the relationship between economics and culture at the present time. One was in

Stockholm in April 1998, when representatives of about 150 governments from around the world agreed that culture should be brought in from the periphery in economic policy-making and given greater prominence in policy formulation. The other was in Florence in October 1999 when the World Bank, one of the leading financial institutions in the international arena, declared that culture was an essential component of economic development, and that henceforward culture would play a stronger role in shaping and conditioning the Bank's economic operations.

For all of these reasons I hope that a book that tries to bring together these two unlikely bedfellows, economics and culture, will be timely. My task has two distinct though closely intertwined aspects. On the one hand I want to consider the relationships between economics and culture as separate areas of intellectual endeavour – in particular to think about the ways in which economics as a social science deals or might try to deal with the phenomenon of culture, taking a broader view of 'culture' than that which has generally characterised work in the field of cultural economics to date. On the other hand, and more importantly, I want also to consider the relationships between economic and cultural activity, that is between the economy and culture as recognisable manifestations of human thought and action, observed in both a macro and a micro context. The book is written as a work in economics – hence economics comes first in the title – but I have tried to make it accessible to a wider range of readers. In particular, I hope that not only economists but also specialists in a variety of cultural disciplines, as well as anyone engaged with cultural production or with the formulation of cultural policy, might find some interest in one economist's approach to cultural issues.

I wish to acknowledge a debt of gratitude to a number of organisations and individuals. First, academics often take for granted the facilities provided for them by institutions of learning which are an essential component of the infrastructure of the scholarly life. Much of this book was written in the Fisher Library of the University of Sydney, whose superb collection and ideal environment for research and writing contributed greatly to my work. In addition I acknowledge the help and resourcefulness of library staff in my own institution, Macquarie University in Sydney. I also spent brief periods working on the manuscript in the libraries of the London School of Economics and Political Science and the Institute of Economics and Statistics at the University of Oxford. As one who finds solace in libraries in much the same way as others seek sanctuary in churches or monasteries, I can only hope that these havens of scholarly endeavour will survive into the new technological utopia as places for real (as distinct from virtual) books and for the people who read them and write them.

In 1999 I was awarded a one-month residency at the Rockefeller Foundation's Study and Conference Center at the Villa Serbelloni in Bellagio, Italy. My specific project there was on the economics of creativity and the outcome of this work forms chapter 6 of the present volume. More importantly, I was able while at the Villa to draw together, re-think and re-draft virtually the entire manuscript for this book, on which I had already been labouring on and off for several years. The superb working conditions at Bellagio and the intellectual stimulus from the small band of fellow residents contributed greatly to the successful completion of my enterprise. I express my thanks to the Rockefeller Foundation and to Gianna Celli and her staff at the Villa for making possible such a period of intense enjoyment and productivity.

Finally, a number of individuals have contributed in various ways to discussions about the substance of this volume over the period of its preparation, and/or have supplied me with comment and criticism. With the usual *caveat*, I express my thanks to Mark Blaug, Tony Bryant, Bruno Frey, Michael Hutter, Arjo Klamer, Craig Macmillan, Graham Madden, Randall Mason, Terry Smith, Michael Tooma and Ruth Towse. I also acknowledge my gratitude to Judith Riordan, who endured the preparation of the manuscript with commitment and unfailing good humour.

David Throsby
Sydney, April 2000

Acknowledgements

Some parts of this book cover topics on which I have written in earlier papers. In several sections I have adapted material from these earlier works, and am grateful to the following publishers for granting me their kind permission to re-use, in edited and adapted form, some short extracts from the works indicated: the American Economic Association, for extracts from 'The production and consumption of the arts: a view of cultural economics', *Journal of Economic Literature* 32 (1994): 1–29; the Australian Key Centre for Cultural and Media Policy, for extracts from 'The relationship between economic and cultural policy', *Culture and Policy* 8 (1997): 25–36; the Getty Conservation Institute, for extracts from 'Economic and cultural value in the work of creative artists', in Erica Avrami *et al.* (eds.), *Values and Heritage Conservation* (2000), pp. 26–31 and from an unpublished paper 'Cultural capital and sustainability concepts in the economics of cultural heritage' (1999); Harwood Academic Publishers GmbH, for extracts from 'Sustainability and culture: some theoretical issues', *International Journal of Cultural Policy* 4 (1997): 7–20; Kluwer Academic Publishers, for extracts from 'Culture, economics and sustainability', *Journal of Cultural Economics* 19 (1995): 199–206, and from 'Cultural capital', *Journal of Cultural Economics* 23 (1999): 3–12; Macmillan Press Limited and St Martin's Press, for extracts from 'Seven questions in the economics of cultural heritage' in Michael Hutter and Ilde Rizzo (eds.), *Economic Perspectives on Cultural Heritage* (1997), pp. 13–30; and UNESCO, for extracts from 'The role of music in international trade and development', *World Culture Report* (1998) 1: 193–209.

I also thank the following publishers for permission to reproduce the extracts indicated: to Jonathan Cape for the passage from Bruce Chatwin quoted on p. 74; to Faber & Faber for the passage from Yasmina Reza quoted on p. 19, the passage from T. S. Eliot quoted on p. 137, and the passage from Tom Stoppard quoted on p. 153; and to UNESCO for the passage from Amartya Sen quoted on p. 61.

1 Introduction

Nothing so difficult as a beginning
In poesy, unless perhaps the end.   (Lord Byron, *Don Juan*, 1821[1])

Definitional issues

It was Farmer Nicholas Snowe in *Lorna Doone* who said, with the insight given to simple rustics in Victorian novels, 'virst zettle the pralimbinaries; and then us knows what be drivin' at'.[2] In an enterprise such as the present one, settling the preliminaries inevitably comprises definitional matters, and this means the two principal objects of our concern: economics and culture.

It might appear that the first of these could be dispensed with quickly. There is apparently so little disagreement among contemporary economists as to the scope and content of their discipline that the introductory chapters of most modern textbooks of economics are virtually identical. The outline of the 'economic problem' always emphasises scarcity, such that the decision facing actors in the economic drama is one of how to allocate limited means among competing ends. Individual consumers have wants to be satisfied, productive enterprises have the technologies to provide the goods and services to satisfy those wants and processes of exchange link the one side of the market with the other. Much of the economics that is taught to students at universities and colleges throughout the western world nowadays is concerned with the efficiency of these processes of production, consumption and exchange, much less is concerned with questions of equity or fairness within the operation of economic systems. As a result, issues such as that of redistributive justice tend to play a secondary role in the thinking of many younger professional economists, if indeed such issues bother them at all.

1

The introductory textbooks also universally make the standard distinction between the study of the micro behaviour of individual units in the economy – consumers and firms – and the macro behaviour of the economy itself. In so doing, these texts lay the foundation for the reification of the economy, a process which has had profound effects on popular perceptions of economics and on the construction of public policy in the present generation. The increasing dominance of macroeconomics as the foundation stone of national and international public policy over recent decades has led to perceptions of the economy as having an identity of its own which seems to transcend its constituent elements. Ironically this view could be seen to parallel the concept of the state as having an independent existence, a concept eschewed by the model of libertarian individualism which is central to modern economics. In some cases the reification of the economy in the media and elsewhere seems to extend almost to personalisation; we speak of economies as 'strong' or 'weak', 'dynamic' or 'sluggish', needing to be nursed when they are sick and requiring the administration of appropriate medicines to bring them back to health.

In considering these texts as providing a definition of the domain and methods of contemporary economics, we should bear in mind that they mostly reflect the dominant neoclassical paradigm which has held sway in economics for the better part of a century and which in the last few decades has been brought to a high level of theoretical and analytical refinement. This paradigm has provided a comprehensive and coherent framework for representing and analysing the behaviour of individuals, firms and markets, and it has yielded an array of testable hypotheses which have been subject to extensive empirical scrutiny. Moreover, the range of phenomena which it has embraced has been continually expanding; the model of rational utilitarian decision-making operating within competitive markets has in recent years been applied to an ever-widening array of areas of human behaviour, including marriage, crime, religion, family dynamics, divorce, philanthropy, politics and law, as well as production and consumption of the arts.

Yet despite its intellectual imperialism, neoclassical economics is in fact quite restrictive in its assumptions, highly constrained in its mechanics and ultimately limited in its explanatory power. It has been subject to a vigorous critique from both within and without the discipline. Furthermore, its supremacy can be challenged if a broader view of the discourse of economics is taken. In common with all great areas of intellectual endeavour, economics comprises not a single paradigm, but a number of schools of thought offering alternative or contestable ways of analysing the functioning of the economy or the actions of individual economic agents. For present purposes, we are quite likely to find such alternative approaches useful in thinking about cultural phenomena.

But while defining economics and the economy may, for the time being, be disposed of relatively easily, defining culture is an altogether different story. Raymond Williams describes culture as 'one of the two or three most complicated words in the English language'.[3] Robert Borofsky suggests that attempts to define culture are 'akin to trying to encage the wind';[4] this picturesque metaphor captures the protean nature of culture and emphasises how hard it is to be precise about what the term means. The reasons are not difficult to find. 'Culture' is a word employed in a variety of senses in everyday use but without a tangible or generally agreed core meaning. At a scholarly level it relates in some way or another to concepts and ideas which occur throughout the humanities and social sciences, but it is often deployed without precise definition and in ways which differ both within and between different disciplines.[5]

As always, an etymological analysis can throw some light on the evolution of meaning. The original connotation of the word 'culture', of course, referred to the tillage of the soil. In the sixteenth century this literal meaning became transposed to the cultivation of the mind and the intellect. Such figurative usage is still in active service today: we refer to someone well versed in the arts and letters as a 'cultured' or 'cultivated' person, and the noun 'culture' is often used without qualification to denote what, under a more restrictive definition, would be referred to as the products and practices of the 'high' arts. But since the early nineteenth century the term 'culture' has been used in a broader sense to describe the intellectual and spiritual development of civilisation as a whole. In turn, this usage became focused onto these same characteristics when evidenced in particular societies, such as nation states. In due course this humanistic interpretation of culture was supplanted by a more all-encompassing concept whereby culture was seen to embrace not just intellectual endeavour but the entire way of life of a people or society.

All of these usages, and more, survive in various guises today. How, then, are we to make progress in defining culture in a manner that is analytically and operationally useful? Some usages are so narrow as to be restrictive of the range of phenomena that are our legitimate concern; others, such as the all-inclusive societal definition where culture is in effect everything, become analytically empty and operationally meaningless. Despite these difficulties, it is possible to refine the range of definitions down to two, and indeed these will be taken to be the dual sense in which the term 'culture' will be used throughout this book.

The first sense in which we shall use the word 'culture' is in a broadly anthropological or sociological framework to describe a set of attitudes, beliefs, mores, customs, values and practices which are common to or shared by any group. The group may be defined in terms of politics, geography, religion, ethnicity or some other characteristic, making it possible to refer, for example, to Mexican culture, Basque culture, Jewish culture, Asian culture, feminist culture, corporate culture, youth culture and so on. The characteristics which define the group may be substantiated in the form of signs, symbols, texts, language, artefacts, oral and written tradition and by other means. One of the critical functions of these manifestations of the group's culture is to establish, or at least to contribute to establishing, the group's distinctive identity, and thereby to provide a means by which the members of the group can differentiate themselves from members of other groups. This interpretation of culture will be especially useful for present purposes in examining the role of cultural factors in economic performance and the relationship between culture and economic development.

The second definition of 'culture' has a more functional orientation, denoting certain activities that are undertaken by people, and the products of those activities, which have to do with the intellectual, moral and artistic aspects of human life. 'Culture' in this sense relates to activities drawing upon the enlightenment and education of the mind rather than the acquisition of purely technical or vocational skills. In such usage, the word is more likely to occur as an adjective than as a noun,[6] as in 'cultural goods', 'cultural institutions', 'cultural industries' or the 'cultural sector of the economy'. To give this second definition more precision, let us propose that the connotation contained in this usage of the word 'culture' can be deemed to derive from certain more or less objectively definable characteristics of the activities concerned. Three such characteristics are suggested. They are:

- that the activities concerned involve some form of creativity in their production
- that they are concerned with the generation and communication of symbolic meaning, and
- that their output embodies, at least potentially, some form of intellectual property.

Of course, any such list presupposes a further set of definitions; words such as 'creativity', 'symbolic meaning' and even 'intellectual property' beg some further elaboration, to which in due course we shall return. For now, let us accept a standard interpretation of these terms to allow us to proceed with a working definition of culture in this functional sense.

Generally speaking possession of all three of these characteristics could be regarded as a sufficient condition in order for this interpretation of culture to apply to a given activity. So, for example, the arts as traditionally defined – music, literature, poetry, dance, drama, visual art and so on – easily qualify. In addition, this sense of the word 'culture' would include activities such as film-making, story-telling, festivals, journalism, publishing, television and radio and some aspects of design, since in each case the required conditions are, to a greater or lesser degree, met. But an activity such as, say, scientific innovation would not be caught by this definition, because although it involves creativity and could lead to output capable of being copyrighted or patented, it is directed generally at a routine utilitarian end rather than at the communication of meaning.[7] Similarly, road signs convey symbolic meaning in a literal sense but fail on the other criteria to qualify as cultural products. Organised sport occupies a somewhat ambiguous position. While sport possibly meets all of the three criteria, some people may still find difficulty accepting it as a cultural activity, especially if it is thought that it does not embody creativity but only technical skill. Nevertheless, there can be little doubt that sport is an element of culture in the first sense defined above, that is as a ritual or custom expressing shared values and as a means of affirming and consolidating group identity.[8]

While the three criteria listed above may be sufficient for providing a functional definition of culture and cultural activities, they may not be the full story when it comes to defining cultural goods and services as a distinct category of commodities for purposes of economic analysis. There has been some debate among cultural economists as to whether a class of goods exists, called 'cultural goods', which can be differentiated in some fundamental way from 'ordinary economic goods'.[9] The above criteria can be seen as a useful first step towards making such a distinction, and indeed they might on their own provide a sufficiently precise definition for some purposes. However, in other contexts a more rigorous specification may be necessary, requiring some appeal to questions of cultural value, a matter to which we return in chapter 2.

It should be noted that no universality can be claimed for these two definitions of culture. Some phenomena that some people may describe as culture will lie beyond their reach. Furthermore, the definitions are by no means mutually exclusive, but overlap in a number of important ways – the functioning of artistic practices in defining group identity, for example.[10] In addition, counter-examples and anomalies can doubtless be suggested. But as a basis for proceeding, the definitions will serve our purpose.

Some qualifications

Three aspects of these definitions of culture require further elaboration. The first is the fact that, although the term 'culture' is used generally in a positive sense, implying virtuous and life-enhancing qualities, there is a spectre at the feast: culture, in the first of the connotations defined above, can also be deployed as an instrument of brutality and oppression. The Soviet state culture that was imposed on artists like Shostakovitch, the cultural underpinnings of Nazism, religious wars, ethnic cleansing, the 'culture of corruption' that may exist in a police force or an organisation, the gang culture that rules on the streets of large cities, mafia culture and other such phenomena, are all examples of shared values and group identification that can indeed be construed as manifestations of culture, if it is defined as we have above.

One approach to the dark side of culture is to ignore it, to make no value judgement as to good or bad cultures, and simply to analyse all cultural phenomena at face value as they present themselves. An alternative that confronts this issue more directly is to admit the possibility of an ethical standard which would outlaw, by common consent, certain characteristics which were universally agreed to be unacceptable. Such a standard might incorporate notions such as fairness, democracy, human rights, free speech and freedom from violence, war and oppression, as basic human values. Acceptance of such a standard would disqualify all the negative examples listed above from consideration as culture, and would prevent certain barbaric and oppressive practices from being excused on the grounds that they were part of the cultural tradition of a particular group. It might be observed that a resolution of the problem of negative cultural manifestations in this way could itself be interpreted in cultural terms. Suppose a minimum ethical standard could be generally agreed upon which accepted as axiomatically desirable such concepts as individual rights, democracy, the protection of minorities, peaceful resolution of conflict and the promotion of civil society.[11] It could be argued in such a circumstance that the values enshrined as universal could be seen to comprise the defining symbols of civilised human existence, and as such could be interpreted as key elements of an overarching *human* culture which transcends other forms of cultural differentiation.

The second issue requiring some further elaboration is whether culture is a thing or a process. In the above definitions, we have emphasised the former, defining a set of characteristics which describe what culture is, rather than who makes it, or who decides how it is used. When the idea of culture as process is entertained, questions are raised about power relationships between affected and affecting groups.[12] Culture may in these circumstances become a contested phenomenon rather than an area of agreement and harmony. So, for example, it becomes possible to speak of a dominant culture, imposed intentionally or otherwise by an elite group in society on an unwilling or unwitting populace. It also opens up the question of defining 'popular culture', an area seen in contemporary cultural studies as being oppositional to the hegemonic and restrictive practices of 'high culture'. Furthermore, concepts of culture as transactional emphasise the fact that culture is not homogeneous and static, but an evolving, shifting, diverse and many-faceted phenomenon. The effect of these considerations is not so much to undermine or replace the concept of culture as an inventory of objects or practices, but rather to suggest that the inventory becomes unstable and its content contestable when the dynamics of cultural processes and the power relationships they imply are brought into account.

The third aspect requiring clarification is the question of how far the definitions of culture as proposed above overlap with ideas about society which are the substance of sociological concern. It might be suggested that a definition of culture which relies on identifying distinguishing characteristics of groups might be seen to parallel a notion of such groups as societies or as social units within a society. Thus, for example, to say that traditions, customs, mores and beliefs comprise the culture of a group might simply describe a set of variables which, to a sociologist, define the basis for providing social cohesion and social identity to the group. Nevertheless, while there will inevitably be some blurring of the lines between cultural and social, and between culture and society, it can be argued that there is a sufficiently clear distinction to allow these domains to be separated, as indeed Raymond Williams was able to do in his influential work whose title, *Culture and Society*, crystallises such a distinction.[13] If culture, in both of the senses defined above, embraces the intellectual and artistic functions of humankind (even if these are exercised unconsciously, as for example in the use of language), its source can be differentiated from those processes of social organisation, both deliberate and spontaneous, which go towards defining society.

Is economics culture-free? The cultural context of economics

The formal precision of modern economics, with its theoretical abstraction, its mathematical analytics and its reliance on disinterested scientific method in testing hypotheses about how economic systems behave, might suggest that economics as a discipline does not have a cultural context, that it operates within a world that is not conditioned by, nor conditional upon, any cultural phenomena. But just as the radical critique of contemporary economics has argued that the sort of economics described above cannot be value-free, so also can it be suggested that economics as an intellectual endeavour cannot be culture-free.

To begin with, it is apparent that the many schools of thought that go to make up the full complement of economic science as it has evolved over at least two centuries themselves comprise a series of separate cultures or subcultures, each defined as a set of beliefs and practices which bind the school together. Just as shared values provide the basis for cultural identity of various sorts in the world at large, so also in the restricted domain of the intellectual discourse of economics we can interpret the coalescence of schools of thought, whether they be Marxist, Austrian, Keynesian, neoclassical, new classical, old institutional, new institutional or whatever, as a cultural process. However, the impact of culture on the thinking of economists goes further, because the cultural values they inherit or learn have a profound and often unacknowledged influence on their perceptions and attitudes. Of course, to argue that cultural considerations affect the way in which economists practise their trade is simply an extension of the well known argument that the ideological standpoint of the observer influences the way he or she perceives the world, and that objectivity in the social sciences generally is impossible since even the choice of which phenomena to study is itself a subjective process. Recognising this in the present context, we might ask, for example, whether the apparent acceptance by the great majority of contemporary Western economists of the dominant intellectual paradigm in their discipline – a belief in the efficacy of competitive markets, the foundation upon which the political system of capitalism is built – derives from a process of intellectual persuasion or simply from an unexamined cultural predisposition shaped by the values of their profession.

Furthermore the cultural context of economics as a discipline relates not only to the conditioning of its practitioners, but also to the methodology of its discourse. The processes by which economic ideas are generated, discussed, appraised and transmitted have been subject to analysis in terms which draw upon the work of theoreticians in literary and critical analysis such as Derrida and Foucault. Turning attention to the textual nature of economic knowledge and to the functioning of rhetoric in economic discourse has been seen by economists such as Deirdre McCloskey as opening up new 'conversations' in the philosophy of economics and in the interpretation of the history of economic thought.[14] Argument, persuasion and other processes involved in conversations among economists or between economists and others have clear cultural connotations, as indicated, for example, in Arjo Klamer's writings on the growth, communication and dissemination of economic knowledge;[15] it is perhaps no coincidence that Klamer occupies the world's first chair in the economics of art and culture, at Erasmus University in Rotterdam.

Let us turn now from the cultural context of economics as a system of thought to the cultural context of the economy as a system of social organisation. The fact that economic agents live, breathe and make decisions within a cultural environment is readily observable. So, too, is the fact that this environment has some influence on shaping their preferences and regulating their behaviour, whether this behaviour is observed at the level of the individual consumer or firm or at the aggregated level of the macroeconomy. Yet in its formal analytics, mainstream economics has tended to disregard these influences, treating human behaviour as a manifestation of universal characteristics which can be fully captured within the individualistic, rational-choice, utility-maximising model, and seeing market equilibria as being relevant to all circumstances regardless of the historical, social or cultural context.[16] Indeed, when neoclassical modelling does attempt to account for culture, it can do so only within its own terms. So, for example, Guido Cozzi interprets culture as a social asset that enters the production functions of labour efficiency units as a public-good input within an overlapping-generations model.[17] While such efforts may capture some of the characteristics of culture in an abstract economy, they remain remote from an engagement with the wider issues of culture and real-world economic life.

At the same time it is important to note that there has long been an interest in examining the role of culture as a significant influence on the course of economic history, arising within several schools of economic thought. Perhaps the most celebrated contribution to the field has been Max Weber's analysis of the influence of the Protestant work ethic on the rise of capitalism.[18] Here the cultural conditions in which economic activity occurs are linked very directly to economic outcomes. Many other specific illustrations of the historical influence of culture on economic performance can be cited. For example, the spirit of individualism inherent in Anglo-Saxon culture, first noted in Adam Smith's discussion of the division of labour, and developed further by the great nineteenth-century political economists, especially John Stuart Mill, can be seen to have provided the conditions for the spread of the industrial revolution in Britain and almost concurrently in the United States.[19] Closer to our own time, there has been much speculation on what it is that explains the 'Asian economic miracle' in the post-war years, beginning with the spectacular industrial dynamism of Japan, and followed by the phenomenal growth rates in South Korea, Taiwan, Hong Kong and Singapore. We shall return to these questions in chapter 4.

Culture as economy: the economic context of culture

In the same way as economic discourse and the operation of economic systems function within a cultural context, so also is the reverse true. Cultural relationships and processes can also be seen to exist within an economic environment and can themselves be interpreted in economic terms. Both of the conceptualisations of culture defined earlier – the broad anthropological definition and the more specific functional intention of culture – can be considered in this light. Let us deal with them in turn.

If culture can be thought of as a system of beliefs, values, customs, etc. shared by a group, then cultural interactions among members of the group or between them and members of other groups can be modelled as transactions or exchanges of symbolic or material goods within an economising framework. Anthropologists have characterised primitive and not-so-primitive societies in these terms, where ideas of markets, exchange value, currency, price and other such phenomena take on cultural meaning. One specific area of interest has been built around the proposition that all cultures are adapted to, and are explicable through, their material environment. Cultures may differ, but their evolution will be determined not by the ideas that they embody but by their success in dealing with the challenges of the material world in which they are situated. Such 'cultural materialism' has a clear counterpart in economics, especially in the 'old' school of institutional economics, where culture underpins all economic activity. Indeed William Jackson sees cultural materialism as providing the means of reintegrating culture into the same material, natural world as economics.[20]

Furthermore, considerations of the role of culture in the economic development of the Third World place the cultural traditions and aspirations of poor people into an economic framework, as a means of identifying ways in which their material circumstances can be improved in a manner consistent with cultural integrity. In fact, as the UN World Commission on Culture and Development (1995) has made abundantly clear, the concepts of culture and of development are inextricably intertwined in any society. Thus, for example, development projects in poor countries such as those financed by international agencies, NGOs, foreign aid programmes and so on, are likely to be effective in raising living standards in such countries only if they recognise that the culture of the target community is the fundamental expression of their being, and that this culture is placed within an economic context that determines the scope and extent of material progress that is possible. We consider these issues more fully in chapter 4.

Turning now to the interpretation of culture in functional terms, we can again identify the notion of culture as economy and the interpretation of culture as residing within an economic milieu. Perhaps the most obvious place to start is with the proposition that cultural production and consumption can be situated within an industrial framework, and that the goods and services produced and consumed can be regarded as commodities in the same terms as any other commodities produced within the economic system. The term 'cultural industry' was coined by Max Horkheimer and Theodor Adorno of the Frankfurt School in 1947 as a despairing indictment of the commodification inherent in mass culture. They saw culture as being transformed by the technology and ideology of monopoly capitalism; for them, an economic interpretation of cultural processes was an expression of disaster.[21] Since then notions of cultural commodification have developed along several different paths indicating different contextualisations of culture within a broadly economic domain.

One such path, leading through to contemporary cultural studies, recognises the pervasiveness of cultural phenomena in everyday life, and investigates popular culture, largely but not exclusively from a left viewpoint, in terms of economic and social relationships in contemporary society.[22] Another line of development might be traced to postmodern thinkers such as Jean Baudrillard who locate culture in a shifting universe of tangible and intangible social and economic phenomena. Steven Connor characterises Baudrillard as arguing that 'it is no longer possible to separate the economic or productive realm from the realms of ideology or culture, since cultural artefacts, images, representations, even feelings and pyschic structures have become part of the world of the economic'.[23] There is a blurring of the boundary between image or 'simulation' and the reality it represents (a 'hyperreality'). Thus, for example, Baudrillard suggests that Disneyland is more real than the 'real' United States which it imitates.[24]

Yet another line of development has been pursued within cultural economics. It concentrates on the production and consumption of culture (mostly the arts) characterised as purely economic processes. The roots of the subdiscipline of cultural economics are firmly planted in economics, and it can now be seen to be established as a legitimate and distinctive area of specialisation within economics, with its own international association, congresses and scholarly journal (the *Journal of Cultural Economics*), and its own separate classification in that arbiter of the taxonomy of economic discourse, the *Journal of Economic Literature*. It traces its modern origins to John Kenneth Galbraith's first writings in economics and art,[25] though identifying its seminal work as Baumol and Bowen's book *Performing Arts: The Economic Dilemma* (1966). Since then a number of good specialised books have appeared, and there is an expanding theoretical and applied literature in cultural economics in academic journals[26] and elsewhere. Within this tradition, the cultural industries are interpreted using the conventional paraphernalia of economic analysis, albeit with some innovative twists and adaptations to account for the peculiarities of artistic demand and supply. So, for example, the work of artists is construed as occurring within a labour market whose operations can be analysed using concepts familiar to economists such as labour supply equations and earnings functions, but whose predictions of behaviour may diverge from the expected because of the idiosyncrasies of artists as a class of workers. When viewed in this way the cultural industries can easily be integrated into a wider model of an economy, such as an input–output model, where the relationships between culture and other industries can be spelled out. The commodification of culture involved in this approach does not crowd out other constructions of cultural production, including the view that art can be rationalised only in self-referential terms. Rather, this economic view of culture simply accepts as a descriptive fact that the activities of producing and consuming cultural goods and services within an economic system do generally involve economic transactions, that these activities can be encircled in some way and that what is contained within the circle can be called an industry and analysed accordingly. We shall return to this interpretation of culture as an industry in chapter 7.

Individualism and collectivism

Our overview of the domain of this book in this introductory chapter has referred to the fact that economic thought as it has evolved over two centuries is founded on individualism,[27] whereas the notion of culture, at least in the senses defined above, is a manifestation of group or collective behaviour. It is useful, in concluding this introduction, to codify this distinction between economics and culture, as a basis for our further consideration of the interrelationships between them. We do this by putting forward the following proposition: *the economic impulse is individualistic, the cultural impulse is collective.*

This proposition asserts, first, that there is behaviour which can be termed 'economic' which reflects individual goals and which is portrayed in the standard model of an economy comprising self-interested individual consumers seeking to maximise their utility and self-interested producers seeking to maximise their profits. The first part of the proposition remains true in an economy where large corporations dominate the production sector, since they represent simply the means whereby their owners and managers can pursue their own economic self-interest more effectively. In the standard neoclassical model of the economy, markets exist to enable mutually beneficial exchange to occur, and according to the theory of general equilibrium such markets will lead under certain assumptions to the maximisation of social welfare, defined only in terms of the individuals who comprise the economy, and given the initial distribution of income.

Of course in this economy collective action may occur. If markets fail or do not exist, voluntary or coercive collective action may be required in order for optimal social outcomes to be achieved. For example, public goods such as national defence or law and order, which cannot be financed directly through individual demand, must be supplied through the state or via voluntary cooperation. Other forms of cooperative behaviour will spring up in an individualistic economy. But all these manifestations of collective action are traceable back to individual demand and, within the economic model, to the self-interest of the economic agents involved. Even altruism is identifiable in this model as an expression of individual utility maximisation.

The above proposition asserts secondly that there is behaviour, distinguishable from the economic behaviour described in the previous paragraphs, which can be termed 'cultural'; such behaviour reflects collective as distinct from individualistic goals, and derives from the nature of culture as expressing the beliefs, aspirations and identification of a *group* as defined above. Thus the cultural impulse can be seen as a desire for group experience or for collective production or consumption that cannot be fully factored out to the individuals comprising the group. These desires range over many types of activities, but we might use the arts as illustration. On the production side, many artistic goods and services are produced by group activity where the outcome is a collective effort acknowledged by the participants as having a value or meaning beyond that which could simply be attributed to the totality of the inputs of the individuals involved.[28] Similarly consumption of the arts – for example, in theatres and concert halls – is frequently a collective activity moved by a sense that the group experience transcends that of the sum of the individual consumer responses. Of course again seemingly contrary cases can be cited. Much art is produced as an individual, even lonely activity, and a person reading a novel or listening to music in the privacy of their own home is engaged in solely individualistic consumption. Nevertheless, artists working alone are generally doing so in the expectation that their work will communicate with others; similarly, lone consumers of the arts are likely to be making some wider human connection. Thus, whatever the artistic products produced and consumed, the processes of producing and consuming them can be seen not only as individual enterprise, but also as expressions of a collective will which transcends that of the individual participants involved.

To sum up, we are suggesting that the economic impulse as specified in the above proposition can be seen as expressing the individual desires of members of society on their own behalf, and the cultural impulse can be seen as gathering together the collective desires of the group or groups within a given society for the sorts of cultural expression referred to in the definitions of culture put forward earlier. This proposition will provide a useful basis for distinguishing the economic and the cultural throughout our subsequent discussion in this book.

Outline of the book

It can be suggested that at some fundamental level, the conceptual foundations upon which both economics and culture rest have to do with notions of value. Certainly theories of value have been central to the development of economic thought since Adam Smith, and whatever the disciplinary starting point for a consideration of culture, whether it be aesthetics or contemporary cultural studies, questions of value are fundamental there, too. Chapter 2 of this volume therefore lays the theoretical basis for the remainder of our work, by considering notions of value in economics and in culture, how they are codified and how they are assessed. The next step then is to propose a means of representing culture in terms which may be capable of bridging whatever divide exists between it and economics, that is to propose a way of conceptualising culture in a form which captures its essential characteristics but which is also amenable to economic manipulation and analysis. This step is taken in chapter 3, where the notion of 'cultural capital' is put forward, as a means of representing both tangible and intangible manifestations of culture. The definition of cultural capital depends on our earlier consideration of economic and cultural value, and allows the characterisation of cultural goods and services, cultural activities and other phenomena in a way which recognises both their economic and their cultural importance. Given the long time-frames within which in practical terms culture needs to be evaluated, we go on to consider the intertemporal characteristics of cultural capital: how it is received as a bequest from the past, how it is dealt with in the present and how it is handed on to the future. Such an agenda can be brought together under the ubiquitous rubric of 'sustainability', in a manner which parallels the treatment of natural capital in an environmental and ecological context.

Chapters 4 and 5 then take up two specific aspects building on the discussion of value and of cultural capital and sustainability. In chapter 4 we consider culture in economic development, looking first at cultural determinants of economic performance, and then broadening our consideration to the role of culture as the means of representing the whole gamut of human development in both developing and industrialised countries. Sustainability questions are important here, not just for the importance of a long-term perspective on economic development, but also because of the need to maintain cultural systems as integrating elements in the development process. Chapter 5 looks specifically at the economics of cultural heritage, perhaps the most obvious manifestation of cultural capital and one where sustainability principles can be most clearly articulated and applied.

In chapter 6 we turn our attention to the process of creativity as a mainspring of cultural growth and development. Economists have long been interested in creativity as a motivating force in innovation and technological change, but have rarely been concerned to venture beneath the surface to speculate about the origins of the creative drive and about the ways in which economic incentives and constraints influence its expression among individual creators, apart from the somewhat sweeping observation that the principal incentive to innovation is the prospect of profit. Again, issues of value are central to our argument; in characterising the work of creative artists, we are able to identify the production of both economic and cultural value in the generation and disposition of their work.

We return in chapter 7 to the notion of the cultural industries as a means of representing cultural activity in economic terms. The approach which has developed as the core of cultural economics over the past thirty years is reviewed and discussed in the context of construing the creative arts as an industry. We then widen the focus to consider the cultural industries more generally, with attention to culture in urban development, tourism and trade. We also discuss the potential for the cultural industries to contribute to economic development in the developing world, using the music industry as a case study.

If cultural activity in the economy is interpreted in an industrial framework, and if the cultural industries so designated lead to economic output and generate employment, governments which may be unconcerned about culture *per se* will begin to take an interest. This leads us directly into chapter 8 where we take up the more general issue of how the state might intervene to affect culture in some way or another. The means of such intervention is cultural policy, an area of government involvement which has emerged as a specific policy arena only in very recent times. Given that in the contemporary world much of public policy is concerned with economic phenomena, it is not surprising that cultural policy raises very directly the relationship between economics and culture. Cultural policy also has significant political ramifications. In our discussion we focus attention on the complementarities and conflicts between cultural and economic policy: again, questions of economic and cultural value emerge as decisive in mapping the territory and in guiding decision-making.

Finally, in the concluding chapter 9, some effort is made to draw the threads together and to point the way ahead. In a contemporary world where we can see juxtaposed the oppositional dynamics of economic globalisation and cultural differentiation, can the twin subjects of this volume, economics and culture, be seen as two organising principles for contemporary society, defining both the scope and limitations for civilised progress into the third millennium?

Notes

1 Quotation is from Canto IV, stanza I, lines 1–2; see Byron (1986, V, p. 203).
2 See Blackmore (1869, p. 82).
3 Williams (1976, p. 76).
4 Borofsky (1998, p. 64).
5 For considerations of the changing concept of culture within anthropology, a discipline where culture is at its very core, see Marcus and Fischer (1986), the appendix to Ruttan (1988), Appadurai (1996, ch. 3), and the further references contained in notes 1 and 2 of Borofsky (1998). For theories of culture in sociology see Di Maggio (1994) and in psychology see Cooper and Denner (1998).
6 Williams (1976, p. 81) notes that the adjectival form dates only from the late nineteenth century.
7 Except insofar as basic scientific research – pure rather than applied – may be

aimed at a general advancement of knowledge and understanding, and as such could be seen as bearing some similarities with art.

8 For a review of the relationships between the economics of sport and of the arts, see Seaman (1999).

9 This debate has focused almost entirely on the demand side, with cultural goods being distinguished by the peculiar nature of tastes for them, a matter to which we return on pp. 114ff. below; see also the delineation of 'creative goods' in Caves (2000).

10 A good illustration is pop music; see Dolfsma (1999).

11 Such a system of 'global ethics' has been proposed by the World Commission on Culture and Development (1995, pp. 33–51); nevertheless, despite the apparent persuasiveness of such proposals, reaching agreement on universal ethical standards remains, both theoretically and practically, a matter of considerable controversy.

12 For discussion of these issues, see Wright (1998).

13 Williams (1958); for a consideration of the society–culture relationship, see Peterson (1976).

14 See McCloskey (1985, 1994); Amariglio (1988).

15 See, for example, Klamer's comparison between the shared values of baseball fans in conditioning their discussions (a cultural phenomenon), and the skills required of participants in economic discourse (Klamer 1988, pp. 260–2).

16 Economists outside the mainstream, however, are less narrowly focused. Institutional economists, for example, take culture as the foundation of economic processes and treat 'all human behaviour [as] cultural behaviour' (Mayhew 1994, p. 117); see also North (1990), Stanfield (1995). For a penetrating appraisal of economics as culture from an anthropological viewpoint, see Escobar (1995, ch. 3).

17 Cozzi (1998).

18 First published in 1904–5; for an English translation see Weber (1930). See further in O'Neil (1995); Armour (1996).

19 See Landes (1969); Temin (1997).

20 Jackson (1996); for the origins of cultural materialism, see Harris (1979).

21 See Adorno and Horkheimer (1947); Adorno (1991).

22 Storey, (1993, pp.6–18).

23 Connor (1997, p. 51).

24 Baudrillard (1994, pp. 12–14); see also Best and Kellner (1991, pp. 111–45), Storey (1993, pp. 162–5).

25 Of which the first appears to be Galbraith (1960, Ch. 3).

26 For reviews of the scope and content of cultural economics, see Throsby (1994b); Hutter (1996); Towse (1997a, vol. I, pp. xiii-xxi); Blaug (1999). Some significant books in the field include Peacock and Weir (1975); Blaug (1976); Netzer (1978); Throsby and Withers (1979); Hendon, Shanahan and MacDonald (1980); Feld, O'Hare and Schuster (1983); Hendon and Shanahan (1983); Kurabayashi and Matsuda (1988); Frey and Pommerehne (1989); Grampp (1989); Feldstein (1991); Moulin (1992); Towse and Khakee

(1992); Heilbrun and Gray (1993); Mossetto (1993); Peacock (1993); Towse (1993); Trimarchi (1993); Farchy and Sagot-Duvauroux (1994); Peacock and Rizzo (1994); Ginsburgh and Menger (1996); Klamer (1996); Hutter and Rizzo (1997); Cowen (1998); O'Hagan (1998); Benhamou (2000); Frey (2000); and many others. Towse (1997a) reprints a large number of important journal articles in this field.

27 For an account of the place of methodological individualism in the history of economic thought, see Infantino (1998); for a discussion relating specifically to the economics of the arts, see Rushton (1999).

28 For a view of the sociological significance of artistic production as collective action, see Becker (1974).

2   Theories of value

YVAN: Of course it's logical, you ask me to guess the price, you know
very well the price depends on how fashionable the painter might be . . .
MARC: I'm not asking you to apply a whole set of critical standards,
I'm not asking you for a professional valuation, I'm asking you what
you, Yvan, would give for a white painting tarted up with a few off-
white stripes.
YVAN: Bugger all.   (Yasmina Reza, *Art*, 1994[1])

Introduction: why value?

In a fundamental sense the notion of 'value' is the origin and motivation
of all economic behaviour. At the same time, but from a very different
perspective, ideas of value permeate the sphere of culture. In the
economic domain, value has to do with utility, price and the worth that
individuals or markets assign to commodities. In the case of culture,
value subsists in certain properties of cultural phenomena, expressible
either in specific terms, such as the tone value of a musical note or the
value of a colour in a painting, or in general terms as an indication of the
merit or worth of a work, an object, an experience or some other cultural
thing. Of course both economics and culture, as areas of human thought
and action, are concerned with values in the plural – i.e. the beliefs and
moral principles which provide the framework for our thinking and
being. But although we must acknowledge the importance of values as an
underlying influence on human behaviour in general and on intellectual
endeavour in the social sciences and humanities in particular, our interest
in the present context is with value in the singular.

In both of the fields of our concern, economics and culture, the notion
of value can be seen, despite its differing origins, as an expression of

worth, not just in a static or passive sense but also in a dynamic and active way as a negotiated or transactional phenomenon. It can therefore be suggested that value can be seen as a starting point in a process of linking the two fields together, that is as a foundation stone upon which a joint consideration of economics and culture can be built. Laying that foundation stone is the task of this chapter. We consider separately the origins of value theory in economics and (as far as we are able to identify it) in culture, and then discuss how these concepts can be applied to the economic and cultural valuation of cultural commodities. We conclude with an application of these ideas to the case of an art museum.

The theory of value in economics

An appropriate point of departure for considering theories of value in economics is, as with most issues in the history of economic thought, with Adam Smith's *The Wealth of Nations* (1776). Smith was the first to distinguish between value in use of a commodity, being its power to satisfy human wants, and value in exchange, being the quantity of other goods and services that someone would be prepared to give up in order to acquire a unit of the commodity. Smith, and the political economists who succeeded him in the nineteenth century, put forward theories of value which were founded upon the cost of production. These writers essentially proposed that the value of an object was determined by the costs of the inputs used in its manufacture, as a basis for their consideration of the laws regulating the distribution of income. Thus, for example, Smith and later Ricardo and Marx formulated labour theories, in which value was determined by the amount of labour embodied in a good. For Marx, other factor rewards (profits, dividends, rent, interest) were surplus value above the labour value. Thus his theory of value was a theory of distribution shaped by the class relations in society; in the Marxian analysis, the labour value accrued to the working class as wages, the residual surplus to the ruling class.

An important element in the eighteenth- and nineteenth-century debate about value was the idea of 'natural value', a set of prices determined by production and cost conditions, which reflected a centre of gravity towards which actual prices would move, free of short-term distortions. Nowadays we would refer to such prices as those obtaining in long-run equilibrium. The idea of natural prices originated before Adam Smith, being discernible in the earlier writings of John Locke, William Petty and others.[2] The underlying tendency was to regard natural value as reflecting the operations of 'natural' forces, determining prices by an orderly process akin to that which regulates outcomes in the natural world.

A related concept was that of absolute or intrinsic value, being a number or a measure which could be attached to a unit of a commodity independently of any exchange through buying or selling and which would be invariant over time and space. Smith defined absolute value in terms of his labour theory, and so did Ricardo.[3] In his later writings Ricardo went further to distinguish between absolute and relative values. But the ideas about absolute value that he and others such as Malthus put forward were strongly challenged at the time by Samuel Bailey (1825) and later by other writers,[4] who ridiculed the idea that there existed any natural or replicable yardstick of value inherent in commodities. Similarly, John Ruskin was fiercely critical of classical value theory, though from a somewhat different perspective. For Ruskin, following Carlyle, the idea that the value of a commodity can be determined by market processes and measured in monetary terms was a violation of the principles of intrinsic value upon which the worth of objects, especially art objects, should be assessed. Instead he related value to the life-enhancing labour of the worker who made the commodity; the worker not only pleased himself by his efforts but also bestowed something of this goodness upon the user of the product. Ruskin applied this theory to explaining why some artworks were more valuable than others, arguing that the creative production process imparted value to a painting or a sculpture which became embedded in or intrinsic to the work itself.[5]

At the end of the nineteenth century, however, came the marginalist revolution[6] which replaced cost-of-production theories of value with a model of economic behaviour built on individual utilities. Jevons, Menger and Walras saw individuals and their preferences as the 'ultimate atoms' of the exchange process and of market behaviour.[7] They explained exchange value in terms of preference patterns of consumers towards commodities that were capable of satisfying individual wants. Yet the idea of utility which the neoclassical economists crystallised was not in fact new. Bentham had used the term utility initially to describe the intrinsic properties of a commodity which 'produce benefit, advantage, pleasure, good or happiness';[8] later he shifted its meaning towards the notion of the pleasure associated with the act of consumption of the commodity, an interpretation further elaborated by Jevons (1888) and accepted as the basis for marginalist theory.

From these origins has sprung the utility theory which underlies the theory of consumer behaviour in modern economics. Individuals are assumed to possess well behaved preference orderings over commodities such that they can state unambiguously that they prefer a given quantity of this good over a given quantity of that (or are indifferent between the two). Under plausible assumptions as to the nature of these preference orderings, including an assumption that marginal utility diminishes as consumption of a good increases, a theory of demand can be derived which is empirically testable in its own right and which can be placed alongside a theory of supply to provide a model for price determination in competitive markets. No questions need be asked of people as to the reasons for their preference orderings. The origins of desire, whether they be biological, psychological, cultural, spiritual or whatever, are of no consequence; all that is required is that preference rankings can be specified in an orderly way.

Despite the self-satisfaction that many economists feel at having arrived at a theory of value which they regard as complete in terms of its universality and elegance, marginal utility analysis has been widely criticised. For our purposes the most important line of attack has been to argue that value is a socially constructed phenomenon, and that the determination of value – and, hence, of prices – cannot be isolated from the social context in which these processes occur.[9] The elaboration of a social theory of value is associated with economists such as Thorstein Veblen, John R. Commons and others of the 'old' institutionalist school, though the lineage extends further back, to John Bates Clark in the late nineteenth century, and earlier. The criticism of the marginal utility theory of value is directed at the foundation stone upon which the theory is constructed, namely the proposition that consumers can formulate orderly preferences based solely on their individual needs, uninfluenced by the institutional environment and the social interactions and processes that govern and regulate exchange. As such, the criticism can be seen as a component of the broader critique of neoclassical economics to which we referred in chapter 1.

The invention of marginal utility may have resolved the so-called 'paradox of value',[10] but it scarcely did away with the need for a theory of value. It is true that neoclassical marginal analysis provided an explanation of price formation in competitive markets which is still accepted today, and that within this model prices can be seen as the means by which market economies coordinate the multiple valuations of the individual actors in the system, imposing an orderly pattern on the chaos of diverse human wants and desires. As a result, for many contemporary economists a theory of price is a theory of value, and nothing more need be said. Nevertheless, it can be argued that market prices are at best only an imperfect indicator of underlying value. They are rarely free of temporary disturbances which may be difficult to distinguish from longer-term tendencies, making it problematical to establish where long-run equilibrium prices might lie. Even without such transient aberrations there are many other ways in which price distortions may occur, such as through imperfectly competitive markets, incomplete information and so on. Further, prices do not reflect the consumers' surplus enjoyed by purchasers of a commodity. Thus it can be suggested that at best prices are an *indicator* of value but not necessarily a direct *measure* of value, and that price theory elaborates on, but is not a replacement for, a theory of value in economics.

Economic valuation of cultural goods and services

We turn now to considering how notions of economic value can be applied to cultural goods and services. To do so we have to distinguish between cultural commodities existing as private goods, for which therefore a set of market prices at least potentially exists, and those which occur as public goods, for which no observable prices are available. We need to bear in mind that many cultural goods and services are in fact mixed goods, having simultaneously both private- and public-good characteristics. A painting by Van Gogh, for example, can be bought and sold as an art object whose private-good value accrues only to those who own or see it; at the same time the painting as an element in the history of art brings wide public-good benefits to historians, art-lovers and the general public. The valuation principles discussed below will be applicable at once to both aspects of such goods.

Individual consumption of private cultural goods

Turning first to private cultural goods, we can readily measure what consumers are prepared to give up in order to acquire such goods and we can construct demand functions for these goods which look much like demand functions for any other commodity. When these demand functions are set alongside supply functions reflecting the marginal costs incurred in producing the goods, a private market might be seen to reach equilibrium. However, as noted in the previous section, the capacity of price to represent a true index of value is at best limited for any commodity. For cultural goods there are added qualifications. On the demand side, the simple timeless utility-maximising consumer is replaced in cultural markets by an individual in whom taste is cumulative and hence time-dependent. As we shall see further in chapter 7, cultural consumption can be interpreted as a process contributing both to present satisfaction and to the accumulation of knowledge and experience leading to future consumption. Thus demand is liable to influence price in ways which ramify beyond the immediate valuation of the good in question.

At the same time on the supply side the standard conditions for price formation in competitive markets are not necessarily met in the markets for cultural goods. In particular, as we shall again examine further in later chapters, producers (particularly creative artists) may not be profit-maximisers, and expected price may play only a minor role – or, indeed, no role at all – in their resource allocation decisions. In addition there are likely to be significant externalities in both production and consumption.

Overall, therefore, we might conclude that price will be only a limited indicator of the economic value of private cultural commodities in market outcomes, partly because of the shortcomings of price as a measure of value for any economic good, and partly because of the additional characteristics peculiar to cultural goods and services. Nevertheless, in most empirical situations when we require an assessment of the economic worth of a private cultural good, its market price is likely to be the only indicator available. Thus considerable effort has been directed at putting together estimates of the value of various cultural goods and services in the market economies of the world. Prices in the fine art market, for example, are continually monitored, and the aggregate value of sales in any period is taken as an indicator of the economic size of the market. Trade statistics can be used as a means of evaluating the economic value of international flows of cultural goods such as music rights, films, television programmes and so on. The economic impact of cultural organisations on local, regional and national economies is evaluated by reference to the market prices and volumes of output produced – box office receipts for theatre companies, revenue from entrance fees for museums and galleries and so on. At a more general level, the size of the cultural sector and its contribution to the economy are measured in many countries by aggregating the value-added or the gross value of output contributed by its various components. In short, despite the theoretical limitations that suggest the exercise of some caution in interpreting market prices as indicators of the economic value of cultural goods and services, the use of data derived directly from market transactions is widespread and widely accepted for such purposes.

Collective consumption of public cultural goods

In the case of public cultural goods, again the application of the standard procedures of economic measurement is possible. Much methodological progress has been made in recent years in economics in valuing intangible phenomena demanded by consumers, such as environmental amenity, using techniques such as contingent valuation methods (CVM), for example. We shall be considering these approaches in more detail in chapter 5 in the context of valuing cultural heritage; for now it suffices to say that CVM and related techniques attempt to assign an economic value to the externality or public good by assessing what the demand function would be if in fact demand could be expressed through normal market channels. These estimates can be aggregated across consumers to reach a total demand price which can be compared with the costs of providing various levels of the good in order to determine whether or not supply is warranted and, if so, how much.

These approaches attempt to mimic a market for the phenomenon concerned, and thus the resulting 'prices' are subject to much the same sorts of limitations as affect the interpretation of ordinary market prices for private goods as discussed above. In addition, however, some further problems are introduced in assessing public-good demand because of inadequacies and biases in the measurement techniques themselves. Thus, for instance, although CVM theory and applications have advanced a long way in recent years, to the point where in 1993 these methods could be given a cautious seal of approval by an independent panel headed by two sceptical Nobel laureates in economics,[11] there remain methodological difficulties which limit the extent to which the valuations they yield can be interpreted as a 'true' economic value. For example, there is likely always to be some concern for the hypothetical nature of the markets created, notwithstanding experimental evidence for the congruity of behaviour in real and simulated markets. Furthermore, although the classic free-rider problem can be controlled, its ultimate importance in conditioning willingness-to-pay responses remains unclear.

Again, however, despite the difficulties in interpreting prices as economic value, economists working on evaluation of the demand for public cultural goods (or for the public-good element of mixed goods in the cultural arena) have had little alternative but to apply the standard approaches and to accept resulting assessments as the best estimates available of the economic worth of the good concerned. Thus, for example, Glenn Withers and I in an early study[12] estimated the willingness of Australian consumers to pay out of their taxation for the public-good component of the arts. Because of the range of assumptions upon which any such estimate could be based, we were reluctant to identify a single 'demand price' as revealed by our study. Nevertheless, we felt able to conclude with reasonable confidence that the average economic value placed by Australian taxpayers on non-market benefits they believed they received from the arts in 1983 exceeded the tax price they were being asked to pay to finance public-sector support for the Australian arts at that time. In a subsequent study William Morrison and Edwin West obtained a broadly similar result in Canada.[13] We shall return in chapter 5 to further contingent valuation studies for cultural goods and services. For now we simply conclude as in the case of private goods above that, despite theoretical and practical limitations, conventional assessment methods can be used to value public cultural goods and that the estimates so obtained have been accepted, for better or worse, as indicators of the economic value of such goods.

Cultural value

As we noted at the beginning of this chapter, to think about culture in either of the senses defined earlier is to think about value. Steven Connor describes value in the cultural discourse as being 'inescapable', not just the idea of value itself but also the

processes of estimating, ascribing, modifying, affirming and even denying value, in short, the processes of *evaluation* . . . We are claimed always and everywhere by the necessity of value in this active, transactional sense.[14]

The agenda for the cultural theorist – value and valuation – is thus strikingly similar to that for the economist.

However, the origins of value in the cultural sphere are quite different from those in the economic, and the means for representing value in cultural terms are therefore likely to be different from those used in economics. What is the nature of the value a community places upon the traditions which symbolise its cultural identity? What do we mean when we say that Monteverdi's operas or Giotto's frescoes are valuable in the history of art? In neither case does an appeal to individual utility or to price seem appropriate. The dimensions of cultural value and the methods that might be used in assessing it are matters which must originate in a cultural discourse, even if at some point it might be possible to borrow from economic modes of thought as one way of modelling them.

At its simplest it can be said that the starting point for an identification of value within a broadly cultural context lies in the irreducible principle that value represents positive characteristics rather than negative, an orientation to what is good rather than bad, better rather than worse. It can be aligned with the pleasure principle in guiding human choices. But at the same time an identification of cultural value with simple hedonism may be insufficient or even inappropriate. For example the formation of value occurs within a moral and social universe which might mediate the understanding and acceptance of pleasure as a criterion and may affect the interpretation of value,[15] as we shall see further below.

A long tradition in cultural thought through to cultural modernism sees the true value of a work of art (for example) as lying in intrinsic qualities of aesthetic, artistic or broader cultural worth which it possesses. Such a humanist view of cultural value emphasises universal, transcendental, objective and unconditional characteristics of culture and of cultural objects. Judgements will differ between individuals, of course, although there may be sufficient agreement on the essential cultural worth of certain items to warrant their elevation into the cultural 'canon'. The museum and the academy become the repositories of this 'high' or 'elite' cultural value. The ground may shift over time, such that works once oppositional to the establishment, such as Picasso's paintings, Stravinsky's music, Joyce's prose, Brecht's drama or Eliot's poetry, are in due course accepted into the canon; but always the eternal properties of absolute cultural worth are in there somewhere and will eventually be discerned and accorded the seal of approval. It might be noted in passing that the assertion of absolute value inherent in cultural objects can be seen as congruent with the ideas of intrinsic, natural or absolute value put forward, in a different context, by the classical political economists to whom we referred above.

In the postmodern period of the last two or three decades, powerful new methodologies from sociology, linguistics, psychoanalysis and elsewhere have challenged and displaced the traditional ideals that harmony and regularity are at the core of cultural value, re-processing these ideas into an expanded, shifting and heterogeneous interpretation of value in which relativism replaces absolutism. Yet it can be suggested that postmodernism, while focusing attention on an expanded view of value, has failed to offer a satisfactory account of how value might instead be perceived and evaluated.[16] Because of the uncertainties thus introduced, many writers refer to a 'crisis of value' in cultural theory today.

It would be a caricature to portray contemporary cultural theorists as having to choose between politically conservative absolutism and left-wing relativism in their search for the truth about cultural value. Yet, like all caricatures, there is a germ of reality in such a picture. If this is so, can the observer without any strong ideological predisposition find a way through? It can be suggested that progress might be possible if the following propositions are acceptable. First, it seems desirable to accept a distinction between aesthetics (for want of a more inclusive term) and the sociology of culture.[17] In other words, it should be possible to separate out the domain of pure, self-referential and internally consistent aesthetic judgement from the broader social or political context in which such judgement is made. Even if such judgements are conditional upon context, the existence of individual aesthetic response cannot be denied. Secondly, and consequentially, it may be possible, with sufficient regularity across individual responses, to find consensual agreements in particular cases which are interesting in their own right. It may be that people agree for the 'wrong' reasons, being hopelessly conditioned by their social environment or by some other external force, but it is equally plausible that their consensus arises from some more fundamental process by which value is generated and transmitted. Indeed it can be said that, whatever the reason for it, the simple fact of agreement on cultural value in particular cases is itself of interest. Thirdly, it should not be difficult to accept that cultural value is a multiple and shifting thing which cannot be comprehended within a single domain. Value is, in other words, both various and variable. Fourthly, it may have to be accepted that measurement may not be possible, insofar as some of the phenomena under consideration may be incommensurable according to any familiar quantitative or qualitative standard. For example, Terry Smith suggests that cultural valuing tends against measurement, whether by reference to external or internally generated scales, because it 'occurs as flows: its modes are generation, concentration, the emergence of channels, strings, sometimes chains of valuing'.[18]

If these broad propositions are accepted for the sake of argument, a possible way forward is to attempt to disaggregate the concept of cultural value into at least some of its more important constituent elements. Thus, without being exhaustive it may be possible to describe an artwork, for example, as providing a range of cultural value characteristics including:

(a) *Aesthetic value*: Without attempting to deconstruct the elusive notion of aesthetic quality further, we can at least look to properties of beauty, harmony, form and other aesthetic characteristics of the work as an acknowledged component of the work's cultural value. There may be added elements in the aesthetic reading of the work, influenced by style, fashion and good or bad taste.

(b) *Spiritual value*: This value might be interpreted in a formal religious context, such that the work has particular cultural significance to members of a religious faith, tribe or other cultural grouping, or it may be secularly based, referring to inner qualities shared by all human beings. The beneficial effects conveyed by spiritual value include understanding, enlightenment and insight.

(c) *Social value*: The work may convey a sense of connection with others, and it may contribute to a comprehension of the nature of the society in which we live and to a sense of identity and place.

(d) *Historical value*: An important component of the cultural value of an artwork may be its historical connections: how it reflects the conditions of life at the time it was created, and how it illuminates the present by providing a sense of continuity with the past.

(e) *Symbolic value*: Artworks and other cultural objects exist as repositories and conveyors of meaning. If an individual's reading of an artwork involves the extraction of meaning, then the work's symbolic value embraces the nature of the meaning conveyed by the work and its value to the consumer.

(f) *Authenticity value*: This value refers to the fact that the work is the real, original and unique artwork which it is represented to be. There is little doubt that the authenticity and integrity of a work have identifiable value *per se*, additional to the other sources of value listed above.[19]

Such a range of criteria may be proposed whether the scales for assessing them are fixed or movable, objective or subjective. Hence whether the guiding principle is absolute or relative, it would seem that some progress might be made in identifying the broad sweep of the concept of cultural value by disaggregating it in this way.

Nevertheless, the problems of evaluation remain, whether the task is an assessment within any one of the components listed above, or whether the quest is for an overall measure or indicator of cultural value in a particular case. Several different assessment methods might be brought into play in evaluating cultural value, drawing on a number of specific valuation methods used in the social sciences and the humanities, including the following:

(a) *Mapping*: A first stage may be a straightforward contextual analysis of the object of study, involving physical, geographical, social, anthropological and any other types of mapping to establish an overall framework which will inform the assessment of each of the elements of cultural value.

(b) *Thick description*: This refers to a means of interpretive description of a cultural object, environment or process which rationalises otherwise inexplicable phenomena by exposing the underlying cultural systems etc. at work, and deepens the understanding of the context and meaning of observed behaviour.[20]

(c) *Attitudinal analysis*: Various techniques may be referred to under this heading including social survey methods, psychometric measurement, etc. and a variety of elicitation techniques might be employed.[21] Such approaches are likely to be useful especially in assessing social and spiritual aspects of cultural value. They may be applied at the individual level to gauge individual response, or at an aggregate level to study group attitudes or to seek out patterns of consensus.

(d) *Content analysis*: This group of techniques includes methods aimed at identifying and codifying meaning, appropriate for measuring various interpretations of the symbolic value of the work or other process under consideration.

(e) *Expert appraisal*: The input of expertise in a variety of disciplines is likely to be an essential component of any cultural value assessment, especially in providing judgements on aesthetic, historical and authenticity value, where particular skills, training and experience can lead to a better informed evaluation. Some testing of such judgements against accepted professional standards via a peer review process is likely to be desirable in some cases in order to reduce the incidence of hasty, ill informed, prejudiced or quixotic opinions.

The above methods may offer some prospect of measurement of aspects of cultural value in certain cases. But in other cases, assessment is fallible not just because of the lack of measuring rods, but because of the non-singular nature of the phenomena themselves. In considering a list of cultural value criteria such as the above, Terry Smith points to a 'doubling' of certain characteristics, where thesis and antithesis are simultaneously present.[22] So, for example, he sees aesthetic value as characterised around concepts of beauty and harmony but also, in another value chain, around concepts of sublimity and the inchoate; similarly he suggests that spiritual value privileges understanding and enlightenment but does so against incomprehension and alienation.

To conclude, there may be a crisis in contemporary cultural value theory, but it should not dissuade us from seeking to articulate more clearly what cultural value is and how it is formed. The radical critique has certainly challenged the methodology and ideological basis upon which traditional positions have been based and has forced a reappraisal of conventional modes of thought. But it does not imply, as its sterner adherents seem to suggest, that the situation is hopeless. Intellectual rapprochement is clearly possible from a variety of standpoints.[23] One approach suggested here is to try to disentangle the notion of cultural value, deconstructing it into its constituent elements as a means of articulating more clearly the multi-dimensional nature of the concept. If such an approach at least gives a clearer sense of the material from which cultural value is formed, it may offer some hope of progress towards operationalising the concept of cultural value in such a way that its importance alongside economic value can be more vigorously asserted.

We shall return to these issues, including questions of measurement, in a more pragmatic vein in chapter 5, when dealing with the cultural value of heritage.

Can economic value encompass cultural value?

Whatever the verdict on the possibilities for identifying and measuring cultural value, the discussion in the previous two sections should be sufficient to indicate that notions of economic and cultural value stand as distinct concepts which need to be separated in considering the valuation of cultural goods and services in the economy and in society. Such a conclusion may be seen to be at odds with conventional economic theory based on individual preferences. It could be argued that all the elements which we have identified as cultural value can be adequately captured within an economic theory of individual utility. Since neoclassical economic theory makes no assumptions about the source of an individual's preferences, such preferences may just as well arise from the person's internal processes of cultural appraisal, influenced by whatever cultural criteria or norms are regarded as important from the external environment, and assessed according to some consistent cultural value scale of their own making. The argument would then run that, if this individual ranks object *A* more highly in aesthetic, spiritual or other terms than object *B*, she will be prepared to pay more for object *A* than for object *B*, other things being equal. The differential in demand prices could thus be interpreted as a measure of difference in cultural value. The proposition that willingness to pay can encompass all that needs to be accounted for in what we have proposed as cultural value, and that therefore a separate concept of cultural value is redundant in economic analysis, is an important one that warrants further examination.

There are a number of grounds on which it can be argued that willingness to pay is an inadequate or inappropriate indicator of cultural value. The most obvious one would be to assert that cultural value is inherent in objects or other cultural phenomena, existing independently of the response to the object by the consumer. If this were so, it would not require an individual to experience the value in order for that value to come into being, and hence whether the individual were willing to surrender other goods and services to acquire the object would be irrelevant to the existence of the object's cultural value. Of course it may be that an individual's recognition of inherent cultural value induces her to pay more for the objects containing such value, but the value exists whether she does so or not.

However, it is not necessary to postulate intrinsic or absolute worth in order to establish an existence for cultural value independently of economic value. Let us leave aside this absolutist argument and accept the notion of cultural value as something experienced, contributing undoubtedly to individual utility but with some distinctive features. There are several reasons why it may not be possible to identify cultural value via individuals' willingness to pay. First, people may not know sufficient about the cultural object or process under consideration to be able to form a reliable willingness-to-pay judgement about it. If such information failure were widespread, it could cast doubt on using the preferences of individuals as a basis for judging the cultural value of the object or process. Secondly, it may be that some characteristics of cultural value cannot be expressed in terms of preferences. Some qualities, essential to some aspect of cultural value, may not be expressible by a fully informed individual as better or worse, but simply as qualitatively different – a painting that is red rather than blue, for example, or an abstract versus a representational work. Thirdly, some characteristics of cultural value may only be measurable, if at all, according to a scale that is incommensurable with, or untranslatable to, a monetary metric. This may arise, for example, because no benefit or utility accrues to the individual from the value in question and hence there is no willingness to pay. Yet the individual may recognise the cultural value of the phenomenon under consideration – an artwork, a musical performance, a movie, a heritage site – and may be able to form a judgement as to its cultural worth according to appropriate criteria. Under these circumstances it is possible that an individual could rank objects in a certain way in cultural terms, but rank them differently in terms of willingness to pay. Finally, some problems may arise in using individual willingness to pay as an indicator of cultural value when the phenomenon in question – a cultural experience, for example – arises because the individual is a member of a group. We refer here not so much to the standard problems of free-riding in revealing willingness to pay for public goods, but rather to cases where benefits accrue to individuals *only* as members of a group – the supposed benefits of national identity, for example, or the sense of connection or group feeling which may arise in a theatre audience. Such benefits may ultimately exist in some collective sense, dependent on the existence of the group, and may not be able to be factored out entirely to the individuals of whom the group is comprised; if so, the sum of individual willingness-to-pay responses for the benefit involved may be an inadequate reflection of its cultural value.

We have discussed these distinctive characteristics of the concept of cultural value from the standpoint of the formation and expression of individual preferences. The points made above are still relevant when we extend the notion of value formation into a transactional context, where assessments of cultural value are formed on the basis of a negotiated process involving interchange and interactions between individuals. People form judgements about cultural value not just by introspection but by a process of exchange with others. We return to this issue in chapter 6, when we consider the formation of the value of artworks.

There remains one point to consider in dealing with the question of whether economic value can encompass cultural value. An economist might be willing to accept that a distinct concept of cultural value does indeed exist, but might argue that it is unimportant to economics and irrelevant to the functioning of economic systems. However, as we have suggested elsewhere, a view of economics which excludes the cultural dimension of the activities of individual economic agents and the institutions they inhabit is likely to be seriously deficient in explaining or understanding behaviour. If concerns about cultural value do have some effect on decision-making at the micro or macro level, affecting resource allocation in some way, then they cannot be ignored in economic analysis.

Thus we continue to maintain the necessity of regarding economic and cultural value as distinct entities when defined for any cultural commodity, each one telling us something different of importance to an understanding of the commodity's worth. If this is accepted, it is useful to ask to what extent the two types of value may be related. For simplicity for the purposes of this discussion let us assume that cultural value, like economic value, can be reduced to a single independent statistic, perhaps identifiable with respect to particular cultural commodities as a consensus judgement which summarises the various elements of which cultural value is composed. If so, it is more than likely that there will be some relationship between this measure of a given commodity's cultural value and its economic value. Take the example of two art works. If one work ranks more highly than the other on the various criteria proposed earlier, such that it achieves a higher score on the assumed singular cultural value scale, it would be expected to command a higher price on the market (through higher willingness to pay) and hence to have a higher apparent economic value. Extending this to many works would suggest some correlation, perhaps even a high correlation, between scores on economic and cultural scales, and indeed such correlations have been demonstrated (using a very restricted interpretation of cultural value) in regard to contemporary art.[24]

But, having proposed such a positive correlation, it is important to note that it is unlikely to be perfect, for the reasons discussed above which make cultural value the distinct phenomenon that it is. Not only will some components of cultural value be incapable of translation across the divide, but also will internal relationships between components be inconsistent. Further there will be cases where the overall relationship between economic and summarised cultural value will lie in the negative direction. In other words, whatever singular or multiple criterion of cultural value is considered applicable, counter-examples can be envisaged, where high cultural value is associated with low economic value and vice versa. For instance, if 'high-culture' norms were adopted (conservative, elitist, hegemonic, absolutist), it might be suggested that atonal classical music is an example of a commodity with high cultural but low economic value, and that TV soap operas are an example of a high economic/low cultural value good. In the context of cultural heritage, many examples of assets with low economic and high cultural value might be identifiable; for example, Nathaniel Lichfield suggests that

former cotton mills have significant cultural value as industrial archaeology but may have no market value as property, since they are no longer useful for their original function.[25]

An application: the case of an art museum

To exemplify some of the concepts discussed in this chapter, we turn finally to a brief illustration of their application to a real cultural phenomenon, the case of the art museum.[26] In doing so, we will observe in a pragmatic context how some of the theory described above might be able to be made operational.

Museums are many things to many people: to the artist they are showcases for their work; to the art historian they are essential repositories of the stuff of their profession; to the museologist they perform a vital function in the transmission of information about art and culture to the community; to the urban planner they are meccas of cultural tourism and recreation; to the architect they are a splendid opportunity for celebrating past traditions or inventing new ones in the delivery of a particular cultural service; and, last but hopefully not least, to the economist they are non-profit firms, motivated by a complex and multi-valued objective function and subject to a variety of economic and non-economic constraints.[27] Let us consider the various ways in which an art museum represents and contributes to economic and cultural value.[28] We consider economic valuation and cultural valuation separately in the following sections.

The economic value of an art museum

Anticipating our more detailed analysis of cultural capital in chapter 3, we can say here that the economic value of an art museum derives both from the asset value of its buildings and contents and from the flow of services that these assets provide.

In regard to the asset value there is little difficulty in conceptualising and measuring the real-estate value of a museum facility, though such values might be purely notional when the museum itself occupies historic premises or buildings of cultural importance in their own right which are never likely to be placed on the market. In regard to the economic or accounting value of the contents of the museums, however, many more problems of interpretation arise when attempts are made to apply standard asset valuation methods and accounting procedures to artworks, archeological resources and so on.[29] But whatever the practical difficulties of concept and measurement in specific cases, the general proposition that the holdings of an art museum have a tangible asset price which measures their stored economic value is not difficult to accept. Within this framework, acquiring and deaccessioning works can be seen as leading to changes in inventory levels, with consequent effects on the cash flow and balance sheet of the institution.

Turning to the flow of services provided by an art museum, we can divide them in economic terms into excludable private goods, non-excludable public goods and beneficial externalities, and consider the economic value of each in turn.[30]

Private goods

Museums produce a range of private goods and services which enter the final consumption of individuals or which contribute in some way to further economic output. Principal among these, in terms of the museum's interface with the public, is the direct value of the consumption experiences of its visitors. In line with our earlier discussion, the economic use value of a museum to its attendees can be measured by the total value of gate receipts (average ticket price multiplied by attendance numbers over some defined period) together with the consumers' surplus enjoyed by visitors. If entrance to the museum is free, then direct use value is measured only by consumers' surplus. Visitors may also buy merchandise at the museum shop, and if so the revenue surplus to the museum over the costs of supplying the goods also comprises a value-added contribution to the institution's output.

Furthermore a museum typically produces other services which accrue to private beneficiaries and whose value forms part of the economic value yielded by the organisation. For instance, the formal education activities of the museum – the instruction of school groups, etc. – yield both private and public benefits; if the stock of human capital of the individuals receiving such instruction is increased, they may enjoy private economic benefits in the future in the form of higher productivity, higher earnings and other consumption benefits. In another direction, the curatorial and conservation services provided by the museum to other organisations or to individuals such as collectors have economic value which may or may not be realised through payments appearing in the museum's accounts. Moreover, the museum may yield direct benefits for practising artists through its function as a means of displaying their work to the public.

A final item appearing in this non-exhaustive list of private goods and services supplied by an art museum is the rewards, both tangible and intangible, which it might provide directly to its donors and supporters. While altruism or a sense of social or cultural obligation might provide the motivational force for the generosity of such people, it is their own utility which is increased as a result, and this has real value in economic terms.

Public goods

Among the range of collective benefits provided by an art museum, the most obvious is the generalised community benefit arising from the museum's presence in the world. The 'community' may be defined at local, regional, national and/or international level, depending on the size and importance of the museum under consideration, ranging from a small-town art gallery valued only by local residents through to the Prado, the Louvre, the Uffizi and the various Guggenheims, which are valued by locals and non-locals alike. The benefits provided by an art museum that might be brought under this heading include, in no particular order:

- the contribution the museum makes to public debate about art, culture and society
- the role the museum plays in helping to define cultural identity, either in specific terms or more generally in its representation of the human condition
- the stimulus the museum provides to the production of creative work by artists, both professional and amateur
- the value to individuals of retaining the option of visiting the museum, an option that they might wish to exercise at some time in the future either on their own behalf or on behalf of others
- the sense felt by people that the museum and its contents have value as a bequest to future generations
- the diffused community benefits of the educational services, both formal and informal, provided by the museum
- the connection with other cultures which an art museum provides either for citizens within its own jurisdiction looking outwards, or for those from outside who wish to learn more of the culture they are visiting, and
- the benefit that people derive from the mere existence of an institution like an art museum – i.e. the satisfaction in knowing it is there as an element in the cultural landscape, whether the individual enjoying such a benefit actually visits the museum or not.

The economic value of all of these public-good benefits is measurable, either separately or (more readily) in aggregate, as the willingness to pay expressed by the beneficiaries to whom they accrue, evaluated using methods such as CVM as discussed earlier. The resulting estimates of the economic worth of the museum's public-good output can be uniquely attributed to the institution if the estimates are derived by comparing 'with' and 'without' – i.e. as the value of the *incremental* output of public goods caused by the presence of the museum.

A further type of non-excludable public good may be produced by an art museum if it engages in research. If the output of its research into art theory, art history, conservation, curatorship, etc. contributes to the public domain, informs other scholars and practitioners and adds generally to knowledge, then it has economic value. But assessment or evaluation of the public-good benefits of research is notoriously difficult; in principle the effects may be identifiable and a price assigned, but in practice these benefits are often measured, if at all, simply as the costs of the inputs used to produce them.

Externalities

Finally, art museums may give rise to externalities, unintended side effects or spillovers which are nevertheless beneficial (or costly) to those who experience them. For example, the presence of a museum within an urban area may generate employment and incomes and have other economic impacts on surrounding businesses and households. Such effects may be important in an economic assessment of the local or regional economy, and are often used by museum directors as a justification for increased financial support from the relevant public funding sources. However, while the net valuation of external effects is in principle a valid component of the total economic value of a facility such as an art museum, there are conceptual difficulties of measurement which have to do precisely with identifying how 'net' the measured values really are. So, for example, the so-called 'multiplier' or 'second-round' impacts of a public investment project involving a museum might be properly disregarded in a cost-benefit appraisal because such impacts would accrue to any other similar project to which the investment capital might be devoted.

The cultural value of an art museum

In accordance with a multi-dimensional concept of cultural value, we could see the cultural value of an art museum as arising from a number of different sources. For the purposes of this analysis, the elements of cultural value might be categorised under two headings, those contained within or arising from the artworks held and/or shown by the museum, and those arising more generally from the institutional setting – i.e. from the museum *qua* museum. Let us consider these two sources of the various constituents of cultural value in turn.

Artworks

The works of art that make up the collection of an art museum may be seen as concentrations of cultural value of various sorts. Those who accept the notion of intrinsic or inherent value believe that cultural value is somehow stored in an artwork like wine in a bottle; it may be drunk from time to time but it is also somehow constantly replenished, so that its amount may even increase with age. In the absence of such a literal concept of artworks as stores of value, it may at least be conceded that their cultural worth is in some way omnipresent, although the valuation that might be placed on them as cultural artefacts may vary markedly between individuals and over time. Whatever the viewpoint, however, it can be said that the function of an art museum in the conservation, restoration and preservation of the artworks in its care does indicate a concern for the nature of artworks as stores of cultural value, and that this value could potentially contain any or all of the various elements – aesthetic, spiritual, historical, etc. – noted earlier.

Furthermore, the exhibition of works, whether from the collection or from shows brought in, provides the museum with a means of realising the cultural value of works as a continuous process over time, a process whereby messages and information are conveyed, meaning is constructed and insights and enlightenment are gained. The criteria for assessing the cultural value created in this way, whether judged at the level of the individual viewer or more generally on behalf of society, may be derived from various discourses, corresponding broadly to the sources or component elements of cultural value discussed earlier. Thus for example, we could identify the fact that an art museum contributes, through the showing of artworks, to the formation of cultural value assessed against aesthetic criteria (the critical assessment of and reaction to the works themselves according to precepts of aesthetic scholarship), historical criteria (the place of works in the history of art), social criteria (the relationship of the works to society and the messages that they convey about social organisation, power relationships, political structures and processes, etc.) and so on.

The institutional setting

At the same time as the artworks on show create cultural value simply as individual works, or as works grouped together which gain something from being seen in association with each other, the art museum also creates cultural value through the fact of its existence and operation as an institution. It may do this, first and foremost, through the ambience and environment it creates within which art can be appreciated. This is more than just a matter of the physical facilities which it provides, although comfortable, convenient, inclusive and non-threatening surroundings do help. It is more particularly a question of the way in which an art museum can convey a sense of the purpose and significance of art and culture deriving from the museum's place in individual and social experience. For example, in its impact on individual response, a museum might foster a sense of shared values, of an egalitarian as distinct from an elitist approach to art.[31] In its broader social context, a museum can affect the formation of cultural value (and values) in the community, through its contribution to the debate about art, society, culture, politics or whatever. It may do so from a position that is identifiable as conservative or radical, right or left, bourgeois or proletarian, traditional or innovative, or it may strive for some sort of neutrality. Whatever the stance, the functioning of an art museum as a potential locus for the formation and provision of cultural value, in the wider sense of the term culture to which we have referred, cannot be denied.

Art museums as cultural institutions may also contribute to cultural value in quite a different way, namely through their function as architecture, especially as vehicles for contemporary architects to do their thing. The list of art museums which have been built in modern times as architectural 'masterpieces' grows longer by the hour. The particular challenge of creating a space which serves the function of showing works of art, but at the same time has sculptural or spatial features which render the building itself an artwork, is one which modern architects clearly relish, and one also to which the public responds. Visitors to some recently constructed museums appear to be motivated as much by a desire to experience the buildings themselves as to see the works they house. Thus do some art museums contribute to creating and conveying cultural value in a manner independent of their more particular cultural purposes.[32]

The way ahead

The case of the art museum illustrates in a practical setting that both economic and cultural value are multi-faceted phenomena which must be deconstructed into their constituent elements in order for them to be understood. In the case of economic value, the various components can in the end be combined, thanks to the existence of a common basis upon which they are assessed. For cultural value, however, no such metric exists, and difficult problems of representing summarised or aggregated judgements remain. It also remains to be shown how economic and cultural value, once they are separately identified, enter the decision processes of agents making choices with both economic and cultural ramifications. We return to these issues throughout the remainder of this book. In particular, we consider problems of identifying and measuring the economic and cultural value of cultural heritage projects in chapter 5, the generation of economic and cultural value in the work of creative artists in chapter 6, and the impact of the different types of value in the policy arena in chapter 8.

Conclusions

We have argued in this chapter that questions of value are fundamental to understanding the relationships between economics and culture, and that economic and cultural value must be separated as distinct concepts in any theoretical construction of value in economic and cultural discourse. It may be that fundamental ideas about preferences and choice, ideas occurring in both economic and cultural theory, can indeed provide a common starting point from which the formation of value might proceed. But it is in the elaboration of notions of value, and the transformation of value either into economic price or into some assessment of cultural worth, where the two fields diverge. Economists are deluding themselves if they claim that economics can encompass cultural value entirely within its ambit and that the methods of economic assessment are capable of capturing all relevant aspects of cultural value in their net. In the many-sided debate about culture in contemporary economic settings, the tendency for an economic interpretation of the world to dominate, deriving from the ubiquity and power of the modern economic paradigm, must be resisted, if important elements of cultural value are not to be overlooked. If we are serious about striving for theoretical completeness, and eventually for operational validity in decision-making, it is essential that cultural value be admitted alongside economic value in the consideration of the overall value of cultural goods and services.

Notes

1 Quotation is from Reza (1996, p. 8).
2 See further in Aspromourgos (1996); Dolfsma (1997).
3 For an account of the concept of absolute value in the labour theories of value of Smith, Ricardo and Marx, see Gordon (1968).
4 For example William Thornton (1869).
5 These arguments are put forward in the Preface to *Munera Pulveris* (1872),

where Ruskin heaps scorn on the 'dull economists' of the 'vulgar' school of political economy; see also in Sherburne (1972, ch. 6) and Grampp (1973).

6 Whether or not the 'discovery' of marginal utility, independently and simultaneously, by Jevons, Menger and Walras, working respectively in Manchester, Vienna and Lausanne, comprises the stuff of revolution is a matter of debate among historians of economic thought; see Blaug (1973) and other papers in the same volume (Collison Black *et al.* 1973).

7 Dobb (1973, p. 33).

8 See Bentham (1843, 1, pp. 1–2); this passage is taken from Bentham's work, *An Introduction to the Principles of Morals and Legislation*, first published in 1789, of which the first chapter is entitled 'On the principle of utility'.

9 See, for example, Heilbroner (1988); Mirowski (1990); Clark (1995a).

10 The paradox of value asks why a diamond, which is a useless luxury, commands a very high price whereas a gallon of water, essential for life, costs virtually nothing. The resolution lies in the fact that it is marginal not total utility which determines price.

11 The panel, co-chaired by Nobel Laureates Kenneth Arrow and Robert Solow, and including Edward Leamer, Roy Radner, Paul Portney and Howard Schuman, found that 'CV studies can produce estimates reliable enough to be the starting point of a judicial process of damage assessment, including lost passive-use values' and that studies can provide a 'reliable benchmark' (Arrow *et al.* 1993, pp. 4610–11) provided that they are carefully carried out, with due attention paid to the biases and other problems affecting the technique; see further in Portney *et al.* (1994).

12 See Thompson, Throsby and Withers (1983); Throsby and Withers (1983, 1984, 1986).

13 See Morrison and West (1986).

14 Connor (1992b, p. 8, emphasis in the original).

15 For a discussion of the evaluation of culture in moralistic as well as hedonistic terms, see Connor (1992a).

16 See, for example, Regan (1992a); Connor (1992b, p. 14).

17 See Etlin, (1996, pp. 7ff).

18 Smith (1999).

19 The question of copies of artworks which challenge the concept of authenticity has long been a matter of interest; see, for example, De Marchi and Van Miegroet (1996). For a discussion of the relationship between aesthetic value and authenticity value, see Meiland (1983).

20 The idea of 'thick description' is usually attributed to Clifford Geertz (1973, ch. 1, pp. 3–30), although Geertz acknowledges his debt to Gilbert Ryle (1971); for discussions of this sort of approach in ethnographic method, see the essays by Richard Shweder and Howard Becker in Jessor *et al.* (1996).

21 For example, contextualisation using narrative methods; see Satterfield *et al.* (2000).

22 See further in Smith (1999).

23 Thus, for example, Steven Connor sets out in his book *Theory and Cultural*

Value to give an account of value which sees 'absolutism and relativism together rather than as apart and antagonistic'; see Connor (1992b, p. 1).

24 Frey and Pommerehne (1989, ch. 6) show a relationship between auction prices for artworks and the standing of the artist according to the consensus views of art critics, other things being equal.

25 Lichfield (1988, p. 169).

26 I use the term 'art museum' here as distinct from 'art gallery' to identify the (sometimes blurred) differentiation between a public and a commercial enterprise. Much of this discussion also applies, *mutatis mutandis*, to science museums, though I confine my attention here essentially to the arts. For an illuminating account of the rise and rise of the art museum in the nineteenth and early twentieth centuries, a period which gave rise to many of the great institutions we know today, see Lorente (1998).

27 For overviews of the economics of museums and art galleries and for collections of papers on the subject, see Frey and Pommerehne (1989, ch. 5); Feldstein (1991); Heilbrun and Gray (1993, ch. 10); O'Hagan (1998, ch. 7); Johnson and Thomas (1998), and the special issue of the *Journal of Cultural Economics*, 22 (2–3) (1998). On the confrontation between economic analysis and curatorial values, see Grampp (1996) and Cannon-Brookes (1996); for a vigorous response to the latter, see Peacock (1998a).

28 For an illustration of an economic evaluation of a specific museum see Martin (1994) who estimates the economic value of the Musée de la Civilisation in Quebec, Canada.

29 See Carnegie and Wolnizer (1995); Carman (1996); Carman *et al.* (1999).

30 Note that we shall be returning to the nature and estimation of these benefits in the context of cultural heritage in chapter 5.

31 Of course not all museums strive for such an ambience, and some may achieve exactly the opposite.

32 See further in Davis (1990) and especially Newhouse (1998).

3   Cultural capital and sustainability

NINA: the only living life is in the past and the future . . . the present is an interlude . . . strange interlude in which we call on past and future to bear witness we are living.   (Eugene O'Neill, *Strange Interlude*, 1927[1])

Introduction

One means of bridging the gap between economics and culture is to propose an approach to representing cultural phenomena that captures their essential characteristics in a manner comprehensible within both an economic and a broadly cultural discourse. Such a means is provided by the concept of 'cultural capital'. Although this term is in use in sociology to describe certain characteristics of individuals, it is gaining acceptance in economics in a somewhat different form, much closer to the ideas about capital which have long been standard in economic thought. As we shall see below, cultural capital in an economic sense can provide a means of representing culture which enables both tangible and intangible manifestations of culture to be articulated as long-lasting stores of value and providers of benefits for individuals and groups. It can be suggested that both cultural theorists and economists should be able to recognise these sorts of attributes in culture from their respective disciplinary standpoints; if so, the concept of cultural capital can provide a common basis from which the analysis of both economic and cultural aspects of cultural goods, services, behaviour and other phenomena can proceed.

In this chapter we put forward the idea of cultural capital by showing how it can be defined alongside other forms of capital in economics, and how it fits in theoretical terms into an economic and cultural universe. Its long-lasting characteristics reflecting the continuing or evolutionary nature of culture can be thought of within a framework provided by the concept of sustainability, an area of analysis where intergenerational issues are especially prominent. Since no single definition is adequate to capture the range of characteristics embraced by the notion of sustainability, we propose a series of principles or criteria by which sustainability can be judged when applied to cultural phenomena. Overall, the ideas developed in this chapter will provide a useful basis for our discussions of culture in development and of cultural heritage to follow in chapters 4 and 5, respectively.[2]

What is 'cultural capital'?

Let us first take an intuitive approach to this question. Accepting the definitions of 'culture' put forward in chapter 1 above, we can suggest that many manifestations of culture so defined can be interpreted as capital assets. When culture is expressed in tangible form – for example as a work of art or a heritage building – the notion of culture as asset is readily comprehensible. Similarly, if broader cultural phenomena, such as traditions, language, customs, etc. are thought of as intangible assets in the possession of the group to which they refer, they too can be brought into the same framework. In chapter 2 we identified the key element in separating cultural from economic phenomena as being one of value formation. Thus we can distinguish cultural capital from 'ordinary' economic assets by appeal to the different sorts of value to which they give rise. Cultural capital gives rise to both cultural and economic value, 'ordinary' capital provides only economic value.

How does this concept fit with conventional interpretations of capital within economics? Contemporary economic analysis identifies three broad forms of capital.[3] The first, *physical capital* – meaning the stock of real goods such as plant, machines, buildings etc. which contribute to the production of further goods – has been known and discussed since the very beginnings of economics. In more recent times, Gary Becker and others have identified a second type of capital, *human capital*, arising from the realisation that the embodiment of skills and experience in people represented a capital stock that is every bit as important as physical capital in producing output in the economy.[4] More recently still, following the increasing awareness of the effect of environmental problems on economic activity, economists have come to accept the phenomenon of *natural capital*, meaning the stock of renewable and non-renewable resources provided by nature, and including the ecological processes governing their existence and use. Although the idea of 'nature' as a provider of services can be seen to derive from the classical political economists' interest in land as a factor of production, and was important also to Marshall and the neoclassicists, as Salah El Serafy points out, the formal analysis of natural capital has been very recent, lying at the core of the emerging subdiscipline of ecological economics.[5] *Cultural capital*, as we shall now proceed to define it more precisely, can take its place as a fourth type of capital, clearly distinguishable from the other three.

Adopting the interpretations of economic and cultural value developed in chapter 2, we can define cultural capital as an asset which embodies, stores or provides cultural value in addition to whatever economic value it may possess. As in the case of other types of capital, it is important to distinguish between stocks and flows. The *stock* of cultural capital, generally or specifically delineated, refers to the quantity of such capital in existence at a given time, measured in terms of any appropriate unit of account such as physical quantities or an aggregate valuation. This capital stock gives rise over time to a *flow* of services which may be consumed or may be used to produce further goods and services.

As indicated above, cultural capital exists in two forms. First, it may be *tangible*, occurring in the form of buildings, locations, sites, precincts, artworks such as paintings and sculptures, artefacts and so on. It includes, but is not limited to, tangible cultural heritage. Such capital may have much the same outward characteristics as physical or human-made capital: like physical capital, it is created by human activity, lasts for a period of time, can decay if not maintained, gives rise to a flow of services over time, can increase through investment of current resources in its manufacture, can generally be bought and sold and has a financial value that could be measured. Its cultural value either as stock or flow could in turn be identified using the sorts of indicators or criteria of cultural value referred to in our earlier discussions.

Secondly, cultural capital may be *intangible*, occurring as intellectual capital in the form of ideas, practices, beliefs and values which are shared by a group, in line with the constituent interpretation of culture put forward in chapter 1. This form of cultural capital exists also in the form of artworks such as music and literature which occur as public goods. The stock of intellectual capital thus defined can decay through neglect or can increase through new investment. It, too, gives rise to a flow of services over time. Both the maintenance of existing intellectual capital and the creation of new capital of this type requires resources.

To summarise so far, we can envisage both tangible and intangible cultural capital existing at a given point in time as a capital stock valued in both economic and cultural terms in its own right as an asset. This stock gives rise to a flow of capital services which may enter final consumption directly, or which may be combined with other inputs to produce further goods and services having both economic and cultural value. These further goods and services may themselves enter final consumption or may in turn be combined with further inputs, and so on. At any stage in this production sequence the cultural goods and services produced may themselves add to the capital stock, augmenting its level or value at the start of the next period. By the same token the capital stock may decay over time and may require the expenditure of resources for maintenance. The net effect of all of these additions to and subtractions from the capital stock within a given time period indicates the net investment/disinvestment in cultural capital during the period, measurable in both economic and cultural terms, and determines the opening value of the stock at the beginning of the next period.

Let us now look more closely at economic and cultural value, and at the relationship between them, in the context of cultural capital. Consider an item of tangible cultural capital as defined above, such as a historic building. The asset may have economic value which derives simply from its physical existence as a building and irrespective of its cultural worth. But the economic value of the asset is likely to be augmented, perhaps significantly so, because of its cultural value. Thus we can see a causal connection: cultural value may give rise to economic value. So, for example, individuals may be willing to pay for the embodied cultural content of this asset by offering a price higher than that which they would offer for the physical entity alone. In other words, a historic building may embody 'pure' cultural value, according to one or more of the scales proposed earlier, and also have an economic value as an asset derived from both its physical and its cultural content. The asset value of other forms of tangible cultural capital may be construed similarly, although the significance of the elements may differ. Artworks such as paintings, for example, may derive much of their economic value from their cultural content, since their purely physical worth (some bits of canvas, some pieces of wood) is likely to be negligible. Similar remarks can be made about the economic and cultural value of the flow of goods and services that tangible cultural capital assets provide.

Intangible cultural capital, on the other hand, has a different relationship between cultural and economic value. The stock of existing music and literature, for example, or the stock of cultural mores and beliefs, or the stock of language, have immense cultural value, but no economic value since they cannot be traded as assets, except insofar as rights to future earnings (e.g. literary or music royalties) can be bought and sold. Rather, it is the flows of services to which these stocks give rise which yield both the cultural and the economic value of the assets. Again, some part of the economic value of such flows exists in purely physical or mechanical terms as public goods demanded for purely economic reasons – the utilitarian function of language, for example, or the use of background music in hotel lobbies and elevators. But, again, the economic value of the flow of services from these cultural assets is likely to be augmented, in most of their uses, as a result of their cultural worth.

These considerations suggest that, since cultural and economic value are independently determined, but the one has an influence on the other, a ranking of individual or collective valuations of cultural capital assets (or of the flow of services they provide) by cultural and by economic value respectively will be likely to yield similar but by no means identical preference orderings. In other words, as we noted earlier, there is likely to be a correlation between the cultural and economic value of items of cultural capital, but the relationship will be by no means a perfect one.[6]

Other usages of the term 'cultural capital'

In popular jargon, the most likely context in which the phrase 'cultural capital' will be heard is with reference to the claims of various cities to pre-eminence in general or specific cultural status. Thus Florence sees itself as the cultural capital of Tuscany, and maybe even of the whole of Italy, while London or New York might vie for the title of cultural capital of the world with respect, say, to live theatre, and so on. But turning to scholarly usage of the term, we can observe that it has been put to service, with greater or lesser degrees of rigour, in several different discourses. As noted in the introduction to this chapter, the most established use is probably in sociology and cultural studies following Pierre Bourdieu, who identifies individuals as possessing cultural capital if they have acquired competence in society's high-status culture. According to Bourdieu, this sort of cultural capital exists in three forms: an *embodied* state – i.e. as a long-lasting disposition of the individual's mind and body; in an *objectified* state, when cultural capital is turned into cultural goods such as 'pictures, books, dictionaries, instruments, machines, etc.';[7] and in an *institutionalised* state, when the embodied cultural capital is recognised in the form of, say, an academic credential. For Bourdieu, the embodied state is the most important. He notes that 'most of the properties of cultural capital can be deduced from the fact that, in its fundamental state, it is linked to the body and presupposes embodiment'.[8] It is thus clear that the concept of cultural capital as developed by Bourdieu is, in its individualistic form, very close to, if not identical with, that of human capital in economics.

Bourdieu's ideas have extended into a number of neighbouring fields, such as literary criticism, where his concept of cultural capital has been invoked in the identification of the literary 'canon'. Similarly, and relatedly, the Marxist concept of cultural commodity production entails an interpretation of cultural capital that has ramified through significant areas of sociology and political economy. So, for example, a Marxist view of transnational corporations sees them as creating capital from culture.[9] In addition, the idea of a society's culture as somehow comprising a capital stock has long had currency in anthropological studies, as evidenced, for example, in analyses of the commodification and valuation of 'primitive' art.[10]

Much of the empirical testing of the sociological concept of cultural capital has looked at the aggregate impacts of education and of Bourdieu's notion of 'habitus' as affecting economic and social outcomes. At this level, when relationships between individuals and groups in society are invoked, the idea of cultural capital becomes entwined with that of social capital, as identified not only by Bourdieu but also elsewhere in the sociological literature, notably by James Coleman.[11] This concept is somewhat difficult to define but it essentially depends on the existence of social networks and relationships of trust between citizens.[12] In a celebrated study, Robert Putnam demonstrated the way in which such social infrastructure has contributed to economic growth in parts of rural Italy.[13] While it is clear that the phenomena encompassed by the idea of social capital are real enough, and do affect economic behaviour in identifiable ways, there is some doubt as to whether social capital should be regarded as a form of capital or rather as something else. Elinor Ostrom points to key differences between physical and social capital, namely that social capital does not wear out with use but with disuse, it is difficult to see and measure and it cannot readily be constructed through deliberate intervention;[14] she sees social capital as an essential complement to physical and human capital. Economists such as Kenneth Arrow and Robert Solow, on the other hand, see these sorts of differences as indicating that social capital is not really capital at all; Arrow suggests abandonment of the capital metaphor in this context, partly on the grounds that social capital does not involve deliberate sacrifice of present for future benefit.[15]

In the end both the Bourdieu concept of cultural capital and at least some interpretations of social capital relate to characteristics of individuals, and as such come close to the idea of human capital as used in economics. Thus, for example, when Richard Zweigenhaft examines the

effect of cultural and social capital on the performance of Harvard
graduates, using 'cultural capital' to mean various forms of knowledge
and skills, and 'social capital' to mean knowing the right people,
networking, etc. the parallel with human capital is almost complete.[16]
Nevertheless, given the close connection between cultural capital as
identified in sociology and human capital as understood by economists,
it is useful to ask whether the connections stretch back the other way –
that is, to what extent human capital has been seen by economists to
embrace culture. Sometimes definitions of human capital within economics explicitly include culture as one of its components. So, for
example, Robert Costanza and Herman Daly speak of human capital as
'the stock of education, skills, *culture* and knowledge stored in human
beings themselves'.[17] Some economists have explicitly extended human
capital to include culture in seeking empirical explanations of various
phenomena. For example, in examining wage differentials among immi-
grant and native-born workers in US labour markets, several writers
have attributed to 'culture' the unexplained earnings gap remaining after
the usual human capital variables have been accounted for. In reviewing
some of these studies, however, Stephen Woodbury concludes that
bundling culture into the human capital framework in this way empties
the theory of empirical content because no independent assessment of
'culture' is possible.[18]

Finally in our brief review of existing usages of the term 'cultural
capital', we consider the proposition put forward by Fikret Berkes and
Carl Folke. These authors consider the relationships between natural and
physical capital from a systems perspective, and argue that a 'third
dimension' is required to account for the ways through which natural
capital can be used to create physical capital.[19] Berkes and Folke use the
term 'cultural capital' to refer to the adaptive capacity of human
populations to deal with and modify the natural environment. The
concept has moral, ethical and religious overtones. Despite the fact that
the paper does not refer to human capital as such, it would seem that the
authors' idea of cultural capital bears at least some resemblance to this
phenomenon, since it relates to innate and/or acquired characteristics of
human beings that affect their productive capacities in both qualitative
and quantitative terms. Given the specificity of Berkes' and Folke's use
of the term cultural capital, referring exclusively to humankind's relationship with the natural environment, it is perhaps unfortunate that they did
not accept instead their alternative terminology of 'adaptive capital',
even though it was less suitable to the systems perspective from which
they were writing. In the end it would seem preferable to allow the term
'cultural' a somewhat wider range.

Parallels between cultural and natural capital

The definition of cultural capital has much in common with the definition of natural capital at a similar stage in its development. Let us briefly review the development of that definition in the ecological economics literature.

The origins of considering the environment as capital go back in fact to the nineteenth-century political economists such as David Ricardo and Thomas Malthus, who were concerned with the contribution of agricultural land to the production of goods and services in the economy. But contemporary formulation of the concept of natural capital to describe 'the free gifts of nature' dates from the late 1980s and the emergence of the subdiscipline of ecological economics during the 1990s. The elements of natural capital are now generally agreed as comprising four components[20]: (i) renewable natural resources such as fish and forest stocks; (ii) non-renewable resources such as oil and mineral deposits; (iii) the ecosystems which support and maintain the quality of land, air and water; and (iv) the maintenance of a vast genetic library, referred to as biodiversity. Within these concepts we can distinguish between the *stock* of natural capital (the fish and forest populations, the mineral deposits, etc.) and the *flow* of environmental services they provide (the harvesting of fish and timber, the recycling of waste materials, erosion control, aesthetic services of landscape, etc.). In some formulations the flow of services is referred to as 'natural income', reflecting the capital/income distinction made earlier this century by Irving Fisher.[21]

The parallels between natural and cultural capital now start to take shape. Tangible cultural capital which has been inherited from the past can be seen to have something in common with natural resources, which have also been provided to us as an endowment; natural resources have come from the beneficence of nature, cultural capital has arisen from the creative activities of human kind. Both impose a duty of care on the present generation, the essence of the sustainability problem to be dealt with below. Further, a similarity can be seen between the function of natural ecosystems in supporting and maintaining the 'natural balance' and the function of what might be referred to as 'cultural ecosystems' in supporting and maintaining the cultural life and vitality of human civilisation. Finally, the notion of diversity, so important in the natural world, has a perhaps even more significant role to play within cultural systems. It is a characteristic of most cultural goods that they are unique; all original artworks, for example, are differentiable from all others, all historic buildings and sites are individually identifiable as distinct. Thus cultural diversity is perhaps even more far-reaching than is diversity in nature.

Apart from the matter of sustainability, there are two important issues raised by the debate over natural capital which are of relevance in the cultural context. The first relates to valuation of capital stocks. In natural capital theory, the valuation question has been a matter of considerable controversy. A recent attempt at quantifying global natural capital attracted much criticism from commentators who objected to alleged double counting and to the apparently infinite price being placed on several items.[22] Nevertheless, the exercise was fruitful if for no other reason than that it focused attention on the difficulty of 'pricing the invaluable'. Similarly, efforts to value the stock of cultural capital are likely to be fraught with danger, and will be compounded by the fact that not only an economic measure but also some form of cultural valuation will need to be sought.

The second issue relates to the relationship among different forms of capital, and the extent to which one is substitutable for another. In the natural capital debate, a great deal of attention has been devoted to the possibilities or otherwise for substituting physical for natural capital. Essentially the argument is that if human-made capital can produce the same goods and services as natural capital, then we need not be so concerned about maintaining levels of natural capital in the future (e.g. preserving stocks of exhaustible resources) since physical capital can be substituted for it. Positions taken in this debate range from zero substitutability at one end through to perfect substitutability at the other. The likely consensus is that while some aspects of the services provided by natural capital may be able to be replaced by manufactured capital, there are other aspects that cannot.[23] In the case of cultural capital, provision of many of the *economic* functions of cultural assets is readily imaginable through substitution by physical capital: the services of shelter, amenity, etc. provided by a historic building could as well be provided by another structure without cultural content. However, since by definition cultural capital is distinguished from physical capital by its embodiment and production of *cultural* value, there would be expected to be zero substitutability between cultural and physical capital in respect of its cultural output.[24]

Sustainability and cultural capital

A view of culture as capital invites consideration of the long term, that is of the dynamic, evolutionary, intertemporal and intergenerational aspects of culture, its supply and demand, its production and consumption. A theoretical framework for such a view is provided by the concept of sustainability, a term most frequently heard in the context of the environment, where the word 'sustainable' is generally linked with the word 'development'. *Sustainable development* marries the ideas of sustainable *economic* development, meaning development that will not slow down or wither away but will be, in some sense, self-perpetuating, and *ecological* sustainability, meaning the preservation and enhancement of a range of environmental values through the maintenance of ecosystems in the natural world. Most thinking and writing about sustainable development over the last decade acknowledges its debt, explicitly or implicitly, to the definition of the term put forward by the World Commission on Environment and Development ('the Brundtland Commission'), which specified sustainable development as being 'development that meets the needs of the present without compromising the ability of future generations to meet their own needs'.[25] Thus a key element of sustainability is the question of intergenerational transfers and the decision-making that surrounds them.

We examine more closely the relationship between culture and sustainable development as such in chapter 4. Here our task is to consider how the notion of sustainability can provide a means of extending our understanding of cultural capital. The aim can be stated as follows. Cultural capital exists as a source of cultural goods and services which provide benefits both now and in the future. As individuals or as a society, we can allow cultural capital to deteriorate over time, we can maintain it, or we can augment it, in short we can *manage* it in a way that suits our individual or collective purpose. What principles should guide our management decisions? By articulating more precisely what sustainability entails when applied to culture, such a set of principles emerges. We do so in this chapter in regard to cultural capital defined in its most general form, relating to definitions of culture in both constituent and functional senses; in chapter 5 we return to these principles and apply them specifically to the assessment of cultural heritage projects.

We identify six principles, dimensions or criteria which define sustainability in its application to cultural capital:

Material and non-material wellbeing

The flow of cultural goods and services produced from cultural capital provides both material and non-material benefits for people as individuals and as members of society. A means of identifying the value of those benefits is provided by the specification of economic and cultural value as their twin components. A first criterion for judging sustainability, then, is the production of *material* benefits in the form of direct utility to consumers, deriving from these economic and cultural value sources. In addition, we might also identify a more general class of *non-material* benefits flowing from cultural capital, the wider public-good benefits accruing to the collective as a result of cultural capital that might be summarised as enhancements to the quality of life to which culture gives rise. We shall return to the nature of these benefits in more detail in chapter 5.

Intergenerational equity and dynamic efficiency

The term *intergenerational equity*, or *intertemporal distributive justice*, is used to refer to fairness in the distribution of welfare, utility or resources between generations. Although the principles of intergenerational equity can be applied to relations between any series of generations at any time, practical interest in it has focused, not surprisingly, on the concern among those of us alive today for the wellbeing of future generations. Intergenerational equity can be considered in relation to cultural capital because the stock of cultural capital is what we have inherited from our forebears and which we hand on to future generations. Intertemporal equity issues arise in regard to access to that capital and to the products of that capital. Equity of access to cultural capital can be analysed in the same way as equity in the intergenerational distribution of benefits from any other sort of capital.

In economics intergenerational equity is defined with reference to the maintenance of an equal level of welfare or utility between generations, expressed as *per capita* consumption, or endowment of resources or capital stock. *Prima facie*, therefore, the intergenerational equity dilemma is a classic intertemporal allocation problem – i.e. a choice between present and future consumption. Casting this problem as one involving fairness or justice makes some economists uneasy, because of their unwillingness to make or assume value judgements on behalf of others; such hesitancy derives from a view of economics (especially neoclassical economics) as an objective or value-free science. So some economists have framed the intertemporal resource allocation question as one of efficiency rather than equity,[26] requiring maximisation of the net present value of benefits which the resources generate. In a series of papers, John Hartwick and Robert Solow have independently shown that if the net income or 'rent' from natural resources can be invested in a certain way, efficient growth paths for an economy can be achieved. David Pearce and Giles Atkinson carry this proposition further by developing a sustainability test for an economy which requires the total capital stock (physical plus natural) to remain constant over time.[27]

However, framing the problem of intergenerational resource allocation in this way raises difficulties, in particular the proper choice of discount rate to apply to future net benefit streams. Even if the conceptual problems of whether the rate is a time preference or an opportunity cost indicator are solved, the determination of a single number to encapsulate the complex processes involved is something of a tall order. Furthermore, if projects are long-lived, involving benefits in the far-off future, the use of a constant discount rate may be inappropriate, and a case may exist for a discount rate which declines over time in order to give greater weight to more distant effects.[28] But, more importantly, it can be argued that seeing intertemporal resource allocation solely as an efficiency question does not dispose of the equity issue entirely. For example, any positive discount rate, however low, will mean that some future benefits will be effectively reduced to zero, inevitably giving what many would regard in ethical terms as undue weight to the preferences of the present generation. Thus there is an inescapable question relating to the fairness of alternative outcomes that cannot be dealt with by an analysis looking only at efficiency.

There are several ways in which the ethical basis of intergenerational judgements can be approached. A utilitarian view might look to the maximisation of total social utility, where individuals' ethical positions are reflected in the measure of their own welfare; in such a case, admitting altruism, disinterested demand, bequest values and other such variables into individual utility functions would allow the self-interest of people alive today to incorporate their interest in the wellbeing of later generations. Alternatively a contractarian approach following John Rawls might be proposed, in which members of future generations are given equal weight in Rawls' 'original position' – i.e. the vantage point from which the choice of a social welfare function is viewed.[29] Nevertheless, despite the theoretical appeal of these sorts of paradigms, they hardly provide operational decision rules to guide social choice when intergenerational equity problems arise.

The foregoing discussion has been framed in terms of intergenerational issues in the treatment of natural resources. How do those issues fall out when applied to cultural capital? To begin with, we can note that both the Hartwick–Solow and Pearce–Atkinson models assume perfect substitutability between natural and physical capital. However, when it comes to cultural capital, this assumption will not hold, because by definition only cultural capital can give rise to cultural value, as we noted above. Indeed because the critical difference between cultural and other forms of capital lies in its generation of cultural as well as economic value, the application of efficiency criteria to intertemporal investment decisions in cultural capital will be incomplete if the generation of only economic value is considered. A proper consideration of such decisions raises the prospect of a dual evaluation of the time-stream of benefits, with both economic and cultural benefits being taken into account, and with perhaps parallel cost-benefit appraisals being adopted, couched on the one side in the familiar economic terms, on the other in the much less straightforward terrain of cultural valuation.

The intergenerational question as an issue of equity rather than efficiency has the same resonances when applied to cultural capital as it does in the context of natural resources. It has to do with the moral or ethical obligation that might be assumed by the present generation on behalf of the future. In cultural terms, this means ensuring that future generations are not denied access to cultural resources and are not deprived of the cultural underpinnings of their economic, social and cultural life, as a result of the short-sighted or selfish actions of those of us alive today.

Intragenerational equity

This principle asserts the rights of the present generation to fairness in access to cultural resources and to the benefits flowing from cultural capital, viewed across social classes, income groups, locational categories and so on. Ideas of equity or fairness, of course, play an important role in general economic and social policy, although they have become overshadowed in recent years as a result of preoccupations in policy-making with questions of economic efficiency. Indeed it can be suggested that in the cultural arena matters such as the distribution of cultural resources, access to cultural participation, the provision of cultural services for minority or disadvantaged groups and so on, are all aspects of equity or fairness in the conduct of cultural life that may be overlooked in the pursuit of efficiency-related outcomes. The principle of intragenerational equity thus requires attention to these questions, if sustainable use of cultural resources is to be achieved.

Maintenance of diversity

We have noted already that, just as biodiversity is seen as significant in the natural world, so also is cultural diversity important in maintaining cultural systems. The diversity of ideas, beliefs, traditions and values yields a flow of cultural services which is quite distinct from the services provided by the individual components. Diversity is an important attribute of cultural capital particularly because it has the capacity to yield new capital formation. For example, to the extent that creative works are inspired by the existing stock of cultural resources, a greater diversity of resources will lead to the creation of more varied and more culturally valuable artistic works in the future.[30]

Precautionary principle

As a general proposition the precautionary principle states that decisions which may lead to irreversible change should be approached with extreme caution and from a strongly risk-averse position, because of the imponderability of the consequences of such decisions. In the natural world this principle is invoked in regard to decisions that might result, for example, in the extinction of species. Similarly the destruction of an item of cultural capital may be a case of irreversible loss if the item is unique and irreplaceable; in such a case the precautionary principle would appropriately be applied if the item were considered of sufficient value to warrant it. The principle does not assert that irrevocable decisions are *never* to be taken in regard to cultural capital, but rather that it is appropriate to exercise a higher level of care in cases where irreversibility is involved, bearing in mind the other principles of sustainability which assist in determining the decision.

Maintenance of cultural systems and recognition of interdependence

An overarching principle of sustainability is the proposition that no part of any system exists independently of other parts. In this respect it can be suggested that cultural capital makes a contribution to long-term sustainability which is similar in principle to that of natural capital. It is now well understood that natural ecosystems are essential to supporting the real economy, and that neglect of natural capital through overuse of exhaustible resources or unsustainable exploitation of renewable capital stocks may cause such systems to break down, with consequent loss of welfare and economic output. A parallel proposition can be put in regard to cultural capital. As we shall see in more detail in subsequent chapters, it is becoming clearer that cultural 'ecosystems' underpin the operations of the real economy, affecting the way people behave and the choices they make. Neglect of cultural capital by allowing heritage to deteriorate, by failing to sustain the cultural values that provide people with a sense of identity and by not undertaking the investment needed to maintain and increase the stock of both tangible and intangible cultural capital, will likewise place cultural systems in jeopardy and may cause them to break down, with consequent loss of welfare and economic output. Thus this final principle, in essence, draws together the entire concept of sustainability when applied to cultural capital, providing an overall framework within which the other more specific principles can be seen to operate.

Conclusions

This chapter has put forward the idea of cultural capital as a sort of fundamental organising principle for conceptualising cultural phenomena in terms recognisable in both an economic and a cultural discourse, and for identifying their various manifestations. We have spelled out some of the characteristics of cultural capital which will be helpful for analytical purposes, and we have gone on to investigate the application of notions of sustainability to cultural capital, deriving a set of principles or criteria by which the sustainability characteristics of cultural capital might be judged.

There are a number of ways in which the concepts of cultural capital and sustainability might now be applied. In the next two chapters we will take up two such avenues. First, in chapter 4 we will be considering the role of culture in economic development. Given that the notion of sustainable development permeates much of contemporary thinking about growth, structural change and social progress in the developing world, it is not surprising that a cultural dimension to these processes can be brought into focus through the use of the same sustainability approach. Second, the matter of cultural heritage provides an obvious specific application of cultural capital ideas and sustainability principles. Already heritage projects are beginning to be evaluated as investment proposals amenable to the sorts of appraisal procedures applied elsewhere in the economy. We will look at the prospects and difficulties in treating heritage as sustainable cultural capital in chapter 5.

Notes

1   Quotation is from O'Neill (1988, II, p. 784).
2   For further discussion of cultural capital and sustainability issues, see Throsby (1997c, 1999).
3   Not including 'financial capital', which is a different form in which capital is held rather than a different type of capital in the productive sense.
4   See especially Schultz (1963, 1970); Becker (1964).
5   See El Serafy (1991) and further in Costanza (1991); Jansson et al. (1994).
6   The direction of causation suggested here is from cultural to economic value – i.e. items of higher cultural worth will generally be accorded a higher economic evaluation. It may be noted, however, that Veblen (1973) proposed the possibility of a reverse causation – i.e. that some people will judge an item's cultural worth according to its price, with a higher price indicating greater aesthetic value.
7   Bourdieu (1986, p. 243).
8   Bourdieu (1986, p. 244).
9   For a treatment of the literary canon as cultural capital, see Guillory (1993); on transnationals and culture, see Ryan (1992).
10 As discussed, for example, in relation to trade in the art of the Côte d'Ivoire by Steiner (1994).
11 See Coleman (1988).
12 For a discussion of definitional problems, see Serageldin and Grootaert (2000).
13 See Putnam et al. (1993); Helliwell and Putnam (2000).
14 Ostrom (1995, 2000, p. 179).
15 See Arrow (2000, p. 4); Solow (2000).
16 See Zweigenhaft (1993); a further illustration is contained in Borocz and Southworth (1996). In Gary Becker's book (1996), ideas about social relationships, networking, etc. are developed further in a human capital context. Becker makes no reference to Bourdieu in this volume, although it is known that he and Bourdieu have discussed informally the similarities between their respective concepts of human and cultural capital. For further reading on these matters see Mahar et al. (1990); Robbins (1991, p. 154).
17 Costanza and Daly (1992, p. 38, emphasis added).
18 See Woodbury (1993); an example of a wage differentials study where cultural differences are discussed is Chiswick (1983).
19 See Berkes and Folke (1992).
20 See El Serafy (1991); Costanza and Daly (1992); Folke et al. (1994); Barbier (1998, pp. 65–95).
21 See Fisher (1927, pp. 51 ff.).
22 The exercise was carried out by Costanza et al. (1997); for criticism, see El Serafy (1998) and Toman (1998).
23 For a discussion of substitution between natural and other capital, see Kaufmann (1995).
24 Note that some counter-examples could be suggested – for example, where a

historic building is replaced by a new one which has little or no cultural value initially but which, for one reason or another, acquires cultural status over time.

25 World Commission on Environment and Development (1987, p. 43).

26 Thus Solow (1986, p. 142) suggests that 'whether productive capacity should be transmitted across generations in the form of mineral deposits or capital equipment or technological knowledge is more a matter of efficiency than of equity'.

27 See Solow (1974, 1986); Hartwick (1977, 1978a, 1978b); Pearce and Atkinson (1993).

28 For discussions of non-constant discounting, see Harvey (1994); Weitzman (1998).

29 See Rawls (1972); for the treatment of future generations in this context, see Page (1977, pp. 200–6) and Becker (1982).

30 Note that Lian and Oneal (1997) show no significant relationship between cultural diversity and economic performance in a cross-national study; however, the measure they use for diversity is one of very limited scope.

4   Culture in economic development

Dedicated development experts, keen on feeding the hungry and banishing poverty, are often impatient with what they take to be premature focussing on culture in a world of manifold material deprivation. How can you (so the argument runs) talk about culture . . . while people succumb to starvation or undernutrition or easily preventable disease? The motivation behind this criticism cannot be dismissed, but the artificially separatist – and stage-wise – view of progress is unreal and unsustainable. Even economics cannot work, as Adam Smith noted, without understanding the role of 'moral sentiments', and Bertold Brecht's note of cynicism in his *Threepenny Opera*, 'Food comes first, then morals', is more a statement of despair than of an advocated priority.   (Amartya Sen, *Culture, Freedom and Independence*, 1998[1])

Introduction

It is a striking fact that one of the leading scholarly journals in economics concerned with the economic problems of developing countries bears the title *Economic Development and Cultural Change*. Few of the articles published in this journal deal directly with culture as such. Yet the acknowledgement is there in the title that in some fundamental sense culture, however it is to be interpreted, underlies the development process and will have some important relationships with economic behaviour in poor countries. The implication is that strategies to alleviate poverty in the Third World and to promote economic advancement will need to have regard for the processes of cultural change which may be critical in determining their success or failure.

In the analysis of economic progress in the *industrialised* world, however, a role for culture in influencing or conditioning economic performance is scarcely recognised. Economic growth, measured in terms of rising material standards of living per head of population, remains a central economic policy objective in all developed countries. Yet the growth process as constructed in contemporary economic analysis has been interpreted solely in terms of economic variables.[2] This may be due in part to the supposition that these variables can capture any cultural influences of importance to economic growth, without need for further specific elaboration of what those influences are. So, for example, it may be thought that the inclusion of human capital as an explanatory variable in economic growth models, allowing technological change to be endogenised, may be sufficient to represent important cultural influences, because those influences will be manifested as characteristics of the individuals making up the labour force.[3] Alternatively, the neglect of culture in explaining economic performance may simply reflect the fact that, to economists, economic variables are all that matter, in other words that so comprehensive a picture of both the causes and the outcomes of economic growth can be gained by consideration of phenomena such as productivity, technology, industrial transition, factor shares, levels of investment, capital flows, etc. that nothing more is required. Indeed this econocentric position might be seen as a further example of the reification of the economy referred to in chapter 1, where the economy is seen as having a life of its own, determined only by, and responsive only to, economic forces.

This chapter considers the role of culture in the process of economic development in both industrialised and developing countries, using 'culture' here in the broad constituent sense of ways of living rather than in the more specific sense of cultural activity (we will be returning to the latter question in chapter 7 where we deal with the cultural industries). The influence of culture on economic performance is considered first by reviewing the relatively small amount of work which attempts to bring cultural factors into an explanation of the relative growth and decline of different economies. We then discuss recent efforts to think more fundamentally about what constitutes the idea of human development, efforts which place the development process squarely into a cultural milieu, and which have some implications for how economic policy might be reinterpreted in a development environment. Finally this chapter looks again at the issue of sustainability, given that sustainable development has become a key concept in the operational world of development assistance. How does culture fit into such a picture?

Culture in economic performance

If we accept the broadly based definition of culture put forward in chapter 1 – that culture can be seen as a set of values, beliefs, traditions, customs, etc. which serve to identify and bind a group together – then it is not difficult to propose that culture will affect the way individuals in the group think and act, and will also have a significant effect on the way the group as a whole behaves. Such a proposition can be put forward for a small group such as a corporation, where the group identity is built around a corporate spirit, or for a large group such as a nation, where shared values may include religious beliefs, social customs, inherited traditions and so on. In either case, an economic version of this proposition might be phrased in terms of the ways in which the group's identity and values shape individuals' preference patterns, and hence their economic behaviour.

It is then possible to suggest that culture may affect economic outcomes for the group in three broad directions. First, culture will perhaps affect economic *efficiency*, via the promotion of shared values within the group which condition the ways in which the group's members undertake the economic processes of production. For example, if these cultural values are conducive to more effective decision-making, to more rapid and varied innovation and to more adaptive behaviour in dealing with change, the economic productivity and dynamism of the group will be likely eventually to be reflected in better financial outcomes (in the case of the corporate enterprise) or in higher growth rates (in the case of the economy).

Secondly, culture may affect *equity* – for example, by inculcating shared moral principles of concern for others and hence encouraging the establishment of mechanisms by which that concern can be expressed. In the case of society as a whole, one significant aspect of this might be seen in intergenerational equity, if a moral obligation to provide for future generations is an accepted cultural value. In general, the effect of culture on equity will be seen in resource allocation decisions of the group directed at achieving equitable outcomes for its members.

Thirdly, culture may be seen as influencing or even as determining the economic and social *objectives* that the group decides to pursue. At the small group level, say that of the individual firm, the corporate culture may be one of concern and care for employees and their working conditions, and these values may mitigate the importance of profit-seeking or other economic goals in the firm's objectives. At the societal level, cultural values may be entirely in tune with, say, the pursuit of material progress, enabling criteria of macroeconomic achievement to be used to distinguish 'successful' from 'unsuccessful' societies.[4] The culture of other societies, on the other hand, may be such as to temper the pursuit of material reward in favour of non-material goals relating to various qualities of life, thus affecting the pace and direction of economic growth; in such cases the criteria defining 'successful' and 'unsuccessful' will be different from the former case.

By these three avenues, the effect of culture on individual behaviour will be reflected in collective outcomes. Thus, for example, at an aggregate level, we might observe the influence of culture on macroeconomic outcomes in terms of *efficiency indicators* such as the rate of growth of *per capita* GDP, rates of technological change, employment levels, rates and directions of structural change and so on, and in terms of *equity indicators* such as patterns of income distribution, social welfare programmes (especially care for the aged and sick), the supply of community services and (reflecting concern for intergenerational equity) the willingness to undertake long-term public investment programmes which may not be of much direct benefit to the present generation.

How far has economics come in viewing economic performance as being mediated by cultural influences along the lines sketched out above? Mark Casson has suggested that:

Economics is making progress in coming to terms with culture. Just a few years ago an economic theorist would typically claim that culture simply does not matter so far as economic performance is concerned; everything that matters is explained by prices – real prices in external markets and shadow prices in internal ones. Today the theorist is more likely to admit that culture matters, but to argue that it is something that economics cannot, or should not, attempt to explain.[5]

Casson goes on to argue that such defeatism is unwarranted, and that indeed economic analysis can make progress in identifying the influences that culture has on economic performance and in quantifying their effects. His own work attempts to specify cultural variables that affect interfirm relations such as cooperation and competition, and intrafirm relations such as organisational behaviour, and to postulate their effects on economic outcomes in different cultural settings.

Nevertheless scepticism among economists still persists, especially at the macroeconomic level where there remains considerable speculation as to whether and to what extent cultural factors have played a role in determining economic performance in different countries. For example, the sources of post-war growth in Japan, and more recently in South Korea, Taiwan, Hong Kong and Singapore, have been widely contested.

It is undeniable that economic factors in these countries have contributed significantly to their rapid growth, including stable macroeconomic management ('getting the fundamentals right'), promotion of competition, strong export orientation, pressure for 'catch-up' technological change, investment in human capital and so on. Even so there is disagreement among economists as to how far targeted industrial policies and strategic government interventions, which have been markedly contrary to the precepts of neoclassical orthodoxy, have been influential in promoting accelerated economic performance. Yet underlying all this, a more fundamental and pervasive role for culture can be proposed, in which certain cultural principles, derived to a significant extent from Confucianism, have helped to create the conditions for economic success. These factors include concern for the welfare and mutual esteem of the group, an achievement-oriented work ethic, regard for the importance of the family, a belief in the need for education, a respect for hierarchy and authority and so on.[6] Looking specifically at the Japanese case, we can observe that such factors as religion, family attitudes, patterns of cooperation within a culturally homogeneous society and so on, have shaped the public and corporate institutions of Japan and the manner of their operation; in this way can the cultural foundations of Japanese society be seen to have permeated all aspects of Japanese economic life.[7]

A difficulty besetting the resolution of various theoretical disputes about the effect of culture on economic performance is the availability of appropriate data for the testing of competing theories. Nevertheless, some progress in assembling and interpreting empirical information on culture and the economy is being made. For example, measurement of relevant cultural traits and their inclusion in cross-country models of economic growth is beginning to show more clearly the quantitative importance of the cultural context in which economic activity takes place. Ronald Inglehart, for example, tabulates a wide range of individual attitudes towards religion, work, the family and social issues across a broad sweep of countries and relates them to economic achievement.[8] In an alternative approach to empirical analysis, Hsin-Huang Michael Hsiao argues that cultural factors should not be interpreted as individual social behaviour *per se*, but should rather be viewed as a set of orderly, institutionalised cultural arrangements at the societal level.[9] Only at that level, he suggests, can one relate cultural behaviour to economic activities. Ultimately, however, whether the approach is micro or macro, neoclassical or institutional, the significant cultural influences do need to be carefully specified and measured if theories about their contribution to economic outcomes are to be properly tested.

Culture in Third World development

Let us turn from the functional role of culture in affecting economic performance to more fundamental issues of what economic development means and how culture, in its broad constituent sense, is implicated in that process. The conceptualisation of economic development as improvement in the material circumstances of the population ('all the necessaries and conveniences of life', in Adam Smith's phrase) dates back to the nineteenth century political economists and beyond. In the mid-twentieth century the theory of economic development as understood by economists still clearly equated growth with material progress. Thus Simon Kuznets wrote in 1966 that 'we identify the economic growth of nations as a sustained increase in per capita or per worker product'.[10] Gradually, however, this restricted view of what comprises progress in the developing world has been replaced with a concept of development reflecting a broader array of society's needs and its aspirations for improved standards of living. 'Development' in this more general sense certainly includes advancement in material wellbeing, measured as increases in *per capita* GDP or disposable incomes, but it also includes changes in an array of social indicators such as nutritional levels of the population, health status, literacy levels, educational participation, standards of public or welfare service provision and a number of non-material characteristics that fall under the heading of 'quality of life', including environmental indicators such as air and water quality. Furthermore, the fact that simple *per capita* measures taken across the whole population conceal inequities in the distribution of income and wealth has been widely recognised, and the importance of redistribution as an element in the development process acknowledged. By and large the theory of development as it stands in economics today has taken these wider interpretations on board. Nevertheless the focus remains clearly on material progress, especially of the poorest groups, as the principal indicator of advancement in the developing world.

Such a view is readily rationalised by reference to the basic needs of human beings for food, shelter and clothing, needs which it is said can be satisfied only by improvement in material circumstances. Further, it is argued that peoples' desires for enhancement in the various aspects of quality of life, including non-material characteristics such as environmental amenity, can be secured only through economic advance measured in material terms. Within this paradigm there is little or no role for culture, either as a mediating influence on the achievement of material progress or as an element in the structure of needs and wants felt by different societies. As a result, as Vernon Ruttan has remarked, cultural considerations have been cast into the 'underworld' of development thought and practice; writing in the late 1980s and early 1990s, he suggested that no development economist would agree to the proposition that cultural variables might be important in explaining political and economic development.[11] Since then, little seems to have changed. Mainstream texts in economic development have no time for culture; taking three such texts more or less at random,[12] an inquisitive reader can find no reference to culture in the subject indexes of any of them.

Despite this orthodoxy, however, there are clear signs of a shift underway in thinking about development, associated with a refocusing on human beings themselves as both the object of development and as the agents by which development is brought about. Thus a commodity-centred notion of *economic* development gives way to a people-centred strategy of *human* development. This shift in focus dates from the late 1980s when the United Nations Development Strategy for the 1990s adopted human development as its key focus, and the United Nations Development Program (UNDP) instituted its annual *Human Development Report*, the first of which appeared in 1991. The objective of human development is interpreted as being to expand the capabilities of people to lead the sorts of lives they desire. Amartya Sen has argued that, although increased output per head may enlarge such capabilities, the ultimate concern of development should not be output as such.[13] Keith Griffin has summarised Sen's argument as suggesting that the focus should be on enhancing

the ability of people to lead a long life, to enjoy good health, to have access to the world's stock of knowledge and information, to participate in the cultural life of their community, to have sufficient income to buy food, clothing and shelter, to participate in the decisions that directly affect their lives and their community, and so on. These are the things that matter – increasing the capabilities of people – and the enhancement of capabilities, not the enlargement of domestic (or material) product, should be the objective of development policy.[14]

A reorientation of development thinking along these lines has obvious cultural implications. People as the object and means of development do not exist in isolation. They interact in a variety of ways, and the framework within which this interaction occurs is provided by their culture – their shared beliefs, values, languages, traditions and so on which contextualise their daily lives. As indicated by the UN World Commission on Culture and Development (1995), re-conceptualising development in human terms brings culture in from the periphery of development thinking and places it in centre stage. In these circumstances notions of economic development, human development and cultural development might become absorbed into a more comprehensive theory of transformation in the developing world.[15]

The rigorous articulation of such a theory remains to be worked out, but it is possible to discern several likely features of a new development paradigm emerging in contemporary thought. First, it is unlikely that a new development model will incorporate strictly uni-directional causalities. Rather the interconnectedness of the elements of the model, with influences flowing in many directions at once, is likely to be emphasised. So, for example, the effect of cultural characteristics and aspirations of a given society on traditional economic variables such as output per worker is likely to be counter-balanced by an account of the influence of labour productivity on changing values. Secondly, and relatedly, it will be acknowledged that neither culture nor economy is a static thing but that each is constantly changing, such that relationships between variables are dynamic processes rather than fixed constants. Thirdly, no single model of development will be appropriate to all circumstances, but rather the differences in development paths between countries which have brought about different economic, social, cultural and institutional conditions, will determine how development prescriptions should be made in each particular case.[16] Fourthly, the new paradigm is likely to see pluralism, not uniformity, as an essential component, in particular an acknowledgement that human development begins at a local level where cultural diversity within and between communities is a vital manifestation of civilised human existence. Finally, a concomitant of pluralism is cultural freedom, both the collective freedom of societies to choose what sort of development they want, and the individual rights which are central to the idea of a free society. These freedoms presuppose an institutional structure, established by collective agreement and operating through the state and civil society, which provides the guarantee that such freedoms will be upheld. Thus attention to institutional arrangements is also likely to figure prominently in this development model.[17]

Within such a broadly based development framework we can suggest, as before, that a means of bringing economic and cultural concerns together is to return to the basic notion of value creation, where the generation of both economic and cultural value can be discerned as outcomes of a development process which balances the desire for material goods and services with the deeper needs and aspirations of human beings for cultural recognition, expression and fulfilment.

Culture, development and sustainability

An invocation of economic and cultural value as components of a development model, together with an acknowledgement of the long-term and evolutionary nature of both economic development and cultural change, render the idea of sustainability a natural frame of reference within which to integrate an analysis of economic and cultural development. Furthermore, given that one of the main connotations of sustainability has to do with the natural environment and its relationship to economic processes, and given the similarities between the natural and the cultural environment and between natural and cultural capital, it can be readily suggested that environmental interpretations of sustainability will have a counterpart in the cultural sphere. We have noted this already in drawing attention to the parallels between the ways in which the ecosystem supports the biosphere and the cultural infrastructure supports the social universe; both in turn provide essential sustenance for the economic life carried on in their respective domains.

The principles of sustainability which we put forward in chapter 3 when discussing cultural capital provide a basis on which to approach the broader issue of culture in economic development. Indeed it can be suggested that they might be capable of specifying a type or pattern of development that is 'culturally sustainable' in the same way as a somewhat similar set of criteria derived for the natural world provides a formula for defining ecologically and environmentally sustainable development. Thus we might accept the principles of material and non-material advancement, intergenerational and intragenerational equity, the maintenance of cultural diversity, the precautionary principle and the recognition of system interdependence as benchmarks against which to assess a cultural development process, strategy or specific project. In the overall scheme of things, a requirement that development be culturally sustainable would extend and complement an expectation that it should be ecologically sustainable.[18]

These sorts of ideas are beginning to be reflected in approaches to development policy in the international community. For example, at the Intergovernmental Conference on Cultural Policies for Development held in Stockholm in April 1998, the first policy objective agreed to by the 150 governments represented was to make cultural policy one of the key components of development strategy. It was proposed that governments should establish policies which recognise the pervasive importance of culture in development 'in such a way that they [the cultural policies] become one of the key components of endogenous and sustainable development'.[19]

Turning to the operational world of development assistance, we may note that the role of culture in sustainable development now appears to occupy the foreground of development thinking. In the World Bank, for instance, which disburses many millions of dollars annually in development loans to poor countries, the notion of sustainable development was introduced about a decade ago, opening out the development paradigm to encompass environmental and social concerns. But the further extension to culture is much more recent, responding in part to the broadly based transformation of thinking about economic development to which we referred in the previous section.[20] Let us review how culture is now being seen in the international arena of bilateral and multilateral development assistance. Three aspects can be highlighted.

First, if it is true that globalisation transmits materialist values and a standardised form of mass popular culture, it can be seen as a potential threat to local cultural differentiation, leading perhaps to social alienation and dislocation. Because of this, an increasingly important target of development assistance in any sector is the nurturing and build-up of local cultural values.[21] Secondly, in formulating specific programmes and projects, attention is now being paid to tailoring such interventions to local traditions and institutions, making use of local expertise and knowledge and emphasising cultural interactions within and between communities. In practical terms this is evidenced in a search for 'bottom-up' processes of strategy formulation and implementation. Thirdly, programmes particularly directed towards the poor can recognise how important cultural legitimation can be in energising communities and improving their self-esteem. Poverty reduction programmes may therefore be more effective if directed specifically towards cultural targets, promoting cultural expression and awareness as being concomitant with improvement in material circumstances.

These sorts of considerations are beginning to have an influence on the way in which development assistance organisations, aid agencies, NGOs and other players on the field perceive their role and carry out their business. For example, the World Bank has now spelled out the fact that culture can contribute directly to its core development objectives. It sees culture in a development context as helping to:

- *Provide new opportunities for poor communities* to generate incomes from their own cultural knowledge and production and to grow out of poverty
- *Catalyze local-level development* through the diverse social, cultural, economic, and physical resources that communities have to work with

- *Conserve and generate revenues from existing [cultural] assets* by reviving city centers, conserving socially significant natural assets, and generating sustainable, significant tourism revenues
- *Strengthen social capital* – in particular, to provide a basis on which poor, marginalized groups can pursue activities that enhance their self-respect and efficacy and to strengthen respect for diversity and social inclusion so that they can share in the benefits of economic development
- *Diversify strategies of human development and capacity-building* for knowledge-based dynamic societies – for example, through support for local publishing, library services, and museum services, especially those that serve marginalized communities and children.[22]

The Bank is pursuing these lines of action in its operational work through efforts, first, to integrate cultural considerations into its lending strategies in all sectors, especially education; secondly, to promote culture in its grass-roots community development work; and thirdly to engage with specifically cultural projects in borrowing countries, such as heritage projects of various sorts.

In the last-mentioned case, where free-standing projects involve the restoration of historic property or some similar line of investment in borrowing countries, the immediate revenues that the project can generate assume a particular importance, since the loan and its repayment have to be substantiated in financial terms. A major revenue source in many heritage redevelopment projects is likely to be tourism. The Bank is careful in its propaganda to emphasise that tourism to cultural sites in developing countries must not degrade the very culture that attracts it and must be developed in a manner respectful of local traditions and cultural sensitivities. In short, it must be culturally and environmentally sustainable. Nevertheless, an emphasis on an economic justification for a cultural heritage project, no matter how well the economic appraisal might encompass non-use values and other indicators of levels of cultural esteem, may orientate the project in directions inimical to the generation of cultural value. It is important that the dual values, economic and cultural, be accounted for in decision-making in such projects. We return to these issues in more detail in chapters 5 and 7.

Conclusions

This chapter has pointed to a paradigm shift in thinking about the nature of economic growth and development. By no means all development economists, still less all growth theorists, would see the shift as important, and a number would not acknowledge its existence at all. Nevertheless a move towards recognising a role for culture in influencing economic performance in small and large groups, and more particularly in underlying and conditioning processes of economic growth and change in developing countries, is gradually becoming more apparent. Central to this movement has been a reorientation of development thinking from a uniform commodity-centred model of development towards a pluralistic human-centred one. Oddly enough, the shift in development thinking is more evident in the practical world of development assistance than in the theoretical arenas where paradigm shifts usually originate. In this respect, we have pointed in this chapter to the acceptance by the World Bank and other development agencies of an explicit role for culture in development as some evidence of the paradigm shift that is taking place. We have suggested, as before, that a distinction between economic and cultural value can help to clarify the nature of the different sorts of value created by the development process.

Notes
1 Quotation is from Sen (1998b, p. 317).
2 See, for example, the pioneering work of Simon Kuznets (1966), who demonstrated uniformities in the patterns of economic growth across a number of countries by reference to an extensive range of economic phenomena. Note that Kuznets did refer briefly to cultural characteristics of different countries (racial and linguistic homogeneity, literacy, adoption of Western values) which he discussed as 'other aspects' of the non-economic characteristics of underdeveloped countries (1966, pp. 454–60). Nevertheless these variables were considered of minor significance and the overwhelming focus was on economic phenomena.
3 For the development of such models, see Lucas (1988); Becker *et al.* (1990); Romer (1994); Barro and Sala-i-Martin (1995).
4 For example, in considering the historical development of the world over the broad sweep of the second millennium, David Landes (1998) characterises nations as successful or unsuccessful on the basis essentially of *per capita* wealth and income. Note, nevertheless, that within this world view Landes recognises the importance of culture in influencing economic performance: 'If we learn anything from the history of economic development, it is that culture makes all the difference' (1998, p. 516).
5 Casson (1993, p. 418).
6 The standard orthodox assessment of the 'Asian miracle' was undertaken under the auspices of the World Bank (1993); for consideration specifically of interventionist interpretations, see Lall (1996) and Masuyama *et al.* (1997). Insightful accounts of the cultural context of Asian economic performance are contained in Berger (1993); Hsiao (1993); Brook and Luong (1997); Sen

(1998a); see also Ozawa (1994) and Gray (1996). For dissenting views see Krugman (1994); Woo-Cumings (1997); Arrow (1998).

7 See further in Munakata (1993); Di Maggio (1994, pp. 33–4); Fukuyama (1995, pp. 161–93); Hayami (1998, pp. 14–17).

8 See Inglehart (1990).

9 Hsiao (1993, p. 20).

10 Kuznets (1966, p. 1).

11 Ruttan (1988, 1991).

12 Gillis *et al.* (1996); Ray (1998); Todaro (2000).

13 Sen (1990).

14 Griffin (1996, p. 233).

15 For a contemporary anthropologist's approach to formulating a more comprehensive development theory and practice, see Escobar (1995).

16 For further discussion of path-dependent and path-independent models of development, see J. Mohan Rao (1998).

17 For an analysis of the importance of institutional structures as they relate to cultural beliefs and the trajectories of developing economies, see Greif (1994).

18 A brief reference is made to culturally sustainable development in the World Commission on Culture and Development Report mentioned in the previous section (WCCD, 1995, pp. 24–5; see also pp. 206–7). For a more elaborate treatment see Throsby (1995).

19 See UNESCO (1998b, p. 14).

20 Two milestones in this progress for the World Bank were a 1992 conference on culture and development in Africa (see Serageldin and Taboroff, 1994), and a conference held in Florence in 1999 organised by the Bank, the Government of Italy and UNESCO under the title 'Culture Counts' (see Wolfensohn *et al.*, 2000).

21 Note that we shall be returning in more detail to the question of globalisation and culture in chapters 8 and 9.

22 World Bank (1999, p. 15).

5 Economic aspects of cultural heritage

A tjuringa – it is worthwhile repeating – is an oval plaque made of stone or mulga wood. It is both musical score and mythological guide to the Ancestor's travels. It is the actual body of the Ancestor . . . It is a man's *alter ego*; his soul; his obol to Charon; his title-deed to country; his passport and his ticket 'back in' . . . If you smashed or lost your tjuringa, you were beyond the human pale, and had lost all hope of 'returning'. Of one young layabout in Alice [Springs], I heard it said, 'He hasn't seen his tjuringa. He don't know who he is.'

(Bruce Chatwin, *The Songlines*, 1987[1])

Introduction

The world is awash with heritage. Every town and village has some historic building or site, some collection of artefacts, or some local tradition or custom the preservation of which provides the inhabitants with a connection to their past. At the other end of the scale, the great museums and galleries of the world housing priceless art treasures, the historic cities, the monuments and sites to which countless tourists make pilgrimage, all represent an international heritage for which there is a vast and ever-growing demand. On the supply side, old buildings jostle for listing as heritage structures worthy of preservation and museums cannot keep pace with the range and number of artworks and other cultural materials queueing up for admission into their collections.

Decisions as to what counts as cultural heritage and how it should be preserved, restored and/or presented to the public have largely been the province of experts: archeologists, art historians, museologists, architects, conservationists, museum directors, urban planners and so on. When economists dare to enter the sacred ground of conservation decisions and point to some of their economic ramifications, their intrusion is often resented, as if matters to do with heritage are beyond the reach of economics.[2] Yet economic analysis, provided it is sensitive to the cultural values with which it is dealing, can engage many questions in this field, ranging from resource allocation decisions within cultural institutions responsible for storing and exhibiting heritage, to policy issues relating to the financing and management of publicly owned heritage at national and international levels.

In this chapter we look specifically at heritage as cultural capital. Treating heritage as asset opens it up to evaluation using the familiar techniques of investment appraisal. Bearing in mind the distinction we have drawn between economic and cultural value, we propose that any meaningful application of such techniques in the study of heritage projects will need to take account of both sources of value. Having done so, we will be able to draw the economic and cultural appraisals together by invoking again the criteria of sustainability in the assessment of heritage decisions.

Definitional issues

The definition of what comprises 'heritage' is a somewhat elastic one. At its broadest, heritage might comprise anything inherited from the past, but such an all-inclusive delineation is scarcely helpful, since almost anything more than a year or two (or a day or two) old would qualify. If interest is narrowed to items of historic or cultural significance, the corresponding definition of heritage is empty without an independent specification of how 'significance' is determined. Shifting the definitional burden to a question of the cultural importance of particular items may suggest that objective criteria for judging degrees of cultural significance could be derived. More likely, however, it will direct the responsibility not to a set of characteristics but to a professional or expert discourse whose practitioners will become the arbiters of what comprises heritage and what does not. This indeed is what has happened, reinforcing perceptions of the heritage game as essentially a self-referential process.

Nevertheless in practical terms, decisions about what comprises heritage have to be made by those engaged in its management and administration, and thus many formal definitions of cultural heritage have been put forward in the drafting of laws, regulations, treaties and conventions designed to protect heritage in some way.[3] For example, the *UNESCO Convention for the Protection of the World Cultural and Natural Heritage* (1972) states at Article 1:

For the purposes of this convention, the following shall be considered as 'cultural heritage':

monuments: architectural works, works of monumental sculpture and painting, elements or structures of an archaeological nature . . . which are of outstanding universal value . . .;

groups of buildings: groups of separate or connected buildings which, because of their architecture, their homogeneity or their place in the landscape . . .;

sites: works of man or the combined works of nature and of man . . .

Such definitions attempt to fix a benchmark by which heritage status can be judged. In some such specifications, an attempt is made to choose a criterion which is capable of unambiguous interpretation, for example a requirement that buildings can be considered as cultural heritage only if they are more than a certain number of years old. More frequently, a degree of subjectivity cannot be avoided in assessing an item's claim. So, for example, the UNESCO Convention cited above goes on to specify that monuments, groups of buildings, etc. must be of 'outstanding universal value from the point of view of history, art or science' to qualify for World Heritage classification. Another convention relying similarly on a measure of judgement is the Burra Charter, originating from Australia's ICOMOS (International Council on Monuments and Sites), which defines heritage in terms of the 'cultural significance' of a building, site or place.[4] What constitutes 'outstanding' or 'culturally significant' in these contexts is a matter for qualitative judgement that can be determined only by agreement on certain cultural criteria. In some cases, such as the World Heritage list, where only the highest-rated applications succeed, broadly based consensus judgements may be possible; there can be little disagreement, for example, that Angkor, Petra or Venice should be included. In most cases, however, the specification of the necessary criteria and their evaluation are strongly reliant on expert opinion in the relevant field.

Heritage as cultural capital

The concept of cultural capital developed in chapter 3 provides a useful means for representing heritage in a way that links these cultural experts' concerns about the value of heritage with the economist's desire for a rational approach to assessing it. In other words treating heritage items as valuable assets and recognising that they give rise to both economic and cultural value may be an acceptable mode of analysis for both sides.

In order to focus the question, let us imagine a heritage project, where a particular item of tangible cultural heritage is under consideration. The project may involve classification, renovation, restoration, modification, re-use, preservation, exhibition or some other discrete process involving the item. For example, the project might involve:

- the restoration of an artwork: the work might be a free-standing single work such as a painting or sculpture, it might be a collection of artworks, or it might be an immovable work or works integral to a building or site such as frescoes, mosaics, rock paintings, etc.
- the expansion or reorganisation of a museum or gallery which is a site for storage and display of cultural objects such as artworks
- the restoration or re-use of a historic building, perhaps involving also a decision as to its possible listing, or
- the redevelopment of a historic or cultural site, precinct, location, urban space, etc.

Other examples of 'projects' might be imagined. In each case the focus of the project is an item, or collection of items, of cultural capital, and the project itself can be conceived of as a process of investment of economic resources and conservation expertise – i.e. an investment involving both economic and cultural inputs. The investment might be interpreted as maintenance investment (as in the case of restoration or preservation) or as new investment (as in a re-use or re-development project) or both. Either way the obvious methodology to call upon is provided by cost-benefit analysis, where the project's net benefits as assessed over time can be compared with its up-front capital costs, as an aid in deciding whether proceeding with the project is justified.

But it has to be remembered that the project under consideration here does not involve a piece of ordinary economic capital for which an assessment of economic costs and benefits could be regarded as a sufficient appraisal. The heritage project is concerned with an item of cultural capital yielding both economic and cultural value. Thus an evaluation of net benefit streams in both economic and cultural terms will be required. Because as noted earlier we would expect some correlation between economic and cultural value, undertaking an economic appraisal of the project should go some way at least to dealing with the cultural value question. But it is unlikely to be the whole story, and moreover there may be individual projects where the expected positive relationship between economic and cultural value does not hold and may even be reversed. Hence we must entertain the likelihood that both an economic appraisal and some form of independent and systematic cultural assessment of the project will need to be undertaken.

In the following sections the application of straightforward methods of economic investment appraisal to heritage projects is considered first, followed by a discussion of a possible parallel process looking at cultural value.

Cost-benefit analysis of heritage projects

The project involves the expenditure of resources now in order to secure benefits both now and in the future. The up-front costs can be regarded as the capital costs of the project. In a project involving restoration of an artwork, these costs would cover the labour of experts and technicians, the costs of materials and so on. For an urban redevelopment project or one including the renovation of a building, significant construction costs might be involved.

The major part of the cost-benefit analysis is likely to be the assessment of benefits. In certain cases this stage can be avoided altogether. If the project relates to a unique heritage item of such unarguable value, and the action proposed in restoration, maintenance, etc. is so obviously essential, that the project is considered self-evidently justified without further ado, an assessment of benefit would be superfluous. In such a case the cost-benefit analysis becomes instead a *cost-effectiveness analysis*, where the benefits are taken as given and the problem is one of finding the cheapest, most efficient and most effective way of achieving the given conservation objective. In most other cases, however, where the resources for conservation are limited, when the range of choices both within and between projects is wide, and where the extent of the benefits involved is contestable, a full cost-benefit analysis is likely to be indicated.

The project benefits may be divided into use values, non-use values and externalities. The first of these categories refers to the economic valuations placed on all the directly used goods and services which the project generates. For example, if the project relates to a historic site visited by tourists, it is the direct consumption experiences of those visitors which provide the use value.

Secondly, the non-use benefits are generally regarded as being of three types:

(a) *Existence value*: People may regard the mere existence of the heritage item under consideration to be of value to themselves or to the community, even if they do not enjoy benefits from it at first hand themselves. For example, citizens of the world may value the existence of the pyramids even though they may never have been to Egypt.

(b) *Option value:* People may wish to preserve the option that some day they, or someone else for whom they have concern such as their children, may wish to consume the asset's services – for example, by visiting a particular cultural site at some time in the future. This option is valuable to such people, and it provides them with recognisable benefit.

(c) *Bequest value*: People may gain benefit from the project through the knowledge that the cultural asset will be passed on to future generations.

Finally, the externalities arising from the project – i.e. beneficial or costly spillovers that affect other economic agents – may be taken into account in a cost-benefit analysis of a heritage project, although as we noted in chapter 2 when discussing the specific case of the art museum, these effects may need to be treated with some caution.

All of the benefits listed above arise from the project over time, and their economic valuation relates to a series of time periods (e.g. years) stretching into the future. The flow of these benefits can be seen as a return to the initial capital investment, and their magnitude, spread over the time period for which the project lasts, can be expressed as a rate of return on that investment. Because a dollar now is different from a dollar in the future, the time-stream of valuations has to be discounted so that it can be aggregated in terms of present monetary values – i.e. to bring financial quantities arising in different periods to a common basis of valuation at time zero. In the cost-benefit analysis literature there has been a long a somewhat inconclusive discussion about the appropriate discount rate to use for different sorts of projects.[5] Should the rate be a means for reflecting the opportunity cost of the capital invested in the project – i.e. should the discount rate be the best available risk-free rate of return that could be earned if the capital were to be invested elsewhere? Alternatively, and especially in the case of public-sector projects, should the discount rate reflect instead the preferences of society for consumption now compared with consumption in the future? Nevertheless, regardless of the discount rate used, when the future time-stream of benefits and costs yielded by an asset is brought back to a single sum measured at time zero the resulting amount is called the net present value (NPV) of the asset's earnings.

There are several alternative methods by which the final outcome of a cost-benefit assessment conducted along the above lines may be represented. These include:

- the *payback method* – i.e. how long does it take for the asset's earnings to repay its initial capital cost?
- the *benefit-cost ratio* and *NPV method* – i.e. do aggregate net benefits, suitably discounted, exceed the capital cost? and
- the *internal rate of return (IRR) method* – i.e. what discount rate just matches aggregate discounted net benefits with the initial capital cost?

Given that the project is an intervention to maintain, restore, protect or re-use the heritage asset under consideration, the appropriate basis for comparison is what would happen if nothing were done. Take the renovation of a historic building, for example. An economic evaluation of the project would assess the costs involved in the restoration work and the *additional* benefit the restoration would bring over and above the benefits yielded by this heritage item in the absence of restoration. In this case the benefits might come as much from averted costs as from increased use or non-use benefits. Either way the appropriate basis for decision can be seen as a comparison between 'with-project' and 'without-project' outcomes. It is important to understand that the valuation involved in such a cost-benefit appraisal is of the *marginal* benefit provided by the project and is not an estimate of the *total* asset value of the item itself, nor of the *total* value of the goods and services to which it gives rise.

Economic evaluation methods

Let us turn now to the ways in which the economic value of use and non-use benefits of cultural heritage may be assessed.[6] The first step in any evaluation is to identify the stakeholders – i.e. to whom do the benefits accrue? In the case of use benefits, the direct beneficiaries from a heritage project may be relatively easy to distinguish. For example, if the project involves the redevelopment of a historic site visited by tourists, these visitors would clearly comprise one of the main interested groups directly affected by the project. In the case of non-use benefits, on the other hand, the project's effects are likely to be more diffuse, and the more significant the heritage asset in question in national and international terms the more widespread these benefits are likely to be. For the Egyptian pyramids mentioned earlier, for example, non-use beneficiaries probably exist all over the world. In practice, empirical investigation will be limited to what is feasible; for historic cities, for instance, residents and visitors can readily be identified but potential beneficiaries from further afield may be difficult or impossible to bring into the analysis.

Once the group of direct beneficiaries has been determined, the assessment of the economic value of their use benefits can proceed. When the project's outputs are sold, the use value can be measured as the expected total net revenue from sales, notwithstanding the limitations on price as an index of economic value to which we have already alluded. Thus, for example, entrance charges levied on visitors to a historic site, net of administration and other operating costs, could be taken as one element of the use values arising from a project to restore or re-develop the site. However, a fuller assessment requires estimation of beneficiaries' demand functions so that changes in aggregate consumers' surplus can be calculated. Such an estimation might be possible if sufficient data on actual consumer demand at a range of prices were available. Alternatively hypothetical demand curves might be able to be constructed using other means.

One such approach is the *travel cost* method of assessment of benefits,[7] which has been widely used in the estimation of the value of environmental amenities such as national parks. It may be applicable to heritage projects presenting as tourist sites, for example, where use benefits are obtainable only by travelling to the site. The travel cost method is based on the proposition that consumers' valuations of such facilities are indicated by how much they say they would be prepared to pay (or how much they actually pay) in travel costs to visit it. If a sample of consumers is surveyed and their willingness-to-pay responses are revealed, a simulated demand curve can be constructed. The area beneath the demand curve and above the admission price (or the total area beneath the curve if admission is free) is the relevant benefit estimate. However, this approach has its shortcomings, including the difficulty of attributing costs in multi-purpose trips, questions surrounding the valuation of time and other problems.

Turning to indirect beneficiaries, we require some means of estimating the non-market value of the benefits they enjoy. One approach is to seek relevant market data which may be used as an indicator or pointer to the non-market effect under consideration. For example, house prices vary systematically with a range of characteristics relating to their environmental amenity such as views, noise, etc.; the demand for aesthetic quality, quietness etc. can therefore be inferred from these variations. This approach is known as *hedonic pricing*, and may have some potential for application to heritage projects. But its use is limited to situations where a reasonably wide spread of market data can be found. So, for example, the influence of heritage values on property prices, including the effects of listing, might be able to be assessed by these means. An illustration is the study by John Moorhouse and Margaret Smith, who investigated the influence of architectural styles on the prices of nineteenth-century terrace houses in Boston. Another application is that of Olivier Chanel *et al.* who used hedonic methods to analyse the auction prices of artworks.[8] Despite the validity of such studies in terms of what they set out to do, the application of hedonic methods in valuing heritage projects is seriously limited in most cases by the absence of any market data from which inference of value can be made.

The principal means for evaluating demand for non-market commodities in economic analysis is *contingent valuation methodology* (CVM), to which we referred briefly in chapter 2 when discussing the economic valuation of public cultural goods. We consider this methodology in more detail now, in the context specifically of estimating the non-use benefits generated by cultural heritage projects.

CVM is one of the most widely used means of measuring non-market benefits in economic analysis.[9] It involves asking people their willingness to pay (WTP) for the benefits received, or their willingness to accept compensation for their loss. The asking may take place under quasi-experimental conditions, or more commonly may be administered through sample surveys of individuals drawn from the population of those experiencing the benefit in question. Thus, for instance, the non-use value of a community cultural centre or museum in a local area might be assessed on the basis of a survey of a sample of residents of the area. The survey might be conducted by telephone, mail or personal interview. Respondents might be asked hypothetically to indicate the maximum financial contribution they would make to a fund to support the cultural centre, or they might be asked whether or not they would contribute a fixed amount to such a fund. Either way an analyst could use the results to estimate a hypothetical demand function for the non-use benefits of the centre.

There a number of biases that may affect responses in CVM studies. The most obvious is the so-called 'free-rider problem' – i.e. people have an incentive not to reveal their true preferences for a public good if they know they cannot be excluded from enjoying its benefits once it is provided. In other words, individuals can escape payment by concealing their true WTP, and yet still enjoy the benefits of consumption. Other biases may arise through the hypothetical nature of the questions, the possibility that responses may be based on insufficient or incorrect information and the difficulties of ensuring that responses on single issues are consistent with an individual's overall budgetary position.[10] There are ways of circumventing these biases, or at least of mitigating their effects, through careful experimental design. For example, the free-rider problem may be controlled for by deliberately providing respondents with incentives to understate or overstate their WTP through altering their assumed liability to pay their nominated amount; by these means those respondents who free-ride can be distinguished from those who do not, and an estimate made of any bias owing to this effect.[11]

Overall the fact that many successful applications of CVM have now been made in the environmental sphere can be taken as indicating considerable further potential for its use in evaluating cultural projects, because of the similarities between the types of non-use benefits that accrue in both of these fields.[12]

Cost-benefit analysis and cultural value

If cultural value is to be taken seriously as an element in the construction of value in heritage projects, and is to be given appropriate weight alongside economic value in decision making, it needs to be assessed in its own right. Although, as noted earlier, a well conducted economic appraisal will tell us something, perhaps quite a lot, about the cultural value of a project, we can never be sure it is anything like the full story until we derive an independent assessment of the components of cultural value. Furthermore, the economic appraisal is founded on an individualistic model of economic behaviour, whereas a cultural appraisal would be expected to address collective benefits which may in some way transcend or augment the cultural value accruing to individuals.

Suppose a unitary measure of cultural value were to hand, akin to the monetary metric used in an economic assessment, enabling expression of the benefits and costs of a heritage project in cultural terms. It would be possible in these circumstances to imagine carrying out a cultural cost-benefit analysis of the project using the same methods as for an economic appraisal. The up-front input of cultural resources in the form of expert time etc. might be regarded as the capital cost, and the flow of cultural returns over time could be aggregated, discounted if necessary to reflect preference for cultural value now rather than later, to indicate a net present cultural value of the project which could be set alongside the economic NPV in making an overall decision on the project's worth.

It need hardly be said that while such a proposition may be sound in a theoretical sense, providing a convenient closure to a fully articulated model of cultural heritage, it remains unworkable until its central measure of cultural value is defined. As noted in chapter 2, such a single measure is very difficult to specify, given the multi-dimensional nature of cultural value. It would seem more sensible to continue to pursue the disaggregation of cultural value into some of its constituent elements, in the hope of treating specific criteria of value as components of a broadly conceived cultural cost-benefit appraisal, with the final choice between the different components being interpreted as a problem in multi-criteria analysis.

Let us consider more closely how cultural value is comprised in a specifically heritage context. For simplicity, consider the heritage asset to be a building, a monument, a historic town centre or a similar entity that we can refer to as the 'site', where the stakeholders can be referred to as 'the community' and where the 'project' involves maintenance or restoration of the site. We look at the possible components of cultural value for the site, who might determine it, and how it might be measured.

Cultural value of a heritage site

We can refer back to the criteria for cultural value put forward in chapter 2 and consider how these values might be attributed to the site, and how individuals and the community derive benefit from such characteristics.

(a) *Aesthetic value*: The site possesses and displays beauty in some fundamental sense, whether that quality is somehow intrinsic or whether it comes into being only in the consumption of it by the viewer. Under the general heading of 'aesthetic value' we might also include the relationship of the site to the landscape in which it is situated – i.e. all the environmental qualities relevant to the site and its surroundings.

(b) *Spiritual value*: Spiritual value conveyed by the site may contribute to the sense of identity of the community as a whole and of the individuals in it. It may provide them with a sense of cultural confidence and of connectedness between the local and the global – i.e. it may help to define the notion of human civilisation and the civilised society. The realisation that similar spiritual value is created by other sites in other communities may promote intercultural dialogue and understanding.

(c) *Social value*: The interpretation of culture as shared values and beliefs which bind groups together suggests that the social value of the heritage site might be reflected in the way in which its existence

may contribute towards social stability and cohesion in the community. The site may impinge upon or interact with the way of living in
the community, helping to identify the group values which make the
community a desirable place in which to live and work.

(d) *Historical value*: This value, however it is received, is unarguably
intrinsic to the site, and of all the components of cultural value it is
probably the most readily identifiable in objective terms. Perhaps its
principal benefit is seen in the way in which historical value assists in
defining identity, by providing a connectedness with the past and
revealing the origins of the present.

(e) *Symbolic value*: The site conveys meaning and information, which
helps the community to interpret its identity and to assert its cultural
personality. The value of the site as a representation of meaning is
important in its educational function, not just for the young but for
advancing the knowledge base and level of understanding of the
whole community.

(f) *Authenticity value*: The site is valued for its own sake because it is
real, not false, and because it is unique. An important concomitant
characteristic is integrity, variously defined in different circumstances; protection of the site's integrity, however interpreted, may
be a significant constraint imposed on project decision-making when
cultural value is taken into account.

Who determines cultural value?

Under each of the criteria listed above an evaluation is implied, leading
to some overall assessment of cultural value for the site. Who should
define what criteria are important and how they should be interpreted?
This question may be posed in terms of finding the appropriate process
for decision-making – i.e. should the evaluation and decision be carried
out as a 'top-down' or a 'bottom-up' process?

In many cases top-down processes are imposed for essentially financial
reasons, because the entity providing funds for the project is allowed to
call the tune or asserts the right to do so. Much publicly funded heritage
work falls into this category, where national, regional and local governments spend money on projects of their own choosing. The values
(plural) in play here tend to be those of elite or dominant groups such as
heritage professionals, bureaucrats and politicians. At the other extreme,
a bottom-up process would seek to allow those most immediately
affected by the site, such as the local community, to assert their own

values; in such a case the ways of interpreting the criteria of cultural value, and the relative importance attached to them, may differ, perhaps markedly, from those obtaining in the top-down case.

Of course not all top-down processes are insensitive to the needs and aspirations of the affected parties, and in practice many enlightened government agencies, NGOs and other groups working on heritage projects strive for an integrated approach, where the necessary top-down expertise and financial inputs are combined with genuine efforts to bring bottom-up values on board.

Measurement

Because of the multi-faceted nature of cultural value, any serious or rigorous attempt to evaluate the project according to the criteria described above will have to call upon a number of different disciplines to provide appropriate assessment methods. This suggests ideally a team approach to cultural value assessment on the site, working alongside the economists engaged in the economic cost-benefit appraisal of the project. The team is likely to utilise some of the assessment methods – mapping, thick description, attitudinal analysis, content analysis, expert appraisal – which we discussed in chapter 2.

It may be possible, in identifying the characteristics of the site which contribute to its cultural value, to devise simple ordinal or qualitative scales measuring the strength or importance of each attribute as exhibited by the site in question. If such judgements can be expressed as, or converted into, cardinal scores, they have the advantage that they can be combined, using any desired weighting system to reflect the assumed relative importance of the individual criteria. Such an approach is clearly no more than an ad hoc means of giving formal expression to judgements which would otherwise be left simply to informal processes. Nevertheless, these methods might be a workable means of systematising an approach to decision-making in regard to the cultural value of the site. In particular, they may be especially useful in comparing or ranking sites, given that the judgements on the various aspects of the cultural value of all the sites would be made in a consistent manner. Thus, for example, Nathaniel Lichfield discusses a checklist with scores for evaluating the cultural quality of heritage buildings, while Peter Nijkamp provides a hypothetical illustration of ascribing cultural value to a number of historic urban districts according to 'profiles' reflecting socio–economic, geographical–environmental and cultural–architectural criteria.[13]

Sustainability in heritage management

In discussing the concept of cultural capital in chapter 3, we suggested that a framework for bringing together the consideration of economic and cultural value generated over the long term by such capital was provided by the ideas of sustainability. The principles for defining sustainability which were put forward there for cultural capital in general can now be reiterated for the specific case of cultural heritage. These principles can provide a means for integrating economic and cultural cost-benefit appraisals of a heritage project carried out along the lines discussed above. The motivation for proceeding in this direction is to provide a set of criteria for formulating sustainable heritage management strategies which recognise both the economic and the cultural value produced by the project. Let us consider the principles briefly in turn.

The first criterion, the generation of material and non-material well-being, is covered by the generalised cost-benefit appraisals of the heritage project as discussed in previous sections. Sustainability would require the analysis of net benefits to take account of both use and non-use values, and of both economic and cultural value generated by the project, in this assessment.

Secondly, the intergenerational equity principle requires the interests of future generations in the project outcomes to be acknowledged. This might be pursued in several different ways. In quantitative terms, respect for intergenerational concerns might suggest adoption of a lower discount rate than might be otherwise accepted on time-preference or opportunity-cost grounds in the process of reducing both economic and cultural benefit streams to present value terms. In qualitative terms, the issue of fairness itself should be explicitly considered in terms of the ethical or moral dimensions of taking account of the likely effect of the project on future generations.

Thirdly, the principle of intragenerational equity would recognise the welfare effects of the heritage project on the present generation. Consideration might be given to the distributional impacts of the capital costs of the investment project under study, to identify whether any regressive effects might be present. Furthermore, intragenerational equity also refers to equity in access to the benefits of the project across social classes, income groups, locational categories, etc. If serious inequities were identified, the possibility of corrective or compensatory action might be raised, if indeed such action were feasible. In addition, an intragenerational equity issue may arise in the processes involved in actually making the investment decision, insofar as it may be appropriate for stakeholders affected by the decision to have some input into these processes via some form of bottom-up mechanism. General considerations of sustainability would suggest attention to the fairness of decision-making procedures in this context, including empowerment of those whose interests are affected by heritage decisions where appropriate and possible. Overall, in regard to this criterion, a sustainable project will be one leading to no adverse distributional consequences in either economic or cultural terms in respect of the incidence of either its costs or its benefits.

The remaining three principles, relating to the maintenance of diversity, the precautionary principle and the recognition of interdependence of economic and cultural systems, can be seen as checks and balances in the overall project appraisal. In particular the last principle provides an opportunity to identify the role of the site as a component of what might be termed the 'cultural infrastructure' of the city, region or country in which it is located, and draws attention to both the economic and the cultural benefits and costs which the project may generate as a consequence of that role.

Policy issues

Governments at national, regional and local levels are significant stakeholders in cultural heritage, as owners or custodians of a considerable slice of the world's heritage or as regulators or financiers influencing other stakeholders in the field. Given that in a number of countries heritage policy forms the major or even the only recognisable arm of cultural policy, and given the considerable capacity of public authorities to influence outcomes in this area, it is useful to consider how the public sector exercises its policy functions in this field.

First, it might be agreed that the objectives of heritage policy could be cast in terms which recognise both the economic and the cultural value of heritage, as discussed in this chapter. If heritage is indeed treated as cultural capital as advocated here, the sorts of assessment measures we have put forward can feed directly into the policy process and can help to articulate policy goals more precisely.

Second, we turn to the question of choice of instruments by which public policy towards cultural heritage can be given effect. The problem of instrument choice is a familiar one in economic policy formulation. For present purposes we could identify four groups of policy measures of use in the heritage area:[14]

- public ownership and operation of heritage institutions, facilities and sites
- financial support for the maintenance, operation and restoration of heritage, either through direct funding or subsidies to private or non-government operators, or through indirect financing via tax concessions and other devices
- regulation limiting or constraining private action in dealing with cultural heritage, and
- education and the provision of information in the hope that better conservation decisions will be made.

Of these, the first two are likely in most countries to be the most significant in financial terms. But it is also worth noting the widespread use of regulation, in the sense of specific constraints or directives affecting behaviour, as a tool of government heritage policy. This is surprising, given that regulation is usually the intervention strategy least favoured by economists. This seeming paradox deserves further exploration. Before doing so, however, we suggest a way of defining regulation in this field.

Regulation in relation to cultural heritage denotes the use of measures which *require* or *enforce* certain behaviour in firms or individuals. We can draw a distinction between what we might call 'hard' and 'soft' regulation.[15] *Hard regulation* comprises enforceable directives requiring certain behaviour, implemented via legislation and involving penalties for non-compliance. *Soft regulation* comprises non-enforceable directives requiring certain behaviour, implemented by agreement and not involving penalties. Both types of regulation seek to change behaviour, the first by involuntary means, the second by encouraging voluntary compliance.

The reasons why hard regulation has been so popular as a tool in heritage policy-making have to do with its direct mode of operation and the apparent certainty of its effects. In contrast, say, to taxes and subsidies, which operate on behaviour at one remove, regulation constrains individual action directly, with a clearer prospect that desired outcomes will be achieved. Thus, for example, if there is an all-or-nothing choice between allowing a building to stand or demolishing it, an order to protect the structure from being interfered with is likely to be the most effective means of securing its continued existence. Similarly, if there is a very high risk of social damage through individual action in respect of heritage properties, direct control of such action may be preferred where other less decisive measures may conceivably fail.

A further advantage of direct regulations is that they may be invoked and removed relatively speedily. Thus direct controls may be a useful supplement to other measures, such as a system of charges, for the continuing maintenance of acceptable environmental, conservation or preservation conditions. Their usefulness arises because of the inflexibility of tax rates and other instruments, and the relative ease with which certain types of regulatory controls can be introduced, enforced and removed. Some crises can at best be predicted only a short time before they occur, and it may be too costly, for example, to keep tax rates sufficiently high to prevent such emergencies at all times. Therefore it may be less expensive to make temporary use of direct controls, despite their static inefficiency.[16] This point is acknowledged in the field of urban conservation through the use of temporary preservation orders – i.e. controls that can be introduced at very short notice to forestall the demolition of historic properties until some due process of consultation or consideration can be pursued.

In all government policy intervention whatever instruments are used, the costs of intervention need to be taken into account. In the heritage case, these costs might include administrative costs incurred in the formulation of standards, in monitoring and enforcement and in collection and disbursements of revenue, and the compliance costs imposed on firms and individuals who have to meet the policy requirements.

Finally the question of the financing of heritage policy must be addressed. In simple terms it can be suggested that the obligation to pay for heritage protection should be assumed by those who are stakeholders in the project under consideration. In many instances such a means of financing heritage projects can be implemented, ranging from local communities supporting the upkeep of their cultural assets via their tax payments, through to contributions by the international community to funds for the preservation of world heritage monuments and sites. Responsibility for initiating and managing such funding mechanisms is not limited solely to the public sector. Third-sector organisations such as NGOs and other voluntary groups can mobilise significant finance for heritage purposes, representing the interests of a variety of constituencies. Furthermore, the corporate sector is becoming increasingly involved in supporting heritage projects, partly through altruism and a sense of ethical responsibility, but more generally because significant payoffs in terms of corporate profile and marketing effectiveness can be gained through association with heritage endeavours. As we shall argue further in chapter 8, new partnerships between the public, private and third sectors are likely to characterise the development of cultural policy in the future, and heritage policy appears at the present time to be a leading example of this trend.[17]

Conclusions

Consideration of heritage as cultural capital can provide a means of integrating the interests of conservationists, who are concerned with the protection of cultural value, and economists, who look at heritage projects as problems of allocation of scarce resources between competing ends. This chapter has argued again that a recognition of both economic and cultural value is essential if the two sides of this division are to be joined. Economic investment appraisal methods, geared particularly to assessment of non-market benefits, can tell us a lot about the value of heritage projects, and can assist decision-makers enormously in their task. But they are not the whole story, and an extension of the cost-benefit framework to accommodate the incorporation of cultural value seems possible in both theoretical and operational terms. We have suggested some potential avenues for development here, and have appealed once more to sustainability principles as a means of finally integrating the economic and cultural assessment. Politicians and bureaucrats may take these considerations on board as they exercise their function of formulating and implementing policy measures in the cultural heritage field.

Notes

1 Quotation is from Chatwin (1987, pp. 286–7).
2 For some representative examples of an economic consideration of heritage issues, see Peacock (1995, 1998a), and contributions to Hutter and Rizzo (1997), Schuster *et al.* (1997), Peacock (1998b) and Getty Conservation Institute (1999); for views from within the conservation profession, see Bluestone (2000) and Mason and de la Torre (2000).
3 See especially Prott (1998).
4 See Marquis-Kyle and Walker (1992).
5 For a discussion in the specific case of heritage projects, see van der Burg (1995); note that such projects are likely to yield benefits into the distant future, suggesting the use of non-constant discount rates as mentioned in chapter 3.
6 See further in Getty Conservation Institute (1999); Serageldin (1999); Klamer and Throsby (2000).
7 The classic methodology is spelled out in Clawson and Knetsch (1966, ch. 5); for an application of the travel cost method to determining the consumers' surplus generated by an art museum, see Martin (1994).
8 See Moorhouse and Smith (1994); Chanel *et al.* (1996).
9 See Mitchell and Carson (1989); Braden and Kolstad (1991); Hausman (1993); Portney *et al.* (1994).

10 This source of bias may lead to overstatement of WTP. For example, if an individual is asked how much she would pay to a fund to preserve the Egyptian pyramids, then subsequently to similar funds for the Taj Mahal, the Great Wall of China and the Leaning Tower of Pisa, the sum of all the nominated amounts may exceed an aggregate amount she would be prepared to contribute to heritage in general.

11 This approach was suggested by Bohm (1979) and was used, for example, by Throsby and Withers (1983) in the CVM study of WTP for the benefits of public support for the arts in Australia referred to in chapter 2.

12 Applications of CVM to the evaluation of cultural projects include studies of the Royal Theatre in Copenhagen (Bille Hansen, 1997), the 'open museums' in Naples (Santagata and Signorello, 1998), the rehabilitation of Fez in Morocco (Agostini, 1998), the restoration of Bulgarian monasteries (Mourato and Danchev, 1999), the benefits from alternative traffic arrangements at Stonehenge (Maddison and Mourato, 1999) and the cleaning of Lincoln Cathedral (Pollicino and Maddison, 1999).

13 See Lichfield (1988, ch. 10); Nijkamp (1995).

14 Compare the five 'tools' for action listed by Schuster *et al.* (1997).

15 See further in Throsby (1997a, 1997b).

16 Such a view has been put by Baumol and Oates in their discussion of policy instruments used in the environmental field; they note that their support for the use in some circumstances of direct controls 'represents a sharp departure from the economist's usual policy recommendations' (Baumol and Oates, 1988, p. 156).

17 An illustration of the mobilisation of private-sector involvement in urban heritage projects can be seen in several Latin American cities; see Rojas (1999). For further discussion of financing mechanisms in heritage protection, see Netzer (1998).

6   The economics of creativity

I am sorry to say that artists will always be sufficiently jealous of one
another, whether you pay them large or low prices; and as for stimulus
to exertion, believe me, no good work in this world was ever done for
money, nor while the slightest thought of money affected the painter's
mind. Whatever idea of pecuniary value enters into his thoughts as he
works, will, in proportion to the distinctness of its presence, shorten his
power. A real painter will work for you exquisitely, if you give him . . .
bread and water and salt; and a bad painter will work badly and hastily,
though you give him a palace to live in, and a princedom to live upon
. . . And I say this, not because I despise the great painter, but because I
honour him; and I should no more think of adding to his respectability
or happiness by giving him riches, than, if Shakespeare or Milton were
alive, I should think we added to *their* respectability, or were likely to
get better work from them, by making them millionaires.
(John Ruskin, *The Political Economy of Art*, 1857[1])

Introduction

The concept of creativity as a dynamic force in human behaviour has
long been a subject for study among psychologists, sociologists, art
theorists and others in fields ranging from child development to business
management. It has been of no interest to economists. Creativity has
entered the discourse of economics only as it may be the generator of
innovation and hence the precursor of technological change.[2] Even there,
the act of creative thought has been seen as essentially exogenous, arising
as a result of processes beyond the reach or interest of economic theory
or analysis.[3] Yet any consideration of the relationship between economics and culture would be incomplete if it failed to pay attention to
the origins of cultural production, that is to the creative process itself. If

93

creative work in the arts and culture results in the generation of both economic and cultural value, then it might be expected that economic as well as cultural influences will affect the way creative ideas are formed and rendered. Are there parallel processes at work here, where economic and cultural worth are generated separately, or is the process of value creation one that can be understood only as a unitary phenomenon?

In this chapter we consider creativity primarily but not exclusively in terms of the work of creative artists such as poets, painters, actors, composers and so on. This is not to deny the importance of creativity in the work of other producers of cultural goods and services such as television directors and journalists, but simply to concentrate attention on a group of workers for whom the creative act, whatever it is, is unarguably of primary importance. Further, because of the fact that some types of artistic production occur as collective activity, the discussion about artists in this chapter might be seen as applying equally to creative work carried on by several or many cultural workers operating as a group. Ignoring intragroup dynamics, we might ascribe to the collective similar motives, incentive structures, decision processes, etc. to those proposed for the individual. If so, the model of the creative process developed in this chapter may be applied as well to the music ensemble or the theatre company as to the individual artist.

The chapter proceeds as follows. After a brief review of theories of creativity, we ask whether the production of artistic works might be able to be modelled as a process of rational decision-making. We proceed to suggest the essence of such a model, built around the production of value in line with a central theme of this book. From simple beginnings we introduce economic variables, and consider the role of economic and cultural value as both incentives to and outcomes of the creative process. Finally, in reviewing the territory covered, we ask whether attempting to see creativity in rational terms is in fact misguided. It may be that the essence of the creative process is a form of conscious or unconscious irrationality which defies any form of ordered or structured formalisation.

Theories of creativity

During the seventeenth and eighteenth centuries, a number of treatises were written on the subject of creative genius. The word 'genius' encompassed not simply the elevation of an individual to exalted status, the most commonly heard usage today, but more generally a mode of thought – i.e. genius as the source of creative inspiration. There was a religious or at least spiritual association with this notion: the artist as channel for a superior power, creativity as a gift from the gods, the imagination as a divine spark. The processes of painting pictures, writing poetry or composing music were spiritual experiences in the service of whatever muse held the artist in her thrall.

Contained within these treatises were many efforts to dissect the concept of creativity and to describe how the process of artistic inspiration occurred. Typical of these was the definition proposed by William Duff in 1767 in his essay on the nature of original genius.[4] Duff identified the principal ingredients of genius as threefold: *imagination*, which takes existing ideas, invents new ones and finds new associations between them; *judgement*, which regulates and controls the imagination, and sorts out the ideas it generates; and *taste*, the artist's internal sensibility which arbitrates between 'grand or mean, beautiful or ugly, decent or ridiculous'.[5] This sort of intuitively appealing account of how the mind works has been replicated many times and in many ways in the years since then, through to the present day.[6]

In recent times the postmodern critique has challenged the idea of creative genius. Two broad lines of attack might be identified. First it is argued that creativity is definable only in individual-specific terms, that there is no way of identifying an absolute standard of genius and that any such judgement is a matter of relativity, impermanence and instability. Second, it is pointed out that artistic creation and its valuation occur in a social and political context which has the effect, among other things, of appropriating matters of taste and judgement to the powerful classes in society. Thus the conferring of canonical classification on certain art works and genius status on certain artists is simply a manifestation of the exercise of the power of the artistic and intellectual establishment.

As in our earlier discussions on value, it is not our purpose here to take sides in traditionalist versus post-structuralist controversies. Rather, it seems preferable to pay heed, as we did earlier, to certain reasonable warnings that the radical critique might point towards, including the fact that subjectivity and relatively can never be banished entirely from considerations of artistic creation either in the making or the receiving, and that the influence on the creative act exerted by the social and political context in which creativity occurs cannot be disregarded.

Creativity as a rational decision process

The picture of the artist at work that springs to mind most readily in the popular imagination is doubtless that of the tortured genius, driven by a relentless inner force and oblivious to anything but the necessity of creative expression; the prospect may seem far fetched that some observer or analyst could impose a logical structure onto the creative thoughts of Hector Berlioz, Vincent van Gogh or Ezra Pound. Yet it is reasonable to speculate that there may be some systematic elements underlying the apparent chaos. If so, we could ask whether it might be possible, for example, to model the production of artistic works as a process of rational decision-making.

To some extent that question is partially answered already by the sorts of dissections of creativity which we noted above. Breaking down the act of creativity into constituent stages, each with a certain function, the whole connected in logical order and leading to a definable goal, is the stuff of contemporary decision analysis, and as such could lead to the construction of a formal decision model along these lines. Alternatively, an approach drawing more directly from a purely economic discourse might envisage creativity as a process of constrained optimisation, where the artist is seen as a rational maximiser of individual utility subject to both internally and externally imposed constraints. It is this latter approach which we pursue here, by suggesting first a 'pure' creativity model and then extending it to incorporate economic variables. The modelling is developed in the rest of this chapter in non-technical terms; a formal statement is contained in an appendix.

A 'pure' creativity model

Let us begin with the creative process as a phenomenon leading from the conception of an idea to the execution of an artistic work embodying that idea, where the sole concern of the artist is for the art, without any extraneous economic or other influences in operation. If the artistic or cultural worth of the work when completed can be defined as its cultural value in the terms we have already discussed, then the artist's aim in making the work might be seen solely as one of maximising this (expected) cultural value.[7] In a rational economising framework, this might be construed not just as the objective function of a decision model but as the artist's utility function with respect to this activity – i.e the utility of the artist is seen as a function of the cultural value of the work, and this utility is the quantity to be maximised.

In essence this is how creativity has been perceived in the formalisations of the process referred to earlier. Cultural value is instilled into works by creative artists who respond to the mysterious leaps of the imagination and transform these stimuli into images, words or sounds. So, for instance, Terry Smith, writing from an art theorist's standpoint, describes this as a process of 'forming flows of value'; the artist's role is to marshal the flows of value and to concentrate them into a configuration which will in due course display them to the world.[8]

As in most decision situations, the objective function in this model is not unbounded; rather the domain over which the decision variables can range is mapped by a series of constraints. In this simple version of the model the constraints are essentially technical, imposed by the 'rules of the game' and the demands of the artform, which serve both to define the artist's expressive scope and to challenge his or her ingenuity. So, for example, playwrights and composers may be commissioned or may choose to write for certain cast or ensemble sizes; painters, sculptors and craftspeople must operate within the technical parameters of their various media; representational artists are bound by the properties of the reality they seek to represent; and so on.

The decision variables in the model – i.e. the variables whose levels are to be chosen by the decision-maker in order to maximise the objective function – might in the first instance be conceptualised as the number and nature of works to be produced over some time period. But suppose the model is applied to a single work. What choices does the artist face which will determine the eventual cultural value of the work? For simplicity and generalisability it is appropriate in these circumstances to specify the decision variables in terms of time spent at various tasks. Such an approach would assume that a unit of work time of a particular sort would yield a certain amount of cultural value in the output; it is the aggregate of value from these various sources which is the quantity to be maximised. However, precise specification of these relationships, even in conceptual terms, may be difficult, indicating perhaps a more general formulation where total cultural value is simply specified as some (increasing) function of labour time spent.

A hypothesis that output of cultural value is expressible as a function of labour time spent by the artist conceals some potentially strong assumptions about the very nature of the creative act. The artist in whatever artform allocates time to different tasks involving thinking and doing. Some require imagination, others the application of technical skills, in still others these ingredients cannot be separated out; all of them come together to constitute creative activity. For the mediocre artist large amounts of time spent at these tasks will still yield work judged to be of little cultural value; for the so-called genius, the reverse obtains. Thus differences between artists in the location of the relationship between time spent and cultural value produced are, in this construction,

a measure, other things being equal, of differences in creativity (or
'talent'), in much the same way as in microeconomic analysis differences
between production functions in input–output space measure differences
in technology. Such a conceptualisation of creativity is consistent with
theories of the creative process requiring spontaneous thinking and rapid
response to intellectual stimuli.

An extended model introducing economic variables

The model outlined above would provide a sufficient portrayal of artistic
creativity if in fact the production of art took place in some sort of a
vacuum, free of the impacts of the mundane necessities of life such as the
artist's need for food, clothing and shelter. In some cases, these ideal
conditions are met; there are many accounts of composers or writers
producing symphonies or novels during a summer spent by a lake in
Switzerland or in some other circumstances where the demands of the
world could be disregarded. Such artists would include those fortunate
enough to be fully and unconditionally supported by a spouse, partner,
or patron – or, in contemporary times, who receive a sufficiently large
grant from a beneficent foundation or government arts agency. But more
commonly the world impinges only too directly upon artistic work,
insofar as the artist, like anyone else, has to earn money to live on. The
history of art is replete with accounts of how important money has been
to many artists, from painters of the Florentine Renaissance, through
Mozart, Beethoven and Stravinsky, to any number of writers, visual
artists and musicians working today.[9]

 Thus the model of artistic production needs to be extended to account
for the ways in which these economic influences might affect the
processes under study. The simplest means of doing so is by specifying
income from artistic work as an explicit variable in the model. The
manner by which income is generated will vary according to the scope
and content of the model. If the production of a single work is being
depicted, the income from the process might be the work's sale price or
the discounted value of the revenue stream it generates in the form of
royalties, etc. In the case of performing artists, on the other hand, income
arises from the sale of their services, paid in the form of wages and
salaries, fees and commissions and so on. Artists also incur expenses in
the pursuit of their work; the costs of materials, the rent of studio space,
and so on are often significant. These expenditures are incorporated in
this model by our assuming that they are netted out of gross revenues,

such that 'income' in this account refers to net income after deduction of operating costs.

There are three ways in which income might be entered into our model of the creative process: as a constraint, as a joint maximand, or as a sole maximand. We consider each in turn.

Income as constraint

In circumstances where the artist needs income only to provide for subsistence or other unavoidable obligations, we can propose that the objective function and technical constraints of the model sketched earlier can remain intact and that the only alteration necessary is the addition of a further constraint – i.e. one requiring the generation of a certain minimum level of income. In such a formulation the earning of income provides no incentive to artistic production, it is simply a necessary element in the decision process that cannot be ignored. The objective remains solely the maximisation of cultural value, but the choices the artist can make in pursuing this goal are now limited to a greater or lesser extent by the newly introduced requirement. In other words we are still focusing here on 'pure' artistic creativity, but now with an acknowledgement that the domain of the decision variables is affected by economic circumstance.

The income constraint may affect the production of cultural value directly in a number of different ways. It may shift the orientation of cultural production towards forms of output that have more income-earning potential than those which would be chosen otherwise. For example, a playwright may have no choice but to write for a small cast or a single set in order to ensure that the work will be performed and the required minimum income earned. Further, the constraint may mean that less costly inputs have to be used by the artist compared with those that would be employed if the constraint were absent. Thus, for example, a painter or sculptor may have to limit the materials used for a particular work to those that can be afforded, so that the net financial outcome will satisfy the minimum income constraint. Nevertheless, in each of these examples, the artist is still assumed to be striving solely for the generation of cultural value but within the limitations imposed by the income requirement.

It can be suggested that this type of model is broadly applicable to most work in the so-called non-commercial theatre, to classical music and to much of opera, jazz and poetry.

Income as joint maximand

For many artists, as for many other human beings, the desire for material goods extends beyond a demand for those things needed merely for survival. For this group of artists, subsistence even at a reasonably comfortable level is insufficient; they need larger quantities of money, to provide not only for higher standards of food, clothing, housing, etc. but also for access to all the other goods and services which income and wealth make possible. Thus the fact that their artistic practice can lead to financial reward is of more than passing interest to them and the generation of income from their artistic labour assumes for them a greater significance than simply being a means of paying the bills.

Let us suppose, nevertheless, that these artists are still strongly motivated by the desire to create art and that the principal reason why they are artists and not bankers or plumbers is that they have something they want to express through their chosen artform. They aspire, as most serious artists do, to produce art of high quality when judged against the professional standards of their discipline, but they differ from those depicted above insofar as money is more prominent in their hierarchy of wants. To apply our model of creativity to this case, we can propose that the artist's utility is comprised of both cultural and financial rewards, such that the objective function in the model can be restated as the joint maximisation of the cultural and economic value arising from the work. The set of technical constraints in the model remains as before. The minimum income constraint could also be retained, though if the artist were halfway successful, it would be unlikely to be binding.

This version of the model provides a specifically commercial orientation to the production of art. It suggests that for these artists money provides an incentive to pursue certain lines of artistic development and not others. The quality of output, measured in terms of the nature and type of work undertaken, is clearly likely to be affected. How much depends importantly on the relative weights the artist assigns to each maximand in the objective function, and on the extent to which the production of cultural and economic value in particular cases are consistent, oppositional or unrelated to each other. Unknown artists working in innovative modes, for example, may find the production of cultural value to be out of step with economic return and, if the weight they place on income in their preference pattern between economic and cultural value is strong enough, they would have to include some more commercially-oriented work in their portfolio. Recognised artists of well established reputation, on the other hand, may find the production of cultural value in their work goes hand in hand with economic return; in such cases the artist may be able to maximise both cultural and economic value simultaneously.

It can be suggested that a model of artistic production where economic and cultural value enter as joint maximands could be applied to some fiction-writing, some film-making, some visual arts and craft, some musicals and a significant amount of popular music.

Income as sole maximand

Notwithstanding the idealised vision that many may have of the creative arts, some artists and other cultural producers are in the game solely for the money. The production of cultural value through their work is by no means absent; it is there, at least potentially, by definition of the terms 'cultural production', 'cultural worker', etc. But it is not something to be maximised. In terms of our model of the creative decision process, the weight of cultural value in the objective function has dwindled to zero, and the maximisation of economic value has become the sole motivation for creativity, subject still to the technical constraints imposed by the conditions of production.

In this construction, virtually all aspects of the quality of output are determined principally by the economic conditions under which it is produced – i.e. by the income-earning potential of the work. If the production of cultural value enters explicitly at all in a manner that affects decision-making, it might do so only as a minimum constraint, specifying a basic requirement for a certain level of cultural content or for the adherence to certain cultural standards.

This model is likely to be most applicable to the following types of cultural production: folk and tourist art, some craft, much of film, commercial television and popular music and the greater part of the output of those cultural industries lying furthest from the artistic core, such as journalism, advertising and most architectural services.

Multiple job-holding

The models constructed above suppose that creative production is the only work that the artist undertakes, and that financial returns can be derived only from the economic value of artistic works created. In reality, two considerations suggest a further elaboration of this simplified approach. First, the return to artistic work may be so low that there is no way in which the artist can organise production to make even enough revenue to satisfy a subsistence constraint, at least at the early stages in an artistic career. Second, there may be other income-earning opportunities available that are lucrative enough to enable revenue to be generated quickly and efficiently, allowing a maximum of residual time for non-lucrative arts work. In these circumstances the possibility must be entertained that the artist might take on an additional job with the sole or primary aim of providing income to support his or her artistic practice.

Such a phenomenon, known in the labour economics literature as multiple job-holding, is by no means new among artists. Trollope, Eliot, Joyce, Gauguin, Borodin and many other well known artists held part- or full-time jobs in fields remote from the arts at various times in their careers in support of their creative practice. In contemporary cultural economics, a number of studies of the economic conditions of arts practice across all artforms have shown that many professional artists hold down non-arts jobs and that the predominant reason for this is the imperative for the artist to earn income to provide for basic needs and to finance his or her creative work.[10]

The model of creative production constructed in earlier sections of this chapter can be extended to account for the possibility of non-arts work. If the general form of the original model is one where the objective function is the joint maximisation of economic and cultural value (where weights ranging from zero to one and one to zero respectively can be attached to these two variables), then it is not difficult to expand the generation of value to include the production of non-arts goods. In such a formulation the artist can choose to produce artistic goods, which yield both cultural and economic value, and non-arts goods, which yield only economic value. The income variable in the model is thus comprised of revenue from both arts and non-arts sources.

Transforming the model as before to one of labour time allocation would enable the hours of work or proportion of time spent in non-arts income-generating activity to be specified alongside the different creative tasks involved in the process of artistic production. At its most basic this version of the model could be presented as one showing simply the choice between arts and non-arts labour supply. As such it would reflect the 'work preference' characteristic of artists – i.e. the fact that unlike most other workers (but in common with some groups such as academics, researchers, etc.), artists generally prefer more work time to less, and derive satisfaction from the work itself. Such a model would predict that artists will respond in an apparently perverse manner to changes in relative wages in arts and non-arts sectors, by virtue of the fact that non-arts work is simply a means of enabling as much time as possible to be spent at the (preferred) artistic occupation.[11]

Value in the work of creative artists

The model of the creative process that we have constructed in this chapter depicts creativity as the creation of value, building on the distinction between cultural and economic value advanced in chapter 2. It is now appropriate to look more closely at how cultural and economic value are formed in the work of creative artists.

Consider an artist who creates an artistic work. It may be a novel, a poem, a musical work, a painting, a sculpture, an installation, a video, a performance. The completed work exists in an embodied form (as is the case of a painting) or as property rights (as in the case of a piece of music). The work itself, or the rights to it, can be traded. The work can be copyrighted and doing so is a means of declaring that the work has economic worth. Indeed the definition of rights in the work enables its owner (the artist initially or a subsequent purchaser of the property rights over the work) to capture its economic value. As we have argued already, the price the work acquires through market exchange is an indicator, though by no means necessarily a perfect indicator, of the work's economic value.

Simultaneously the work also exists as an idea. (I use the singular here as an abstraction to simplify the exposition; of course most artworks contain and convey multiple ideas.) The idea comprising the work cannot be copyrighted but it can be exchanged. The process by which the idea is exchanged is a continuous one, such that in due course the idea has many owners (although there was only one originator). In this process of exchange, consumers determine their individual valuations of the cultural worth of the idea. Their valuations may be singular, summarising their opinions into a condensed measure (the work is 'a good book', 'a rather poor painting', etc.), or they may be multiple, reflecting perhaps the sorts of criteria for articulating cultural value that we put forward in chapter 2 above. Since the idea is a pure public good, the aggregation of individual valuations can be thought of as comprising the total cultural valuation of the idea within the sphere of its circulation. Again despite its limitations, this aggregate could be thought of as indicating the cultural value of the idea and hence of the work. Because of the continuous circulation of the idea, individual valuations (and hence the aggregate value) may change over time, and it may take a long time for an 'equilibrium' cultural value for a work to be established. Even then, it may still not be stable over time.

The essence of these propositions is that there exists both a physical market for artworks and a parallel marketplace for the ideas which are a necessary attribute or product of those works. The physical market determines the work's economic value, the market for ideas determines its cultural value. It is the fact that the physical work is the vehicle for conveying the idea that transforms the work from an 'ordinary economic good' into a 'cultural good'. As such it possesses not only economic value (in common with all economic goods) but also cultural value. As we have noted already, the two values are not unrelated, because consumers' demand functions for artworks are likely to contain some measure of cultural value as a significant argument.

We might summarise the above speculations as suggesting that artistic work might be interpreted as supplying a dual market. The artist's vision, springing from the complex conjunctions of the creative process, drives the production of ideas; his or her technical skill enables the realisation or embodiment of those ideas into actual works. These works will (hopefully) realise an economic price through market exchange, and (also hopefully) a cultural 'price' through the reception, processing, trans- mission and assessment of the ideas which they convey.

The formidable task then remains of determining how the market for ideas processes the raw material supplied to it by artists into some measure of cultural value or cultural price. The articulation of the constituent elements of value in particular cases, as discussed above, would seem to offer hope for some progress, especially since in the first instance, as noted, this would seem to be an approach that could be taken regardless of the ideological standpoint of the observer.

Creativity as an irrational process

Having proposed in this chapter that creative activity can be modelled as a rational decision process, where the maximisation of value guides the artist's hand and choices are made in a systematic way, we can now turn around and ask whether instead creativity is in fact the very antithesis of a structured process. Perhaps truly creative ideas are generated not by complying with the rules of an ordered universe, but by subverting them. Perhaps the very characteristic that makes artists different from others is that they are willing to overthrow logic and reason and to seek new connections in a manner that defies systematic analysis.

There might be several ways in which the process of artistic creation might be thought of as irrational. First, the choices made by artists may be arbitrary and random, not answerable to any definable criterion and not guided in their execution by any conscious sense on the artist's part that they are leading anywhere in particular. Finished works created under such conditions may be accorded cultural value in due course by those who consume them, through the circulation of ideas as described above, but the value has not been imparted by the artist as a deliberate act. Therefore the process of creativity itself could not be represented in any systematic way as the determined creation of cultural value, and its outcomes as a process would remain unpredictable.

Second, creativity might be construed as irrational if it is a deliberately anti-rational process – that is, if it works by establishing or identifying a set of criteria and then acting in a manner which is intentionally contrary to those criteria. Some revolutionary art such as the Dada movement could be seen in these terms, where the explicit aim is to undermine established artistic norms.[12] But such behaviour is 'irrational' only when measured against the criteria it seeks to overthrow, and can be interpreted as perfectly rational, and possibly even systematic, orderly, logical, etc. when the objective is revolution. Pursuing these lines of reasoning may rapidly empty the words 'rational' and 'irrational' of any content at all.

Nevertheless we might conclude that to construe creativity as an irrational process is at least a testable proposition if, for example, we accept as a benchmark a rational model such as the one of constrained maximisation of value put forward in this chapter. Such a conclusion clearly indicates that the next step would be empirical – to what extent can the reality of creative work be seen to be consistent with the assumptions and predictions of such a model, or to what extent does the model fail? In the absence of comprehensive evidence we can simply offer several illustrations which might in fact indicate that no clear-cut resolution of this question will be possible – i.e. that different artists may conform to one or other model, or to none of them, and that no systematic pattern is evident.

The first example is Johann Sebastian Bach, whose music was composed by a process that appears to have been systematic and regular. His creative genius is now beyond dispute, but in his time he worked to write music which he understood to have value for the purposes for which it was written: cultural value in the service of the church and in the spiritual enlightenment which it conveyed, economic value in its capacity to earn him an income to support himself and his family.[13] A somewhat different illustration is Samuel Beckett who wrote *Waiting for Godot* as 'a relaxation', without any apparent sense that he was creating cultural or any other sort of value, let alone a masterpiece; indeed he regarded it as a 'bad play' and expressed continuing amazement that people found so much in it. It is something of an irony that this work has given rise to more books, articles and opinions than any other drama of the twentieth century.[14]

A further example is that of an artist for whom the actual process of creativity itself was all-important: the composer Sergei Prokofiev, who fits the 'work-preference' model very well. His wife wrote that

Sergei would not and could not imagine a single day without work . . . He was capable of composing without table or piano, in a railway carriage, a ship's cabin or a hospital. He would work no matter what mood he was in, in moments of euphoria or when he was in the doldrums . . . Being very strong-willed, he found it easy to do without many of the joys of life for the sake of the one he considered supreme: the joy of creation.[15]

Two more examples illustrate the creation of particular works whose economic value was an important motive for their production. The Impressionist artist Edgar Degas painted *A Cotton Office in New Orleans* in 1873 because he believed (wrongly) that it would appeal to a particular client in England, and he even changed his style to suit what he thought the market would like. In the event, the painting was sold in 1878 to a small museum in France, providing a much-needed boost to the insecure Degas family finances.[16] A similar concern about the economic return to particular works was shown by Igor Stravinsky, a composer who, though by no means poor, was often anxious about money; for example, his correspondence concerning the commissioning of a work for tenor, baritone, chorus and orchestra for the Venice Biennale in 1956 reveals a detailed preoccupation with the financial aspects of arrangements for the work's composition and first performance.[17] In both of these examples, then, the artist's objective function with respect to the works in question clearly contained the generation of both economic and cultural value as essential arguments.

Conclusions

Creativity remains an elusive phenomenon. This chapter has explored the possibilities for constructing creativity as an orderly process susceptible to analysis in rational terms. We have suggested that within the sphere of cultural production it can be sensibly understood in its real-world manifestations only if economic considerations are taken into account. In order to link a concept of creativity as a cultural phenomenon with the observable economic realities that impinge upon it, we have proposed a model based on the creation of cultural and economic value. In modelling the process of artistic production, where these values originate, we have suggested that not only do artists allocate their time in a dual labour market (arts/non-arts), they also sell the products of their labour into a dual market (the market for physical goods/market for ideas), where economic and cultural value provide distinct and separate measures of the success of their efforts.

Appendix: a model of artistic production

The model spelled out in this chapter can be specified in formal terms as follows. Assume that the artist can produce commercially-oriented artistic work or non-commercially-oriented artistic work. Both commercial and non-commercial artistic work yield both economic and cultural value, but commercial work yields primarily economic value and non-commercial work yields primarily cultural value. (It is assumed that both economic and cultural value can be measured by separate single-valued variables.)

The artist may also undertake non-arts work which yields only economic value. The artist's utility is a weighted function of the production of economic and cultural value. The decision variables are the amounts of labour time devoted to commercial artistic work, non-commercial artistic work and non-arts work. The sum of these labour inputs is constrained by the number of hours of work time available.

The artist's income consists of earned and unearned components. Earned income is a function of the economic value produced, unearned income is exogenous. There is a minimum income constraint which ceases to affect the decision variables if unearned income is sufficiently large. All variables are measured for a given time period.

Let v_c = level of cultural value produced

v_e = level of economic value produced

L_{ax} = arts labour time devoted to commercially-oriented artistic work (hours)

L_{ay} = arts labour time devoted to non-commercially-oriented artistic work (hours)

L_n = non-arts labour time (hours)

H = working time available per time period after allowance for a fixed amount of leisure time (hours)

Y = total income per time period

Y_u = unearned income per time period

Y_z = earned income per time period

Y^* = minimum income level required per time period.

Then the artist's decision problem is

$$\max u = u(wv_c, (1-w)v_e) \quad 0 \le w \le 1 \tag{6.1}$$

where

$$v_c = v_c(L_{ax}, L_{ay}) \tag{6.2}$$
$$v_e = v_e(L_{ax}, L_{ay}, L_n) \tag{6.3}$$

with

$$\partial v_c/\partial L_{ax} < \partial v_c/\partial L_{ay} \tag{6.4}$$
$$\partial v_e/\partial L_n > \partial v_e/\partial L_{ax} > \partial v_e/\partial L_{ay} \tag{6.5}$$

The constraint set is

$$L_{ax} + L_{ay} + L_n = H \tag{6.6}$$

and

$$Y \ge Y^* \tag{6.7}$$

where

$$Y = Y_u + Y_z(v_e) \tag{6.8}$$

with

$$\partial Y_z/\partial v_e > 0 \tag{6.9}$$

The equilibrium conditions for the polar cases of $w = 1$ (an artist concerned only with the production of cultural value) and $w = 0$ (an artist concerned only with the production of economic value) indicate that labour would be allocated so as to equate the marginal products deriving from (6.2) and (6.3), respectively. Given the relationships specified in (6.4) and (6.5), this suggests that when $w = 1$, $L_{ay} > L_{ax}$ and $L_n = 0$, and when $w = 0$, $L_n > L_{ax} > L_{ay}$. If (6.2) and (6.3) are linear, equilibrium will occur at $L_{ay} = H$ when $w = 0$ and at $L_n = H$ when $w = 1$. In the intermediate cases (where $0 < w < 1$), the outcome depends on the functional forms assumed, with interior solutions possible in both linear and non-linear specifications of (6.2) and (6.3).

Notes

1 Quotation is from Ruskin (1857, pp. 136–7).
2 On innovation in economic theory, see, for example, Mansfield (1995). The question of how innovations arise and are used is also a subject of interest in evolutionary economics; see, for example, Nelson and Winter (1982).
3 A pioneering exception is Bruno Frey's work on intrinsic and extrinsic motivation of economic behaviour; see Frey (1997b). Another exception is

Roger McCain's approach to creativity through 'cognitive economics'; see McCain (1992, chs. 18–19).

4 Quoted in length in Etlin (1996, pp. 38–9).

5 Etlin (1996, p. 39).

6 For a detailed example, see Etlin (1996, pp. 39–70).

7 As always it is expectations which govern behaviour, and the present case is no exception. In the following exposition value should be read as expected value when it enters an *ex ante* decision function. The specification of an expectations model here would present challenges, especially since in this field the gap between expected and actual is likely to be wide.

8 See Smith (1999).

9 For a comprehensive account of the commercial incentive to artistic output in both high and popular cultural forms, see Cowen (1998). William and Hilda Baumol suggest that the profusion of talented composers in the Vienna of Mozart's time can be explained by the proliferation of courtly jobs available to them; see Baumol and Baumol (1994).

10 See Throsby (1992); Wassall and Alper (1992); Towse (1993); Throsby and Thompson (1994); several papers in Heikkinen and Koskinen (1998); Jeffri and Greenblatt (1998); Caves (2000).

11 A 'work-preference' model of artist behaviour is constructed in Throsby (1994a).

12 Hans Richter, one of its participants, describes the Dada movement as 'an artistic revolt against art' (Richter, 1965, p. 7).

13 See Wolff (1991, chs. 1–4). On cultural value, note Bach's statement of 1738 that 'the ultimate end or final goal of all music . . . is nothing but for the honour of God and the renewal of the soul' (see Poulin, 1994, p. 11); see also Butt (1997, chs. 4–5). On Bach's interest in earning money, see Bettmann (1995, pp. 131–3).

14 See Bair (1978, pp. 381–3).

15 Quoted in Samuel (1971, pp. 118–19).

16 See Brown (1993). In working to a particular market, Degas reflected a characteristic of the French Impressionist *avant-garde* of the late nineteenth century, who specifically aimed to please an expanding middle-class capitalist clientele.

17 See Pozzi (1999).

7 Cultural industries

A chief source of the high prices paid to writers and, perhaps, the most profitable literary novelty of the nineteenth century [in Paris], was the newspaper serialization of their novels. Alexandre Dumas *père* wrote 100,000 lines a year for *Le Siècle* at 1.50 francs a line. Eugène Sue was paid 100,000 by *Le Constitutional* for *The Wandering Jew* . . . In turn serialized literature proved a tremendous circulation builder . . . An inevitable outgrowth of this was the use of publicity stunts and the fabrication of customer intrigue and anxiety as a means of merchandising literature. At times the publication of a serial novel was interrupted without explanation in order to create the impression that the author was ill and, perhaps, unable to produce the next installment when, in fact, the novel had been written and delivered in advance . . . 'Industrialised literature' . . . happens to describe well the methods of its greatest practitioner, Alexandre Dumas, *père*, who kept a stable of ghost writers readying manuscripts for his signature. In one of the literary jokes of the period the elder Dumas asks his son, also a novelist, 'Have you seen my latest work?' and Dumas *fils* answers, 'No, father, have you?'   (César Graña, *Bohemian versus Bourgeois*, 1964[1])

Introduction

Many creative artists resent the thought that their activities form part of an industry. Such a proposition, they believe, emphasises the commercial aspects of artistic production and subjugates the pure creative impulse to the demands of the market place. For those artists represented in chapter 6 as being motivated solely by the desire to create cultural value in their creative work without thought of economic gain, such a view is understandable. The heavy-footed economist, brandishing words such as 'market structure', 'concentration ratios', 'labour demand' and 'value-added', must indeed seem insensitive to the finer purposes of art.

Yet the fact that individuals and firms produce goods or services for sale or exchange, or even simply for their own pleasure, creates a grouping of activity around particular products, types of producers, locations, etc. which can be encircled in conceptual terms and labelled an industry. As we noted briefly in chapter 1 when introducing the term 'cultural industry', such a delineation need not imply any ideological or pejorative judgement, nor does it necessarily impose any economic or other type of motive on the industry participants. The paraphernalia of industry analysis comprise simply a convenient box of tools for representing and analysing the way in which the processes of production, consumption and exchange occur for given commodities.

Nevertheless, it has to be conceded that in practice the application of the word 'industry' to art and culture does focus attention on the economic processes by which cultural goods and services are made, marketed, distributed and sold to consumers. The term 'cultural industry' in contemporary usage does indeed carry with it a sense of the economic potential of cultural production to generate output, employment and revenue and to satisfy the demands of consumers, whatever other nobler purpose may be served by the activities of artists and by the exercise of the tastes of connoisseurs. Indeed many within the cultural sector, including presumably those artists whose objective functions contain some component of economic gain, welcome the idea that cultural activity makes a significant contribution to the economy. The argument here is that if culture in general and the arts in particular are to be seen as important, especially in policy terms in a world where economists are kings, they need to establish their economic credentials; what better way to do this than by cultivating the image of art as industry, bigger (in the Australian case, at least) than beer and footwear.[2]

Thus the field of the cultural industries comprises somewhat contested territory. For present purposes let us sidestep the value-loaded debate and concentrate on the ways in which the cultural industries may be defined and studied in contemporary economic analysis. We consider first the sorts of definitional issues that beset any industry study, and that are especially important in considering the cultural industries. We then look specifically at the core arts as an industry, and go on to widen the focus to deal with the cultural industries in urban and regional growth, in the economies of developing countries, in tourism and finally in international trade.

Definition of the cultural industries

Any self-respecting university course or textbook on industry economics spends some time at the outset discussing the difficulties of defining an industry – i.e. whether the concept of industry can be delineated according to groupings of producers, product classifications, factors of production, types of consumers, location, etc. What is problematical for industries in general is especially so in the cultural sphere because of uncertainties in the definition of cultural goods and services. We have noted in earlier chapters some of the ways in which cultural goods and services can be distinguished from other commodities in the economic system. In terms of industry definition, the categorisation of cultural commodities which we put forward in chapter 1 is probably the most useful – that cultural goods and services involve creativity in their production, embody some degree of intellectual property and convey symbolic meaning. Such a definition would enable specific industries to be defined around particular cultural products such as music, with the aggregation of all such products enabling reference to 'the cultural industries' as a whole. In some usages one or other of these character-istics on its own might be looked to as the principal definitional base. For example, creativity might be emphasised, as in the 'creative industries', a term used by a UK minister in 1998 to describe the arts sector's dynamic contribution to British economic performance.[3] Alternatively, the gener-ation of intellectual property might be seen as a sufficient criterion, enabling the terms 'the copyright industries' and the 'cultural industries' to be used more or less synonymously.[4]

Accepting the general definition of cultural commodities noted above allows us to propose a model of the cultural industries centred around the locus of origin of creative ideas, and radiating outwards as those ideas become combined with more and more other inputs to produce a wider and wider range of products. Thus at the core of this industry model lie the creative arts as traditionally defined: music, dance, theatre, literature, the visual arts, the crafts, and including newer forms of practice such as video art, performance art, computer and multimedia art and so on. Each of these artforms on its own can be regarded as an industry, and is frequently referred to as such, although such a usage generally embraces more than just the original producers. So, for example, the 'music industry' refers to an enormous range of partici-pants, including composers, performers, publishers, record companies, distributors, promoters, retailers, collecting societies and so on; even so the core of the industry can still be seen to be the original creative musician. An aggregation of all the artforms within a region, a nation, etc., together with their attendant service providers, can then be seen to comprise the arts industry as a whole for that region, nation or for whatever other unit is the focus of study.

The next group in the widening pattern of concentric circles defining the cultural industries comprises those industries whose output qualifies as a cultural commodity in the terms outlined above but where other non-cultural goods and services are also produced, such that the proportion of what might be termed 'primary cultural goods and services' is relatively lower than in the core arts case. Although precise boundaries are difficult to draw, this group can be thought of as including book and magazine publishing, television and radio, newspapers and film. In all of these cases both cultural and non-cultural goods and services are produced side by side. The inclusion of the film industry in this category may, however, be problematical. Some would place film clearly in the core arts group, others would see it as falling more into the media and entertainment category; in reality a subdivision into types of film would be required to assign sectors of the film industry into one category or the other.

Finally, in some interpretations the boundaries of the cultural industries are extended further to catch industries which operate essentially outside the cultural sphere but some of whose product could be argued to have some degree of cultural content. These industries include advertising, where creative input is required in some aspects of its operation; tourism, where some market segments are built on a cultural base; and architectural services, where design may strive for qualities beyond the purely functional. However, it is apparent that these industries could be thought of as a component of the cultural industries only if a very broad definitional basis were adopted.

The above scheme thus represents a concentric-circles model of the cultural industries, with the arts lying at the centre, and with other industries forming layers or circles located around the core, extending further outwards as the use of creative ideas is taken into a wider production context.[5] As in many other industries, the identification of key indicators of the size, nature and extent of economic activity for the cultural industries can present problems. In regard to *output*, for example, the means of measurement of the volume or value of production will vary according to the purpose required and the nature of the product produced. In the performing arts, output might be measured in different circumstances as the number of performances staged by a theatre company over some time period, the number of seats available or sold for a symphony concert series, or box office revenue for an opera or musical production. In the visual arts, on the other hand, one possible indicator of output might be the aggregate value of sales over a given month or year; however, this would have to be adjusted to account for the resale of works if a measure of the value of initial output were required.

When it comes to *employment* in the cultural industries, further difficulties of classification arise. A number of cultural producers such as many writers and composers are self-employed individuals who may not be picked up by employment or enterprise surveys or who may finish up in some other job or industry classification in census data. The definition of artist as an occupational classification for census purposes varies widely between jurisdictions, such that persons who would be regarded as eligible according to appropriate criteria may be excluded while ineligible ones are counted in. Many employees in the cultural industries work at what might be termed 'non-cultural jobs': accountants, technicians, administrators and so on. Yet again the line between, say, an artistic and a non-artistic job may be blurred for purposes of data collection; for example, are film editors, lighting technicians or sound recordists creative or technical workers?

In the area of *trade* in cultural goods, definitional problems also arise, exacerbated by the fact that much cultural trade is in rights rather than in physical commodities. In music, for example, the value of exports for a given country must compile the foreign royalty payments due to composers, performers, publishers and record companies on account of the musical works in which they hold rights, and add to that amount the value of physical products exported such as CDs, musical instruments and music scores, the revenues from the export of live performances and so on.

The creative arts as an industry

Let us now look at the core components of the cultural industries as defined above and consider the way in which the creative arts may be seen as an industry, or as a series of industries organised around the separate artforms. We consider in turn the characteristics of demand and supply, technology and the nature of factor and product markets.[6]

Demand for the arts

In economic theory the origins of demand are the tastes and preferences of consumers. Economics has not had a great deal to say about the formation of tastes, and indeed the new consumer theory goes so far as to do away with differences in tastes altogether, with variations in consumption behaviour being caused by differing shadow prices of commodities produced according to household production functions in which material goods and services enter as inputs; in this model the relative consumption of commodities rises and falls over time, not because of a shift in tastes but because the shadow prices of various goods and services change as experience, understanding and other human capital characteristics change. Notwithstanding the theoretical plausibility of such a model, however, economists studying differences between consumers' preference orderings for commodities are more likely to accept that tastes do indeed differ between individuals and that changes in tastes do shift demand functions; they are also likely to agree that questions as to how those tastes are formed are not a matter for economists but are better left to sociologists, psychologists and other behavioural scientists to explain.[7]

Whatever the theoretical underpinnings, there is one aspect of tastes as a force in determining demand that has particular relevance to the arts – the fact that taste for artistic goods and services is cumulative. It is apparent that a person's enjoyment of music, literature, drama, the visual arts and so on, and hence her willingness to spend money on consuming them, are importantly related to her knowledge and under-standing of these artforms. Such cultural competence is acquired through education and experience, and hence stronger and more discriminating tastes for the arts are likely to be shown by the better educated and by those who have already become consumers. The latter point can be traced back to Alfred Marshall, who recognised that enjoyment of what he referred to as 'good music' was an acquired taste that would increase over time with exposure; in chapter III of book III of his *Principles*, Marshall wrote: 'It is therefore no exception to the Law [of diminishing marginal utility] that the more good music a man hears, the stronger is his taste for it likely to become'.[8] In recent times these ideas have been formalised into a theory of rational addiction covering consumption of a range of goods from heroin to rock music.[9] Whether one calls it addiction or the cultivation of taste, it is clear that if any progress is to be made in explaining demand for the arts, the endogenisation of tastes in economic models will be essential, going at least as far as linking present to past consumption.[10]

For the rest, the specification of demand for the arts as an economic commodity can follow a fairly conventional route. So, for example, a demand function for attendance at live events in theatre, opera, dance and music would be expected to contain own price, price of substitute entertainments, consumer income and quality characteristics of performances as explanatory variables. The diversity of the product, and the discernment of consumers in deciding their attendances at particular performances, suggests that the qualitative characteristics of events (what work(s) are being performed, who is playing, what the critics have said) are likely to dominate price in determining demand. Furthermore, consumption of the live arts is highly time-intensive, indicating that the price of leisure time is likely to be more influential in determining demand than the ticket price itself.

Empirical studies of demand for the arts across the various artforms, from opera to literature, have derived price and income elasticities conforming broadly to *a priori* expectations. For example, demand is more price elastic for popular cultural forms than for the higher arts; in the latter case quality characteristics of the good or service provided do tend to outweigh price in influencing consumption decisions. Income elasticities, in turn, are found to be relatively higher for the arts than for many other commodities, because of the luxury nature and leisure content of some arts consumption, and also because of the association of tastes with education and hence (at one remove) with income.

Supply of the arts

The supply side of the arts industry comprises a very wide array of production units, ranging from global corporate enterprises down to individual self-employed producers. But a distinction can be made in analysing the arts between the profit-making and the non-profit sectors of the industry. Although clear-cut lines cannot be drawn, it can be broadly stated that profit-oriented supply in the arts embraces popular entertainments and cultural forms where demand is strong and widespread and where financial motives dominate over artistic values in the organisation of production. Supply characteristics in this sector of the arts industry can be analysed in terms similar to those applicable to any commercially-based industry in the economy, with the difference only that there may occasionally be grounds for asserting the public interest in some way or another if the cultural content of output warrants it – for example, in regard to trade. The non-profit sector, on the other hand, embraces the more esoteric art forms such as classical music, jazz, 'serious' drama, poetry, opera, classical and modern dance, the fine arts, contemporary visual art and so on. Production activities within these product groupings tend to be more concerned with artistic values than with financial gain, as indeed the designation 'non-profit' indicates. Suppliers may be unincorporated individual artists (dealt with further below), firms incorporated as not-for-profit enterprises under appropriate corporations law or publicly owned and operated firms organised on a non-profit basis.

Some scholars in contemporary cultural studies regard the drawing of a distinction between the high arts and popular culture as demonstrating an old-fashioned elitism, conservatism and a privileging of hegemonic forms of cultural practice. It is certainly true that lines between different forms of cultural expression have become blurred over time such that sharp divisions between the high arts and popular culture are increasingly difficult to draw. It is also undeniable that a term such as 'high culture' has long been associated with the cultural consumption of the wealthy and privileged classes in society. But for present purposes, when we are looking at the arts as an industry, it is possible without ideological overtones to identify the production and consumption of the core artforms in economic rather than in cultural terms, and to observe the distinctive characteristics of their economic organisation.

Returning to the non-profit characteristic, we note first that most of the explanations for the existence of voluntary not-for-profit firms in a market economy can be applied to the arts. For example, the hypothesis that such firms exist in response to unsatisfied demand for public goods could be readily invoked if the arts give rise to beneficial externalities or to public goods where consumers believe that existing government supply, if any, of such goods is inadequate. Alternatively, it can be suggested that arts firms can extract additional consumers' surplus from their customers – e.g. through voluntary donations – only if they are organised on a not-for-profit basis. Indeed when arts organisations are in receipt of government grants and subsidies, and/or look to individual and corporate donors for financial support, as many do, the not-for-profit form is the only realistic corporate structure available to them.[11]

As noted in chapter 6, the behaviour of non-profit firms in the arts such as theatres, opera and dance companies, symphony orchestras, smaller musical ensembles, non-commercial museums and galleries and so on, can be modelled in similar terms to those applied to individual creative artists. The goals of such firms can be seen to comprise primarily the production of cultural value, subject to both economic and cultural constraints. In more specific terms, the generation of cultural value by non-profit arts firms can be portrayed via an objective function wherein the quality of work produced (however 'quality' is defined) and the audience reach (numbers of attendees or consumers of the product) are the joint maximands, and a break-even financial requirement is entered as a minimum constraint on the generation of economic value. As would be expected, this model would predict that such an enterprise will tend to produce more output and devote more resources to quality than a corresponding profit-maximising firm.[12]

Technology

Technological change has profound effects on both production and consumption patterns within the arts industry. On the production side, one of the most obvious of contemporary influences has been the effect of computer technology and advances in video and sound reproduction on the process of artistic creation and on the nature of products produced. While it is tempting to hail such developments as a thoroughly modern phenomenon, an artefact of the twentieth and twenty-first centuries, technological advance has always characterised the arts industry, with many innovations over the centuries having significant effects on production processes and on the type of outputs produced, such as the development of fresco painting in the thirteenth century, or the invention of the fortepiano in the eighteenth.

Nevertheless, one of the most persistent debates in the economics of the arts has been the role of technology in the live performing arts. In a pure sense productivity improvements in the live arts, and to a lesser extent in some other areas of artistic production, are not possible in the same way as they are in, say, manufacturing. The physical output per unit of labour input in the latter sector has risen by several thousand per cent over the last 200 years, whereas the labour requirement to give a live performance of a Haydn string quartet has not changed in the slightest over the same period. As Baumol and Bowen (1966) originally pointed out using a two-sector model comprising a productive (manufacturing) and an unproductive (arts) sector, wage rises in the economy as a whole cannot be offset by productivity gains in the arts industry in the same way as they are in manufacturing, leading to the potential for an ever-widening gap between costs and earned revenue in arts organisations.[13]

The implications of the Baumol and Bowen hypothesis for the arts have been clarified over the thirty-five years or so since it was first put forward. We may draw attention to at least half a dozen ways in which the live arts have withstood the pressures imposed by stagnant productivity. First, technical changes have occurred in areas such as venue design, sound and lighting facilities, etc., enabling larger audiences to participate as immediate consumers of live performance. Secondly, media reproduction technology has extended consumption much further, and has enabled significant new revenue sources for companies to be accessed. Thirdly, factor use has been adjusted by many companies in response to cost pressures, such as performing plays with simpler sets and smaller casts, notwithstanding the possible ramifications of such strategies for the quality of the companies' output. Fourthly, factor price adjustments have not occurred in the arts to the full extent suggested by the two-sector model; in particular, arts companies have not always found it necessary to match wage rises elsewhere in order to attract or retain an adequate supply of labour, and furthermore widespread use of voluntary labour is evident in some areas of the arts, notably the museum and gallery sector. Fifthly, rising consumer incomes and changing tastes have maintained some secular growth in demand for the arts, although the benefits of such demand shifts have been unevenly spread among different types of artistic product. Finally, a widening range of public- and private-sector sources has been called upon to fill the income gap over time; for example, new models for mutually beneficial partnerships between arts organisations and corporate enterprises are constantly being developed and refined. As a result of these various mitigating influences, empirical studies of the so-called 'cost-disease phenomenon' in the arts have by and large found little evidence of differential rates of inflation in the performing arts compared with other sectors of the economy.[14] These studies have shown that the combined impacts of production adjustments, increased demand and generally rising levels of unearned revenue have countered any tendency towards a secular rise in deficits among arts companies, suggesting that although the cost disease will doubtless continue to present such companies with difficult problems, it is unlikely to be terminal.

Technological change also affects the demand side of the arts industry. Scale economies in consumption in some artforms reduce the marginal cost of adding a consumer to close to zero, and make available a far wider range of consumption experiences to individual consumers in the market. One outcome of these trends has been the creation of super-stars whose rise to fame may not be entirely explicable in terms of their talent.[15] The advent of the internet as a locus for arts consumption, and of the broader digital economy as a principal domain of cultural interchange, is likely also to have significant effects on many aspects of structure, conduct and performance in the arts industry in the future.

Labour markets

Artistic labour markets present some intriguing challenges to a labour economist seeking to understand the standard variables usually considered in models of labour market behaviour – labour supply, wage determination, earnings distributions, career paths and so on. Some aspects of the arts labour market seem to conform to conventional theory, others are more complex.

To begin with, there are problems of definition to which we alluded above – is there a distinction between cultural and non-cultural workers in the arts industry, and if we confine attention to creative artists (as most analytical work has done), can we regard them as a homogeneous group for purposes of analysis? In regard to the first question, it is probably true that non-cultural workers in the arts industry do conform to conventional labour market theories of wages, earnings, etc. and hence may not present any particular puzzles to economic analysis; accountants or electricians working in theatre companies, for example, are probably little different from accountants or electricians working in any other industry in terms of their labour market behaviour. But if we focus attention on cultural workers, taken here to be synonymous with creative artists, we find considerable diversity of occupational status and behaviour. In the case of employment status, for example, only a relatively small proportion of artists work as employees, receiving a regular wage or salary and enjoying the benefits that regular employment brings. By and large, it is only performing artists – actors, dancers, singers, instrumental musicians – who have the opportunity to work in this way. Some such artists are fortunate enough to be employed by an established company, and receive not only regular pay but also leave entitlements, superannuation benefits and security of tenure. But in most cases they are in the minority, and the reality is that most performing artists, even though formally speaking they are employees, are likely to work on a sporadic or short-term contract basis. If they are unionised, as they often are, they are at least able to look forward to minimum rates of pay for the period they are lucky enough to be in work, but they are likely to enjoy few accompanying benefits and no guarantees of continuity of employment.

Indeed many performing artists are better regarded as self-employed freelancers, and this occupational category also describes the great majority of non-performing creative artists – writers, visual artists, craftspeople, composers, directors, designers and others. Among these, those whose work entails producing things for sale – i.e. writers, painters, sculptors and so on – do not earn wages from their artwork at all (except when working to commission); hence they are better regarded as small business people, whether incorporated or not, rather than strictly as workers. Nevertheless, despite all these variations among the artistic labour force, analysis of artistic labour markets has tended to look at all creative artists through the one lens of labour market theory, although a distinction between initial creative artists and interpretive artists (i.e. essentially between non-performing and performing artists) is occasionally made.

Four characteristics of arts labour markets can be highlighted as distinctive. First, the labour force comprises relatively few workers who choose, or who are able, to work full-time at their creative occupation. The industry thus contains a predominance of part-time workers, the majority of whom hold other jobs either elsewhere in the arts industry (e.g. as teachers) or in some other industry altogether. We have referred in chapter 6 to the incentives towards multiple job-holding among creative artists, deriving from the need to earn a minimum income for survival and from the desire for some financial security. Empirical studies have confirmed the intuitive hypothesis that multiple job-holding among professional artists arises mostly out of necessity rather than by choice. The second feature of arts labour markets to be noted is the extreme skewness in earnings distributions, with the great majority of practitioners earning very low rewards, but with a handful of stars attracting very large rents. These latter wealthy artists may raise mean incomes across the industry marginally, but generally average annual earnings from practice as an artist are well below what would be predicted for any other group of workers with similar human capital attributes. Yet, despite the low expected rewards, there is generally – in most artforms in most countries – an oversupply of labour. This apparent paradox is discussed further below.

Thirdly, although the human capital model has had some success in explaining earnings differentials among artists, its findings have shown up some peculiarities. It appears, for example, that formal training is not as significant a determinant of eventual financial success in the arts as it is in other occupations and, as artists' careers progress, learning-on-the-job plays a stronger role. In fact it can be shown that the traditional human capital variables of education and accumulated experience have differential effects on the three different types of occupation that artists characteristically pursue (often simultaneously): creative arts work, arts-related work such as teaching, and non-arts work.[16] Even so, many believe that success as an artist is entirely explicable in terms of a single quality, the individual's 'talent'; however, in formal analytical terms the role of talent in contributing to a successful artistic career remains undetermined as long as independent and reliable measures of this quality continue to be elusive. Finally, risk is acknowledged to be a factor in influencing career choice and subsequent earnings levels among artists, but its impacts are debatable. Certainly a greater degree of uncertainty attaches to expected rewards in the arts than in most other careers, but it is unclear whether the prospect of a gamble attracts or deters new entrants. For some, the lure of becoming famous is irresistible, despite the very low probability of success. For others, uncertainty is simply accepted as an inevitable concomitant of an artistic career. Risk-averse artists are likely to manage risk through multiple job-holding and other strategies.

In the end, it tends to be issues of art-for-art's-sake, the inner drive of the creative spirit, art-as-a-way-of-life and other aspects of the non-pecuniary attractions of artistic work which contribute to the distinctive differences between arts labour markets and those in other industries. In terms of our discussion in chapter 6, some sense can be made of some of the peculiarities of labour markets in the arts by reference to the notions of economic and cultural value in influencing the work of creative artists. In particular, reference to the non-monetary rewards of being an artist places the issue of oversupply of artistic labour in a wider perspective. As Pierre-Michel Menger has pointed out, an oversupply of artists has historically been characteristic of the industry, from the glut in Parisian novelists and poets in the early nineteenth century to that of musicians in England over a long period through to the present day.[17] Some part of the excess supply of labour is attributable to the actions of arts organisations in seeking to keep as large a pool of talent available as possible, but the flexibility in individual behaviour – moving in and out of the profession as circumstances change – and the psychic income generated from creative work may suggest that the importance of disequilibrium in the arts labour market can be overstated.

Goods markets

Models of demand, supply and price determination in voluntary exchange markets can be applied to any cultural good or service, and demand functions and supply decisions have been formalised and analysed for a number of artistic products, especially in the performing arts. But nowhere in the arts have market processes been more extensively or rigorously studied than in the markets for art objects —

paintings, *objets d'art* and other collectibles. The reasons are twofold. First, most of these markets, such as fine art auctions, come close to the ideal of a freely functioning market process with little or no market distortion, and even where irregularities such as information asymmetries appear, they may be able to be taken into account in analytical work. Secondly, comprehensive and reliable data of the sort to make an econometrician's eyes light up with delight are frequently available, not just for contemporary times but for historical periods as well.[18]

Just as in the labour markets discussed above, so also in goods markets do the arts display some distinctive features. Confining our attention to the market for physical artworks (paintings, pieces of sculpture, other artefacts), we can note that the goods traded are unusual as a generic commodity group in that they are created only by individuals. Every unit of output is differentiated from every other unit of output, an extreme case of a non-homogeneous commodity. For the work of artists no longer living, supply is non-augmentable. Artworks can be copied but not reproduced, in the sense that ultimately there is only one unique original of every work of art.[19] They provide clear consumption benefits to purchasers through their utilitarian characteristics as durable private goods. At the same time, artworks form part of the cultural capital of a nation or of the world (some more so than others), and thus have, to a greater or lesser degree, public-good characteristics, especially when they are acquired by galleries or collections for public showing. Because artworks can be resold, and their prices may rise over time, they have the characteristics of financial assets, and as such may be sought as a hedge against inflation, as a store of wealth, or as a source of speculative capital gain.

For the purposes of economic analysis of market behaviour, the essential features of artworks that animate the utility functions of buyers can be captured by distinguishing between art as *decoration* – i.e. art providing immediate consumption services through its aesthetic or decorative qualities – and art as *asset* – i.e. art providing financial services through its potential for price appreciation. Thus the price of a particular artwork realised in the marketplace could be expected to be influenced partly by the buyer's desire to have the piece on display for the pleasure it provides, and partly by the expectation that on resale it may provide a handsome capital windfall. Studies of art prices have imputed the observed spread between average rates of return on artworks and returns on other financial assets of comparable riskiness as measuring the consumption value of the art. To put it more clearly, an average portfolio of artworks is likely to return less over time to its owner than will an average portfolio of stocks and bonds; the difference can be construed as the price the investor pays to enjoy the artworks on her dining room wall. Ultimately, however, the analysis of markets in artworks may be most plausibly carried out within a cultural capital framework, where the works traded can be interpreted as assets embodying and generating both economic and cultural value. By articulating the latter, the distinctive characteristics of investment and trading in artistic goods can be identified.[20]

Cultural industries in urban regeneration and regional growth

The role of culture in an urban context is becoming more clearly recognised as increasing concern is felt in all parts of the world at the relentless growth of cities and at the economic, social and environmental problems which accompany such growth. The importance of the arts in the economic life of the city and as a catalyst for urban regeneration was first recognised several decades ago. More recently, interest has widened to embrace broader issues of the urban cultural fabric, community values and the prospects for re-thinking urban design along environmentally and culturally sensitive lines.[21]

Culture, in both of the senses in which we are using the term, is importantly implicated in the process of urban development. At least four non-mutually-exclusive roles for culture in the life of cities can be observed. First, a specific cultural facility may comprise on its own a significant cultural symbol or attraction affecting the urban economy: the Leaning Tower of Pisa or the Alhambra Palace in Granada are examples. Second, and more often, a 'cultural district' may act as a node for development in the local area, such as occurs in Pittsburgh or Dublin. Third, the cultural industries, especially the performing arts, may constitute a vital component of a city's economy, not just in major centres like London or New York but also in smaller regional towns and cities as well. Fourth, culture may have a more pervasive role in urban development through the fostering of community identity, creativity, cohesion and vitality, via the cultural characteristics and practices which define the city and its inhabitants.[22]

The economic ramifications of these manifestations of culture are well known. They include, first, the direct revenue impacts of cultural activities on the local economy through spending on cultural goods and services by local and non-local consumers; such expenditures may be seen as a contributor to regional growth under conditions of secularly rising consumer incomes and shifts in tastes towards cultural and leisure activities. Second, there are the indirect or second-round spending effects on the incomes of related businesses and individuals such as restaurants and transport services. Third, employment effects, both direct and indirect, of expanded cultural activity may be significant. In some cases the cultural sector can provide a replacement for jobs lost in the processes of industrial transition; in most cases, the quality of the jobs provided is seen as advantageous, since employment in arts-related businesses or in cultural institutions may provide a more interesting and satisfying working environment for employees than work in some other areas. Fourth, culture may have wider economic implications for urban revitalisation through the opportunities it affords for diversification of the local economic base; this may be particularly important for regions suffering industrial decline in a post-Fordist age. Finally, there may also be longer-run externalities with real economic potential if the enhancement of the cultural environment of a city leads to greater social cohesion, a stronger sense of civic pride, lower crime rates, increased economic dynamism and so on. These sorts of factors may be important in improving the profile or image of the city as a desirable location for in-migration of capital and establishment of new businesses.[23]

The above phenomena have been reflected in urban policy formulation at national, regional and local levels over the past several decades in a number of countries. The European experience is broadly typical.[24] By and large we might see the 1950s and 1960s as the time when the arts, especially the elite arts, began to be recognised more clearly as important in urban life. During the 1970s a period of policy consolidation occurred around notions of personal and community development, participation, egalitarianism, democratisation of urban space and the encouragement of a stronger sense of the cultural, social and environmental aspects of city life. During the 1980s and 1990s, however, these softer ideas about culture in the urban setting have tended to yield to harder notions of the economic potential for urban cultural development: maximising the economic returns in revenue and employment terms to the local economy, promotion of cities' 'images' as dynamic economic centres, and co-opting culture as a positive economic force in the social and physical regeneration of declining urban areas.

At the present time the policy focus could be seen as one of trying to come to terms with the phenomenon of globalisation and its impact on the economic and cultural life of the city.[25] In this process the various antecedents to urban policy described above can still be discerned. These include a concern for the importance of the arts and creativity and an acknowledgement of the significance of cultural pluralism and diversity within the global context, alongside a recognition of the powerful economic forces at work. The current period could therefore be characterised as one searching for a holistic model wherein both cultural and economic considerations can be properly represented, and policies can be developed which balance the multiple economic, cultural, social, environmental and other objectives of urban development, and which assert a role for local cultural differentiation in a globalising international economy. Such a model is provided by the notion of the 'sustainable city', an urban form which combines attention to environmental concerns through measures such as improved public transit, energy efficiency, recycling and waste management, use of open space, etc. with a recognition of the cultural values of identity, belonging, creativity and participation that can be enhanced through culturally enlightened urban planning.

Within this context the concept of cultural capital is a useful way of depicting the place of culture in the urban setting. Heritage buildings, cultural institutions, facilities such as theatres, concert halls, craft workshops, artists' studios and so on can all be seen as capital assets, and the people who produce cultural goods and services in these facilities – actors, musicians, craftspeople, writers, technicians, designers, administrators and many others – all contribute to the generation of economic and cultural value over time. Furthermore, the fostering of social cohesion and identity through local cultural development can be interpreted as being directed at the intangible web of cultural connections and interactions which supports the urban community and gives it meaning. These phenomena are examples of intangible cultural capital – the stock of practices, customs, traditions, etc. which the present generation has inherited, and which it will adapt and add to before passing on. Urban development projects and strategies can be seen as implicating all of these types of capital, with long-term payoffs being measured in both economic and cultural terms.

Cultural industries in the economies of developing countries

In the Third World, the concept of culture as industry has some particular connotations. In primitive societies, as we noted in chapter 4, culture and economy are to a considerable degree one and the same thing. As development proceeds and the economy becomes more differentiated, cultural factors may continue to exert a significant influence on the methods of production and the types of products produced. In this process, some specific cultural industries will emerge, defined in the terms set out on pp. 112–14 above. It is useful to ask to what extent the cultural industries *per se* can be a force for development in the economies of the developing world. To throw some light on this issue, we take the particular case of the music industry.

The importance of music as a corner-stone of cultural life in developing countries is well understood.[26] The production of local popular music has grown from its roots in long-established local culture, and has emerged in many countries in the developing world to become a significant economic industry through the wider spread of live music practice, local and national broadcasting, the establishment of a domestic recording industry and eventually, for some participants, access to the international music market. This process originates with the fact that production of music for economic gain can provide a relatively accessible avenue for individuals and groups to move into the cash economy. Many of the performance skills will already have been acquired, and capital requirements and barriers to entry are relatively low. Typically individuals or groups begin with live performance for payment and, if they are successful and motivated, they may move into broadcasting or recording for the local market. In many countries throughout the developing world, small-scale recording companies have sprung up over the years, serving local broadcasting networks and retail outlets. Since there is often no effective copyright regime in force, the costs to users can be quite small, and of course this also means that the returns to composers and performers of the music are likely to be similarly constrained.

Eventually, however, the emerging local music industries of developing countries are affected by the international market, through two avenues. First, the production sector of the music industry in these countries becomes increasingly a target for the large transnational record companies. Secondly, consumers' demands for the sort of music that circulates internationally grows as such music becomes more readily available, as incomes rise and as tastes change; thus the proportion of domestically produced music in a country's total music demand tends to decline as development proceeds.

What, then, are the chances that artists and music styles from developing countries might break into world markets and hence might contribute to the local economy through the generation of export revenue? Some local music genres have grown over time to dominate the international scene, beginning with jazz and moving on to rock'n'roll, rap, hiphop, reggae and other musical forms. Nevertheless, despite the apparently rapid uptake of musical style and fashion by the international recording industry, artists from the South have found it very difficult to be recorded and to gain exposure in the international marketplace. In most cases, music from the Third World has been brought to wider attention through the activities of independent record producers, standing somewhat apart from the major transnational companies, and through the development of the specific category known as World Music representing a range of specific musical genres or styles originating in various parts of the world, including such musics as *salsa* from Cuba and Puerto Rico, *zouk* from the French Antilles, *rembetika* from Greece, *raï* from Algeria, *qawwali* from Pakistan and India and many more.[27]

It is apparent, then, that while music can be a significant contributor to economic life in developing countries as an important industry in the domestic economy, its role cannot be assessed without reference to the impacts on it of the global music industry, which becomes inexorably a more and more significant force as development proceeds. The globalisation of music has seen a dominating role played by the publishing and sound recording industries centred in the United States, Europe and Japan, with a handful of transnational corporations gaining an ever-growing control over the market. In these circumstances, the scope for independent artists and music producers, especially from the developing world, to gain a share of the market is severely constrained. While some local musical genres and styles have been taken up on the international circuit, establishing a means for cultural interchange and diffusion and leading in some cases to substantial economic rewards for a few individuals and for some developing economies, the penetration of local music into the world sphere has been very slow. Where it has occurred, it has generally been under the control of the global industry; in many cases it has happened without any payment whatsoever accruing to the originators of the music. A stronger copyright regime in the future will be important in dealing with this problem and in ensuring appropriate rewards to musical creators, not just in developing countries but throughout the world.[28]

Cultural tourism

Tourism occupies a somewhat unusual position in relation to the cultural industries. In the broadest sense all tourism, whether domestic or international, has a cultural dimension. The motives of consumers in travelling to new places may simply be leisure or curiosity, but the experiences they have when they get there are undeniably located within a cultural context and are replete with cultural messages which may or may not be comprehended or appreciated. Even tourists holidaying at resorts which present a standardised tourism experience with no reference to the locality or region in which the resort is situated are caught within some sort of cultural milieu, even if it provides them only with a pre-packaged and homogenised experience. Furthermore, tourism in broad cultural terms is a two-way process, with a number of different types of cultural interaction, some positive and some negative, occurring in both directions between visitors and host community.[29]

In a more specific sense, however, tourism can be seen not so much as a cultural industry in its own right but rather as a user of the products of other industries within the cultural sector – the performing arts, museums and galleries, heritage sites and so on. At a local or regional level these cultural industries may be strongly tied to tourism, supplying the tourist industry with a range of products and in turn depending to a greater or lesser degree on tourists for their economic livelihood. The phenomenon of mass tourism, brought about by the falling real cost of international travel and increased consumer spending on leisure, has led to large-scale expansion of tourist infrastructures in many parts of the world. The cultural impacts of mass tourism are well known, ranging from the physical pressures imposed by large numbers of tourists on heritage sites to the damage that may be caused to local community cultural values if an area is constantly being invaded by crass and insensitive visitors.

In a still more specific sense, tourism and culture come together in the niche market that has come to be known as 'cultural tourism'. Whereas mass tourism is high-volume, low-cost and provides a pre-packaged commodity, cultural tourism is low-volume, high-cost and tailored to individual demands. Typical cultural tourism experiences include purposive visits (whether individually or part of a group) to cultural festivals or specific cultural sites, or longer tours constructed around a cultural theme – opera, places with literary associations, indigenous communities, archeological sites, art galleries, etc. While some enthusiastic tourism promoters hail cultural tourism as a new phenomenon, in fact it has been around for a long time – the European Grand Tour of the nineteenth century, for example, was a form of cultural tourism undertaken, then as now, by the wealthy and privileged for purposes of education and self-improvement.[30] Of all the types of tourism noted above, cultural tourism is clearly that with the closest relationship to the cultural industries of host locations and/or to the cultural practices and ways of living of host communities.

The economic benefits and costs of tourism, both large- and small-scale, are well documented.[31] The principal issues lying at the intersection of the economic and cultural aspects of tourism have to do with possible conflicts between the economic incentives driving the tourist industry and the cultural values upon which tourism impinges or relies. While it is true that tourism provides an economic stimulus and financial support for much cultural activity, it may also have adverse cultural impacts. Damage to cultural sites, congestion of cultural facilities, inappropriate hotel or resort development in culturally sensitive areas and so on, are all examples of ways in which pursuit of the financial rewards from tourism provision may have negative cultural ramifications. Thus tourism strategies which seek to maximise the economic gains from tourist expansion – as proposed, for example, by regional development authorities and other public agencies – may require consideration of such cultural impacts if they are to be successful.

An appropriate framework within which to consider both the cultural and the economic consequences of tourism is again that provided by sustainability. Indeed the notion of sustainable tourism is now well established,[32] deriving primarily from the concerns about the impacts of tourism on the environment. In fact there is a close parallel between tourism that can be judged sustainable with respect to environmental amenity and that which is sustainable in cultural terms. In both environmental and cultural contexts, such tourism would be expected to be sensitive to local values, non-intrusive and non-degrading of affected sites. Instead of seeking to extract short-term profits from the exploitation of tourist demand, it would aim at preserving and enhancing the very environmental and cultural amenities which have attracted the tourists in the first place. It can be suggested that sustainable tourism strategies can lead in the long term to win–win outcomes, with positive effects on both cultural values and economic profitability.[33]

Trade policy and the cultural exception

During the 1990s the word 'culture' began to crop up more and more frequently in the context of international trade. There has always been trade in cultural products of one sort or another, including a long history of illicit trade in cultural property. There has also been a degree of intervention in trade in cultural goods, particularly in order to prevent national heritage items such as artworks (so-called 'national treasures') from leaving the country in which they are located. But the revolution in communications technologies and the apparently relentless forces of economic globalisation which have appeared over the last decade or so have cast cultural considerations in international trade into an entirely new context.

Three different arenas can be seen as the principal focal points for these developments: negotiations leading up to and consequent upon the replacement of the General Agreement on Tariffs and Trade (GATT) with the World Trade Organisation (WTO) in 1994; the implementation of the North America Free Trade Agreement (NAFTA) between Canada, the United States and Mexico also in 1994; and the negotiations within the Organisation for Economic Cooperation and Development (OECD) for a Multilateral Agreement on Investment (MAI), begun in 1995 and never concluded. Although the detail of the concerns within each of these forums has differed, it is convenient for our purposes here to consider them together, drawing attention to the broad issues common to them all.

The economic imperative driving the world trading system towards a reduction in protectionism and a freeing up of global markets is based, of course, on the simple proposition that free trade maximises world welfare. In a world where comparative advantage promotes specialisation in production and mutually beneficial international exchange, inter-vention to distort the free flow of goods and services will result in a loss of efficiency and a reduction in economic welfare.

The appearance of cultural commodities such as films and television programmes in international trade exemplifies the two different aspects of culture which we defined in chapter 1. One aspect relates to the production of such goods and the other is concerned with the cultural impacts in consumption. On the production side, it is culture in the functional sense which is involved; the export of cultural product into the international trading system constitutes a significant economic contri-bution which the cultural industries in a given country can make to the national economy. Many countries earn valuable foreign exchange from the export of such cultural goods and services, most notably the United States, which is overwhelmingly the largest exporter of cultural goods in the world. On the receiving end, on the other hand, it is the notion of culture as ways of life and as an expression of group identity that is implicated. Imported cultural product brings with it symbolic messages that may be seen as detrimental to local cultural identity. Thus the positions of the two sides of the market can be identified. On the one hand, the producers of certain cultural goods and services see lucrative trading opportunities in many parts of the world which they wish to exploit. They have access to scale and other economies in production which enable product to be supplied at highly competitive prices, and there is often a strong demand from consumers in importing countries for the material they supply. Exporting countries are thus opposed to any intervention which will limit their market access. On the other side of the fence, importing countries see their local culture being swamped by foreign product, against which the local cultural industries are unable to compete without some form of protection.

The argument in trade circles has centred on the question as to whether or not cultural goods are different from other goods. If they are, then cultural exceptions may be included in trade agreements, allowing some form of protection of domestic cultural industry. Just as quarantine laws prohibit the import of disease-bearing plants and animals, so does cultural protection seek to shield the community from infection by foreign cultural influences. Thus, for example, both France and Canada have argued strongly for a cultural exception in trade agreements affecting them, because of fears of cultural dominance from the United States. Other countries, such as Australia, impose regulations on radio and television stations to provide for a minimum content of locally generated material in their broadcasts which might otherwise contain nothing but imported programmes.

To some, such interference with the free flow of goods, services and information comprises an illiberal and authoritarian restriction on consumer choice. Many economists, to whom any form of market distortion is anathema, would point to the economic costs and inefficiencies induced by such protection. But a broader view of the matter might indicate a tempering of this position. Two arguments might be suggested. First, it may be true that French consumers, say, would watch nothing but American television programmes and attend foreign rather than French movies, if given a free choice. But there may be doubts as to whether their choice would be fully informed, or whether it would reflect a genuine expression of fundamental preferences. There is some evidence that people are willing to pay something to protect expressions of local cultural identity, even if they do not always consume such cultural product directly themselves.[34] In other words, if specifically domestic modes of cultural expression produce some public goods such as feelings of national pride and solidarity, or some beneficial externalities such as a pool of trained local talent, there may be sound economic reasons for some degree of government intervention in the market to support such activities; if so, protection may in some circumstances be an appropriate instrument to use, and the efficiency costs imposed may be seen as the price paid to secure the external benefits or the public goods in question.

The second point goes beyond economic concerns and brings into play the notion of cultural value as a desired aspect of human existence. It may be argued that the preservation of a national cultural identity, as is clearly the aim in the French and Canadian positions noted above, generates cultural value for the respective communities which stands somewhat apart from the economic gains and losses arising within the trading system. Trade negotiations are traditionally all about economics, and any suggestion that cultural value might be taken into account in determining the 'rules of the game' would be likely to be scorned or dismissed as special pleading, especially by economists. Yet the fact that cultural identification, self-recognition and self-esteem are important to people, and that these values are impacted upon by trade, should give pause for thought. Economic policy-making in this area may need to accept that the ultimate goals of different societies extend beyond immediate economic concerns, and that cultural values might therefore be specifically admitted into the policy-making process in this area. No doubt it was considerations such as these which prompted nations at the Stockholm Conference in April 1998 to agree to 'promote the idea that cultural goods and services should be fully recognized and treated as being not like other forms of merchandise'.[35] The United States was represented at this Conference, despite its not currently being a member of UNESCO; it would seem unlikely, however, that its delegates would have agreed with this proposition.

Language, in this area as everywhere else, both reflects and influences prevailing opinion. The use of the word 'exception' to describe the treatment of cultural goods in international trade conveys a somewhat negative sense, that culture is the misfit, a hindrance to the achievement of an otherwise perfect uniformity in the world trading system. If the protection of cultural values and the pursuit of other cultural objectives were accepted as a legitimate element alongside the pursuit of economic value in influencing trade policy at an international level, perhaps the term 'cultural recognition' would provide a more positive orientation in describing efforts to deal with this matter in negotiations between countries.

Conclusions

This chapter has ranged widely over the ways in which culture is implicated in the industrial structure of the economy, from the central role of the creative arts industries in the economies of developed and developing countries to the wider ramifications of the cultural industries, including their contribution to urban revitalisation, tourism and trade. In all of these various manifestations, culture emerges as a potential source of economic dynamism in a local, national or international setting. While care must be taken not to oversell the economic importance of the cultural industries, it is nevertheless true that these industries are placed in many respects at the leading edge of development into the twenty-first century. Such a statement can be rationalised on several grounds, including the following:

- changing patterns of consumption and rising real incomes are leading to secular increases in the demand for cultural goods and services
- the cultural industries are important content-providers in the development of new information and communications technologies
- the cultural industries foster creative thought and expression, which are important to processes of innovation and technological change, and
- the cultural industries can have a strong impact on employment levels, and as they grow they can contribute to absorbing labour released from declining sectors of the economy.

In the midst of all the enthusiasm about the potential economic dynamism of the cultural industries, however, we should not lose sight of the fact that the creation of economic value is not their only *raison d'être*. Processes of production and consumption in the arts and culture, and the broader role of culture in articulating essential values by which human beings express their identity and work out ways of living together, have a crucial content of cultural value, defined against different yardsticks from those we use to measure economic success. Any consideration of the cultural industries, at the micro or the macro level, cannot afford to overlook or downplay this critical dimension.

Notes
1 Quotation is from Graña (1964, p. 34).
2 See Australia Council (1996, p. 32), where the value of the total supply of goods and services to the Australian economy in 1993–4 was estimated at $A4.8 billion for the arts industry group, $A3.7 billion for beer and other alcoholic beverages and $A1.3 billion for footwear. For British studies of the size and impact of the arts sector, see Myerscough (1988); Rolfe (1992). Cultural economists have been critical of 'impact' studies in which the economic importance of the arts industries or of specific arts events or institutions have been overstated; see Seaman (1987), Bille Hansen (1995) and van Puffelen (1996).
3 The Minister was the Rt. Hon. Chris Smith, Secretary of State for Culture, Media and Sport; his collected thoughts on this subject have been published as Smith (1998). The same term 'creative industries' has been used by Richard Caves (2000) as the title for his book.

4 See, for example, a study of the cultural industries in Australia identified on the basis of copyright (Guldberg, 1994).

5 This economic view of the cultural industries as a nested set with the creative artist at the core might be compared with Bourdieu's mapping of the fields of cultural production in a different discourse; see Bourdieu (1993, especially chs. 1 and 3).

6 For an application of the standard industry-economics concepts of structure, conduct and performance to the performing arts, see Throsby and Withers (1979, ch. 4).

7 For an essay touching on economists' attitudes to the study of tastes, see McPherson (1987); for a discussion of these issues as they relate to cultural goods, see Blaug (1999).

8 Marshall (1891, p. 151).

9 See Becker and Murphy (1988); Becker (1996).

10 For a discussion of the cultivation of taste and its effects on demand for the arts, see McCain (1979, 1981).

11 From among the large non-profit and third-sector literature, see especially Hansmann (1980, 1981); Powell (1987); Weisbrod (1988); Salamon and Anheier (1996).

12 See Throsby and Withers (1979, ch. 2); Heilbrun and Gray (1993, ch. 6); Throsby (1994b, pp. 11ff).

13 William Baumol's papers on this topic are collected together in Towse (1997b).

14 See, for example, Netzer (1978); Peacock et al. (1982); Baumol and Baumol (1984).

15 See Rosen (1981); Adler (1985); MacDonald (1988).

16 For example, one study showed that experience was the most important determinant of earnings in creative work, formal art qualifications were more relevant in arts-related work, and general education and age played the expected roles in non-arts work; see Throsby (1996).

17 See Menger (1999, pp. 566ff). For an account of labour supply to the literary market in nineteenth-century Paris, see Graña (1964). The English music industry is treated in Ehrlich (1985); see also Towse (1993).

18 Note, however, that the reliability of some such data may be questionable; see Guerzoni (1995).

19 Though it must be conceded that notions of uniqueness and originality become blurred in some artistic media, including print-making and computer art.

20 Bruno Frey cites Baumol's 1986 paper on art investment as sparking contemporary interest in the economics of the art market; see Frey (1997a, p. 165). The treatment of this subject by Frey and Pommerehne (1989, chs. 6–8) must also have acted as a stimulus to further work. See contributions to Ginsburgh and Menger (1996) and to a special issue of the *Journal of Cultural Economics*, 21 (3) (1997).

21 An early example of the study of the economic role of the arts in urban planning is Perloff (1979). For discussions of urban renewal through creative

activity see Landry *et al.* (1996); Lorente (1996). For a consideration of heritage conservation and tourism in urban regeneration, see Stabler (1996).

22 A somewhat more special case is the 'city of art' where cultural value permeates the entire urban fabric and affects all aspects of urban operation. A paradigm case is Venice, where the concentration of tangible and intangible cultural capital is intense and all-pervasive; see Mossetto (1992a, 1992b) and Borg and Costa (1995).

23 A contemporary illustration is the effect of the new Guggenheim Museum on the urban economy of Bilbao; see Vidarte (2000).

24 See, for example, Bianchini and Parkinson (1993); McGuigan (1996, ch. 5); European Task Force on Culture and Development (1997, pp. 73–9).

25 See further in Jelin (1998).

26 Wallis and Malm (1984); Robinson *et al.* (1991); Nettl (1997).

27 See Broughton *et al.* (1999).

28 For a more detailed discussion of the issues raised in this section, see Throsby (1998b). See also Hannerz (1991); Rutten (1991); Mitchell (1996); Rice (1996).

29 For an anthropological view of the host–guest relationship and other aspects of tourism and culture, see contributions to Chambers (1997).

30 A historical account of cultural tourism is contained in Bendixen (1997). For further discussion of contemporary cultural tourism, see Boniface (1995); Herbert (1995); contributions to Robinson *et al.* (1996).

31 For an overview see Tribe (1995); Vellas and Becherel (1995).

32 In fact a *Journal of Sustainable Tourism* was established in 1991.

33 See further in Commonwealth of Australia (1991); France (1997).

34 See a study by Franco Papandrea (1999) which demonstrated a willingness to pay among the Australian community for domestic content regulation of television programmes.

35 UNESCO (1998b, p. 16). For discussion of culture in trade in France, see contributions to Flynn (1995). For some of the cultural ramifications of NAFTA, see contributions to Dallmeyer (1997); Acheson and Maule (1999). A detailed treatment of the 'cultural exception' is contained in Farchy (1999).

8 Cultural policy

> We observe nowadays that 'culture' attracts the attention of men of
> politics: not that politicians are always 'men of culture', but that
> 'culture' is recognised both as an instrument of policy, and as something
> socially desirable which it is the business of the State to promote.
>
> (T.S. Eliot, *Notes Towards the Definition of Culture*, 1948[1])

Introduction

There is perhaps no other area where the relationship between economics
and culture is more direct that in the arena of public policy. Not that
there is much evidence of this in most of the world's economies; the
concept of an explicit cultural policy as a specific government portfolio
has had little or no prominence in most countries until quite recently,
even though public-sector involvement in cultural activity of one sort or
another in these countries goes back further, and broader interactions
between culture and state go back further still.

One of the reasons for the lack of interest in culture in contemporary
public policy has had to do with the ascendancy of the economic
paradigm in the conduct of national and international affairs, which we
discussed in chapter 1. The dominating influence of economic ways of
thinking on the process of policy formation in many democratic countries has meant that public policy and economic policy have become
almost synonymous. For example, much of social policy in areas such as
education, welfare, public health and community development is now
cast in terms of service delivery with emphasis on efficiency and cost-
effectiveness. Yet while such aims are laudable in themselves, it is
gradually becoming recognised that they may be inimical to the pursuit
of broader social objectives of equity, quality of service and so on. In

137

turn, this prominence of economics in the public arena has had a profound effect on policy towards culture. Recalling the distinction between individualism and collectivism noted in chapter 1, we can argue that in a society where government policy emphasises the pursuit of an economic agenda, the balance in the policy mix will tend to favour individualistic at the expense of collective goals. Among the former category we include satisfying the demands of individuals for food, clothing, shelter and other private goods and services, and the individual component of their demand for public goods,[2] while in the latter category we include the collective goals of society covering a wide variety of aspirations including freedom, justice, non-discrimination, fairness, social cohesion, peace and security and so on, as well as the collective component of demand for public goods, and goals relating to specific cultural concerns such as the arts.

At best, a policy focus on individualism might be defended as being consistent with the libertarian ideals of individual freedom, autonomy and self-determination; at worst, it can be seen as leading to an exploitative, materialistic and uncaring society. In other societies, this situation might be reversed such that collective goals predominate. In these circumstances the resultant form of social and economic organisation might be seen either as expressing noble aspirations for egalitarianism, or alternatively as involving an abrogation of individual rights and an authoritarian imposition of state culture on society. What constitutes the 'right' balance between the two extreme positions described, and how that balance is chosen in particular societies, is essentially a political matter to which we return below.

Thus the contemporary economic condition has a significant influence on the relationship between the state and culture. Of course much has been written about culture and state in different discourses, including philosophy, political science and cultural theory. Some of these writings, and especially those in critical cultural studies, have drawn attention to the economic forces which have shaped cultural policy. Our task here is not to review this literature but to see the economics and politics of cultural policy in a context where the relative claims to attention of economic and cultural concerns can be considered in comparable terms.

Culture and the state: the economics of cultural policy

If the importance of economics to the formulation of public policy is accepted as a fact, it is appropriate to ask how far an economic approach to policy-making might be able to incorporate culture within its frame of reference. Beginning with the broad definition of culture as signifying shared traditions, beliefs and ways of life, we might expect that little engagement would be possible. Culture in this sense provides a context for economic activity, as we have noted, and may affect economic performance in some way, but there is no apparent basis for deliberate policy intervention. In other words governments in liberal democratic societies are unlikely to see an explicitly *economic* motive for policy measures to affect culture in this broad sense, unless they were persuaded, say, that the encouragement of shared values through government action could affect economic outcomes.

Turning to the more specific interpretation of culture, however, we *can* see an economic basis for policy. There are clear economic dimensions to activities such as the arts, heritage, public broadcasting, film-making, publishing and so on which are certainly of interest to public policy, and this fact is reflected in the extent to which governments actually do make economic interventions in these areas, using instruments such as provision of subsidies, public ownership of enterprises, investment incentives, tax concessions, regulations, provision of information, education and training and so on.

Taking the arts as an example, we might ask, as a question in positive economics, whether the fact that legislators vote funds for this area is consistent with an economic model of a free-market economy. Their actions might be construed in one of three ways. First, we might suggest that if in fact the community were indifferent or hostile to the arts, the imposition of government preferences for the arts through subsidies and other measures would be dictatorial or, at best, paternalistic in a world where consumer sovereignty is supposed to guide the allocation of resources. Secondly, and alternatively, we might hypothesise that governments are simply acting on a belief that voters share their view that the arts are good for society and that there is a proper role for the public sector in supporting them; if so, and if their belief were correct, the actions of governments could be argued to be broadly in line with individual preferences. In some countries opinion polls and similar indicators of popular opinion have lent some support to this proposition, although its validity is called into question from time to time by reaction to cases of obscenity or profanity in publicly funded arts events. Thirdly, government subsidies to the arts could be seen as the outcome of rent-seeking behaviour by individuals and enterprises in the arts industry who succeed in capturing the grant-making process and turning it to their own advantage.[3]

A more interesting question from the viewpoint of finding an economic basis for cultural policy is the normative one; is there an economic rationale for arts support within the free-market model of the voluntary exchange economy? Much interest has focused on this question in the literature of cultural economics.[4] The most plausible rationale framed in these terms is the proposition that the arts manifest some characteristics of market failure, including possibilities that the arts give rise to external benefits in production and consumption, that there are non-market demands for the arts for existence, option and bequest values, and that the arts exhibit public-good characteristics alongside the private benefits conferred by individual consumption. Of course such speculations, if valid, would provide only a *prima facie* case for corrective government action. Before such action would be warranted in normative terms, it would need to be shown that at the margin the social benefits gained from intervention would outweigh the direct costs involved, in comparison to alternative means of achieving the same ends. Further, an assurance would be required that obstacles such as political corruption or bureaucratic inefficiency in delivery mechanisms ('government failure') will not prejudice an optimal outcome.

Moving beyond standard efficiency considerations raises the possibility that the arts might be deemed a merit good,[5] and that, if so, this would provide normative grounds for collective action. At first glance, the arts would seem to fit the 'merit want' description rather closely: society apparently sees the arts as 'meritorious', yet people do not demand them in private markets to the extent that such a view would suggest, providing a presumptive case for corrective intervention. Closer examination, however, suggests that a number of the characteristics that might be ascribed to the arts as a merit good can actually be explained as generalised externalities or social goods. For instance, a belief that the arts are socially beneficial when held by people who do not themselves consume the arts directly, or an acceptance by some individuals of the desirability of others' consumption, can be accounted for as cases of interdependent utility functions and hence explicable according to the standard theory of externalities. In such cases what appears at first sight to be 'imposed choice' turns out to be ultimately consistent with the principle of consumer sovereignty.

Nevertheless, this may not be the complete story. Are there aspects of a normative case for intervention in arts markets that still lie beyond the standard welfare analysis based on rational action in accordance with individual preferences? Let us consider three possible alternatives. First, the efficient operation of market processes requires fully informed consumers. If individuals lack the necessary information on which to base their market choices, or at a more fundamental level are ignorant of their own welfare, then they may take decisions that are not in their own best interests, and corrective action, at the least through provision of information and education, might be justified. Thus, according to this argument, the fact that people do not consume the arts is because they don't know what is good for them; provision of the arts by an enlightened and better informed government will soon transform the philistine public into cultural connoisseurs.

Secondly, a scrutiny of the relationship between preference and action, interpreted unquestioningly in conventional welfare analysis as a direct linkage, indicates that there may be significant cases where the observed behaviour of individuals is inconsistent with their underlying values, for reasons such as misperception, weakness of will or fluctuations in preferences over time. Such cases of apparent irrationality present a challenge to the accepted definition of consumer sovereignty, suggesting that a broader and more carefully articulated interpretation of consumer sovereignty might be warranted.[6] Government action which appears initially to restrict consumer choice might then be seen to be normatively consistent with a broader sovereignty notion. In the case of the arts, the public sector's capacity to take a longer view might indicate provision of the arts in order to smooth out myopia, indolence and other short-term irrationalities among the population.

Thirdly, it is possible that a traditional social welfare function that admits only individual utilities as its arguments may be too restrictive in the context of socially meritorious goods such as the arts. The suggestion of an 'augmented' social welfare function, where society expresses desires that are additional to those of its members as individuals, has been around for some time. More recently Charles Taylor has drawn attention to the specific possibility of 'irreducibly social goods' – that is, goods which contain some element of benefit that cannot ultimately be attributed to some individual.[7] Such a possibility would transpose the motive for intervention to one of seeking collective rather than individualistically-based outcomes, and could thus be readily applied to cultural policy.

Culture and the state: the politics of cultural policy

Turning from economics as a basis for interpreting the relationship between culture and the public sector to broader conceptions, we can observe that in social and political discourse there has long been interest in the relationship between culture, society and the state. In regard to ideas about culture's role in society, it was during the nineteenth century that the word 'culture' acquired its full meaning encompassing the whole way of life of society, the intellectual development of the population and the practice of the arts. Thus developed the linkage between the cultural flowering of the individual and the societal context wherein that flowering occurred. Writers such as Samuel Taylor Coleridge and William Wordsworth speculated about the ideal of the 'exemplary person', the individual of refined sensibility and cultivated taste who epitomised the highest expression of culture and who might act in some sense as a model towards which the unenlightened might strive. The process of transformation was, of course, to be education, and this in turn brought into focus a role for the state in bringing the transformation about.[8]

At the same time a more overtly political relationship between culture and state might be discerned, deriving from notions of representativeness that preoccupied a number of nineteenth-century thinkers, including John Stuart Mill and Matthew Arnold. Whether 'culture' is construed in the broad sense of the system of traditions and mores governing society, or in the more specific connotation of the civilising virtues of art, one of its functions can be seen to be the shaping of citizens for active participation in democratic society. As the operation of democratic political institutions was refined during the late nineteenth and early twentieth centuries, the idealised concept of the representative individual, fashioned by culture, could be seen to become personified as the key element in representative democracy. In this way a role for culture might be perceived in helping to legitimate the functioning of the modern state.[9]

In contemporary times, the relationships between culture, society and state referred to above can still be seen to have relevance. Certainly, they provide much room for debate within the disciplines of cultural studies, philosophy, political theory and sociology. At the same time, the period since the Second World War has also seen a more direct manifestation of the relationship between culture and state in the emergence of cultural policy as an identifiable mechanism for the assertion of the state's role in regard to culture. It is useful to ask how the political climate and institutional framework have determined the direction and orientation of public policy towards culture over this period. Let us look first at the international context in which cultural policies have evolved, and then consider the more specific ways in which national governments have dealt with culture.

At the international level, the optimism and social idealism that prevailed in the wake of the Second World War looked forward to a positive role for culture in the reconstructed world. So, for example, there are cultural dimensions in the charter of the United Nations, formed in 1945, and the right to cultural participation was incorporated into the Universal Declaration of Human Rights in 1948. Further, a formal institutional context for cultural matters at the international level was provided by the establishment of the United Nations Educational, Scientific and Cultural Organisation (UNESCO) in 1946.[10] At a series of conferences, notably in Venice in 1970 and in Mexico in 1982, the UNESCO member states acknowledged the pervasive importance of culture in national affairs, and especially in development, and agreed to guidelines for the development of cultural policies. At the same time specific agreements and international treaties were being formulated for adoption by national governments covering particular areas such as the status of the artist (Belgrade, 1980) and the protection of movable and immovable heritage, including the Word Heritage Convention (Paris, 1972).

In more recent times, the declaration of UNESCO's Word Decade for Culture (1988–97) was intended to focus international attention on culture in national life, especially in the developing world. This ambitious project aimed specifically to shift the existing narrow concept of economic development towards a broader one where the individual human being became the object and instrument of development, a transformation we discussed in chapter 4. The Decade was organised around four main objectives: placing culture at the centre of development; asserting and enhancing cultural identities; broadening participation in cultural life; and promoting international cultural cooperation.[11]

Pursuit of these ideals was given a more substantive form by the work of the UN World Commission on Culture and Development (WCCD) (1992–5), to which we referred in chapter 4. One immediate outcome of the WCCD process was an international conference on cultural policies held in Stockholm in April 1998. This conference led to a declaration adopted by all countries present embracing many aspects of cultural policy formation within their jurisdictions. The resolutions adopted by the conference do indeed provide a comprehensive framework for bringing cultural concerns into the mainstream of policy formation in both developing and developed countries. Recognising that sustainable development and the flourishing of culture are interdependent in all countries from the least developed to the most advanced, the conference identified the essential aims of cultural policy as being to 'establish objectives, create structures and secure adequate resources in order to create an environment conducive to human fulfilment'.[12] Accordingly the conference recommended that states adopt five policy objectives:

- to make cultural policy one of the key components of development strategy
- to promote creativity and participation in cultural life
- to reinforce policy and practice to promote the cultural industries and to safeguard and enhance the cultural heritage
- to promote cultural and linguistic diversity in and for the information society, and
- to make more human and financial resources available for cultural development.

It may be observed that this set of objectives for cultural policy brings together a number of aspects of the relationship between culture and economics. It attempts to integrate cultural policy into the wider context of economic policy formation, it acknowledges the resource implications of such a move and it recognises the potential contribution of the cultural industries to the economy, especially in the new communications environment. At the same time, the objectives, and the more detailed statements of purpose which underpin them,[13] accept that cultural considerations (cultural value, in the terms used here) are distinct, important and complementary to the economic objectives and constraints which affect the conduct of national affairs, and should be given appropriate consideration if the overall process of policy delivery is to be effective in meeting society's needs.

A serious hindrance to the international endeavour to advance the status and understanding of cultural policy is the lack of data and documentation about the cultural characteristics of various countries, making it difficult to carry out soundly-based empirical research in this field. A number of efforts to overcome this problem are evident in the expanded and better informed collection of cultural statistics now in place in many countries, facilitating a substantial increase in interest in cultural policy issues among scholars, bureaucrats, politicians, administrators and others.[14] One significant step towards providing a resource for cultural policy research has been the inauguration of UNESCO's biennial *World Culture Report*, first published in 1998 (UNESCO 1998a). This Report, complementary to other major international reports such as the World Bank's annual *World Development Report*, the UNDP's *Human Development Report* and others, is an outcome of the WCCD process referred to above. The *World Culture Report* is designed to inform the debate about culture and to assist those engaged in cultural policy-making through the publication of internationally comparable statistical data on culture[15] and independent analysis of cultural development issues.

So much for the international context within which cultural policies have been formed. Let us turn now to the evolution of policies towards culture in nation states themselves. This account relates principally to the European countries and to the former British Dominions of Canada, Australia and New Zealand. It has only occasional relevance to the United States, which has pursued an essentially non-interventionist policy stance on culture in the post-war years, and to developing countries, which have faced particular problems of their own in this field, some of which we have touched upon in chapter 4.

Accounts of the development of cultural policy in the countries under consideration have discerned various periods in the evolution of policy since the Second Word War.[16] The delineation of stages varies from case to case, but the overall trends observed are similar. In the decades of the 1950s and 1960s, the rise of the welfare state embraced egalitarian notions of culture for all. Mechanisms for supporting artistic production and participation were established, social programmes encouraged the development of creativity within communities, education strategies recognised the importance of exposing children to the arts at an early age. During this time, too, a growing awareness of threats to cultural heritage consolidated a practical policy effort around protection, preservation and restoration of art collections and historic buildings and sites. Then in the 1970s the focus began to shift towards a more functional view of culture, with the emerging recognition of the cultural industries as engines of economic dynamism and societal transformation. These developments continued through the following decades, with the increasing awareness of the economic importance of the cultural industries: their employment potential, their role in local and regional economic development, especially in an urban environment, and their involvement in the phenomenon of mass tourism. By the close of the 1990s, these industrially derived motivations for cultural policy formation were firmly established.

Three broad shifts might be identified as characterising these developments in the post-war period. The first has been a transition from an essentially monocultural basis for the provision and dissemination of culture by the state to a more diverse and inclusive position. This shift is interpreted in contemporary cultural studies as a breaking down of the hegemonic position of the high-culture norms of the upper and middle classes in society in favour of a construction of culture as arising from the transactions of 'ordinary' people, with a strong component of concern for minority and disadvantaged groups in society. In policy terms this shift might be perceived to a greater or lesser degree in areas like the weakening of 'elite' criteria in the definition of artistic excellence in arts support programmes, emphasis on cultural access and participation rather than on pursuit of 'quality' in the high arts, promotion of multiculturalism and cultural diversity, greater recognition of local and community cultural values in determining policy directions and so on.

The second transformation that can be seen in cultural policy development in the post-war period is a shift from public-sector to private-sector dominance. Although the state has retained the capacity to direct and manage cultural change by means of its cultural policies, its power to do so has been inexorably weakened over the period because of reductions in government budgets, withdrawal of state involvement in a number of areas and increased recognition by the corporate world of commercial opportunities in the cultural sector. As a result the nature of cultural change and the direction of growth in the arts, for example, are now determined less by purposive public-sector intervention than by the pressures of commercial sponsorship and private patronage. These trends reflect the general move towards deregulation, privatisation, *désétatisation* and market liberalisation which have occurred across the board during the 1980s and 1990s in liberal democratic countries and in the transformation of the economies of Eastern and Central Europe in particular. The cultural sector has been affected by these processes in a number of ways. Decreasing public budgets, especially in the former communist countries, have prompted a search for new sources of support for culture. The United Kingdom, for example, has led the way in using gambling revenue for such purposes through the establishment of national lotteries to yield funds for cultural and other such projects.[17] In addition, new forms of corporate organisation for cultural institutions have been sought as a means for disconnecting them from total public ownership and control. For instance in the Netherlands national museums and galleries have been re-established as autonomous and independent business units, whereby the state retains ownership of buildings and collections, and continues to provide financial support on agreed terms, but the governance and management of the institutions are freed up to be more flexible, responsive, dynamic and entrepreneurial in the operation of the facilities and in the delivery of services to the public.[18] In these contexts the scope of cultural policy shifts towards a more open and flexible exercise of fiscal and regulatory responsibility by the state, while clearly maintaining its fundamental role in asserting and protecting the public interest in the cultural sphere.[19]

The third shift affecting cultural policy formation in the late twentieth century has been the inexorable progress of globalisation in the world economy. We consider these issues in more detail in chapter 9; for present purposes it is sufficient to note that the increasing mobility of capital, the communications revolution and the growing interdependence of national economies within a global market structure have had profound cultural ramifications. Some see these forces as having a homogenising influence on culture around the world, diluting cultural diversity via the penetration of the internationally recognised symbols of a standardised commercial culture generally associated with brand-names such as Coca-Cola, McDonald's, Levi jeans and so on. Yet there is also evidence of community resistance to the subjugation of national or local modes of cultural expression by some impersonal global imperative. Indeed it can be argued that greater economic integration has been frequently associated with greater rather than lesser cultural differentiation. In Europe, for example, where nations are moving more and more closely together in economic terms within the European Union, the symbols of national cultural identity appear to be becoming more sharply defined. This is even true of language, despite the growing ubiquity of English as a means of commercial communication.[20]

Whatever the ultimate verdict about the cultural impacts of regional or global integration, the very processes at work do have a significant effect on the landscape within which cultural policy operates. Some writers, such as Nestor Garcia Canclini, go so far as to argue that cultural policies can no longer be seen as a national prerogative implemented by national governments; Canclini cites the predominance of the global mass communications industries over traditional local forms of production and circulation of culture as evidence for a weakening of the state's capacity to assert a national cultural policy.[21] Others would see the disappearance of the nation state altogether, as the power of governments to influence economic activity is progressively eroded. Such extremism would, however, seem to be unwarranted, especially given the slowly evolving prospects for multilateral agreement on issues of national sovereignty. But the fact remains that global markets, and especially new information and communications technologies, are more and more strongly implicated in affecting the nature and scope of cultural policy-making in the contemporary world.[22]

In political terms, all of these three developments taken together suggest a realignment of powers and responsibilities in the processes of cultural policy formation and delivery at regional and national levels. It is true that the state remains the most effective means for implementing the collective will in the modern mixed economy, through its coercive powers of taxation and regulation of social and economic life. But there is little enthusiasm anywhere in the developed world for a return to the state as a monolithic centre of gravity as it was in the former communist countries of Central and Eastern Europe, and the importance of private market activity as a concentration of economic power throughout the world cannot be ignored. An enlightened cultural policy in the modern age is therefore likely to be one that seeks to forge a cooperative coalition in the pursuit of society's cultural objectives, a partnership where public agencies, NGOs and the corporate sector have an incentive to act together rather than independently. It is possible to imagine in such a policy scenario that sovereign governments can play a leading role, protecting and advancing the collective interest, not through assertion of elite or partisan values, but by recognition of the fundamental import-ance of broadly-based notions of culture in society. In this way a genuinely democratic cultural policy might emerge, providing a context where the private sector can be constructively involved without the public interest being subverted, and looking to manage processes of cultural change in society rather than trying to direct them.

Economic and cultural value in policy formation

We have stressed repeatedly the underlying importance of value in considering the intersections of economics and culture. The area of cultural policy is no exception. The fact that there is an economic dimension to the cultural activities and behaviours that cultural policy seeks to address indicates that the economic value of culture will be an important policy concern. At the same time, cultural policy has an obvious mandate to address the cultural aspirations of society, seen in all the various manifestations of culture, including shared values and beliefs, community traditions, identity, the production and consumption of cultural goods and so on. It is clear that the cultural value arising from these phenomena is a critical dimension to their existence, in some cases the only significant dimension. Thus it is possible to identify a basic principle for the formulation and implementation of cultural policy, namely that if the interests of both the economy and the culture are to be served, cultural policy should take account of both the economic and cultural value of the outcomes it seeks to attain. Whether the cultural policy is a broadly directed one, aimed at enhancing cultural identity, diversity, creativity or other aspects of the cultural life of the community, or whether it is made up of specific measures directed at particular areas such as the arts, regional development, heritage, tourism, etc., the importance of balancing economic and cultural value considerations in the formation and implementation of policy is essential.

This proposition may seem so self-evident as to be trivial. Yet in a policy environment dominated by the economic paradigm it may be a difficult proposition to sell. For policies to gain acceptance in such an environment they must be keyed to observable economic and social outcomes, and any appeal to inchoate and in some respects perhaps unmeasurable phenomena like cultural value is unlikely to be taken seriously by hard-headed policy-makers accustomed to dealing with quantifiable bottom lines. As we have noted, the cultural sector can indeed find policy justification in the sorts of tangible economic benefits it brings, but to leave it at that not only sells culture short, it may tend to promote cultural development in directions contrary to broader societal goals. Thus the assertion has to be explicitly pressed that cultural value has a significance that stands distinct from economic value as a component to be taken into account in policy-making.

Within the discourse of contemporary economics, a recommendation such as this may be dismissed as special pleading, or as rent-seeking by those who stand to gain from the allocation of public funds to culture. Such a position is understandable especially when placed within a model of the policy-making process as one dominated by a hegemonic cultural elite. Nevertheless, the ultimate appeal in a liberal democratic society must be to the goals and aspirations of the people at large, and not to the values either of the cultural establishment or of the economic bureaucrats. What little we know of public attitudes to economic, social and cultural influences on their lives would seem to suggest that there is more to human happiness than can be encompassed in terms of economic measures alone.[23] Thus we might accept that the notion of cultural value as promulgated here might have some currency in the satisfaction of human desires.

All of this suggests a two-pronged approach to cultural policy formation, where both economic and cultural value outcomes are placed side by side in the evaluation of policy initiatives – i.e. where the cultural policy objective function is construed as seeking the joint maximisation of economic and cultural value. The weight on these two components of value will clearly vary from case to case. For example, policy towards the cultural industries as such may well emphasise economic value creation, though subject to cultural constraints, while policy directed at more overtly cultural ends, such as support for creative artists, would be expected to weigh cultural value more heavily, though possibly in turn subject to economic constraints. The point to stress is that the policy objective function is not adequate or complete if it contains only economic value, on the supposition that that captures all that matters.

In summary, the above considerations suggest two shifts in emphasis in the formation and delivery of cultural policy in the modern mixed economy. The first is towards a recognition that not all of the aspirations of those whom policy is supposed to serve can be captured within a measure of economic value. The corollary requires the acceptance of the validity of alternative concepts of value, here corralled under the rubric of cultural value, and the incorporation of cultural value into the process of public policy formation. The most obvious locus for introducing cultural value into the policy-making process is in the drafting of cultural policy itself, but these propositions also have wider implications and indeed we can observe that cultural value has entered the policy debate in other areas as well, such as employment and trade policy. The second shift, relevant especially in the cultural policy arena, is towards creating partnerships in policy delivery which bring in voluntary and corporate cooperation alongside the public-sector representation, but without losing sight of the state's inalienable responsibility for protecting and enhancing the public interest.

Conclusions

We began this chapter by suggesting that in societies where the policy agenda is determined predominantly by economic considerations and where the form of economic organisation is based on a market economy, the pursuit of individualistic goals of economic wellbeing and advancement will be favoured over the pursuit of collective goals such as those of cultural preservation, achievement and growth. The greater the relative importance attached to the economic agenda, the more difficult will the process of cultural policy formulation and implementation become. We concluded the chapter by reasserting the importance of value as the underlying principle with which public policy is concerned, and emphasising the distinctive concepts of economic and cultural value as the twin focal points of cultural policy formation.

These considerations carry with them some significant implications for the development of policy in all of the specific areas we have considered – development, heritage, trade and so on. In the central area of the arts, where economic and cultural values jostle for attention perhaps more sharply than anywhere else, our discussion points to a consolidation of a policy focus around the arts' essential role in cultural value formation. Policy-makers might then recognise more clearly how economic constraints limit the creation of cultural value and direct their efforts to loosening those constraints, using the policy instruments at their disposal in new ways and in new partnerships with other stakeholders. This in turn suggests a de-emphasis in arts policy on the economic earning power of the arts *per se* and a shift of that policy focus to where creative cultural activity has the greatest scope to generate economic rewards – i.e. to employment policy, regional and urban development policy, industry policy affecting the arts and wider cultural industries, tourism, etc. Even so, however, the legitimacy of cultural value creation in these areas has still to be recognised – that is, the composite objective function with economic and cultural value as its principal dimensions is still the appropriate means of expressing the policy goals.

Notes

1 Quotation is from Eliot (1948, p. 83).

2 Though the difficulties of quantifying individual demands for collective goods has meant that they have tended to be downplayed in importance in the individualistically-oriented economy.

3 See further in Stigler (1971); Tollison (1982); Ricketts and Peacock (1986); Rowley *et al.* (1988). For the pursuit of private benefit from public policy in the arts, see Withers (1979); Seaman (1981); Schneider and Pommerehne (1983); Throsby (1984); Grampp (1989).

4 A full statement of the standard theory is contained in Throsby and Withers (1979, chs. 10 and 11). Some of the main contributions to the debate are reprinted in Towse (1997a, II, part V). Contrary positions are argued in Grampp (1989) and Cowen (1998).

5 For the original exposition of merit goods, see Musgrave (1959); for a reassessment thirty years later see Musgrave (1990) and Head (1990).

6 See further in Hamlin (1990).

7 See Taylor (1990).

8 See further in Williams (1958).

9 See further in Lloyd and Thomas (1998).

10 For an account of the origins of UNESCO, see Pompei *et al.* (1972), including the essay on 'Culture' by Jean d'Ormesson (pp. 95–122).

11 See UNESCO (1987, pp. 13–25).

12 UNESCO (1998b, p. 13).

13 UNESCO (1998b, pp. 14–18).

14 This interest is particularly evident in Europe: see, for example, work carried out under the auspices of ERICarts (the European Research Institute for Comparative Cultural Policy and the Arts); the Cultural Policy and Action Division of the Council of Europe in Strasbourg (see Council of Europe, 1997); CIRCLE (Cultural Information and Research Centres Liaison in Europe); and the Boekman Foundation in Amsterdam (see Boekman Foundation, 1999). Evidence for a spread of cultural policy interest beyond Europe can be seen in the fact that the *European Journal of Cultural Policy*, first published in 1994, changed its name after a year or two to the *International Journal of Cultural Policy*, in recognition of the broader coverage of its contents.

15 For a discussion on the problems and possibilities for the statistical derivation of cultural indicators, see McKinley (1998); Pattanaik (1998).

16 See, for example, Mulgan and Worpole (1986); Lewis (1990); Bennett (1995); McGuigan (1996); Volkerling (1996); Blokland (1997, pp. 202–72); European Task Force on Culture and Development (1997); Bradley (1998); Quinn (1998); for an account of government arts policies going considerably further back – to the Ancient Greeks, in fact – see Pick (1988).

17 See Creigh-Tyte and Ling (1998).

18 For further discussion of these issues, see Throsby (1998a).

19 For an extensive discussion of the nature of privatisation in the cultural sector, see contributions to Boorsma *et al.* (1998); this volume contains case studies of experiences in France, Greece, Italy, Hungary, the Czech Republic, the United Kingdom and elsewhere.

20 The issues of national identities within Europe and of a specifically 'European culture' are discussed in a vast literature, to which a useful entrée is provided by Wintle (1996).

21 See Canclini (1998).

22 For a wide variety of perspectives on these issues, see contributions to UNESCO (1998a).

23 There is a surprisingly long literature on the relationship between economics and happiness, adroitly surveyed by Andrew Oswald (1997). Concern for 'happiness' as a consideration in economic progress (Easterlin, 1974) stemmed originally from dissatisfaction with the rate of growth of output as an indicator of growth in human welfare (Abramovitz, 1959). More recently, its relationship with 'utility' has come under scrutiny (Frank, 1997; Ng, 1997). See also Frey and Stutzer (1999) and, at a more applied level, contributions to Eckersley (1998). The overall conclusion of these writings is that economic measures such as *per capita* consumption and rate of economic growth are very inadequate as indicators of human welfare and happiness.

9　Conclusions

SEPTIMUS: When we have found all the meanings and lost all the mysteries, we will be alone, on an empty shore.
THOMASINA: Then we will dance.　　　(Tom Stoppard, *Arcadia*, 1993[1])

The historical moment

Works of art and scholarship are informed by the historical moment in which they are created. So, for example, the nineteenth-century writers who grappled variously with problems of economics and culture – Carlyle, Coleridge, J.S. Mill, Matthew Arnold, Ruskin and many others who dealt with aspects of the material circumstances and the cultural manifestations of human existence – were inevitably conditioned by the nature of the society in which they found themselves – that is, by the values, concerns and state of development of the world at the moment in time at which they happened to be studying it.

Such an observation is no less true today than it was 100 or 200 years ago. Thus, in embarking on the present project of examining the relationships between economics and culture at the beginning of the twenty-first century – the chasms which divide the two domains and the linkages which might be forged between them – our task is inexorably contextualised by the condition of the world as it stands today. And it is a world in which economics and culture, both as intellectual disciplines and as systems of societal organisation, have undergone profound changes; both look very different now from the way in which they would have appeared to scholars and to citizens a century or even a decade ago.

Both discourses have been subject to a vigorous radical critique from within. Economics has more or less shrugged it off, in part at least because economists have been able to characterise the attack as ideologi-

153

cally driven from the left and therefore not to be taken seriously by a largely conservative profession. The study of culture, on the other hand, has shifted ground significantly, notwithstanding a stout defence in some quarters of traditional positions.

In regard to economics as a system of thought, the apparent universality of the economic model of individual behaviour and of the transactional relationships which that behaviour engenders has pushed economics into centre stage among the social sciences. The paradigm of the rational utility-maximising individual is thought to be so comprehensive in its coverage of human motivation and action that there remain few if any phenomena that cannot be caught within its ambit. Likewise the representation of human interaction provided by the model of voluntary exchange markets is believed to give us, in normative terms at least, such a thoroughgoing picture of the way in which the macro organisation of society should work that we need nothing more. Little wonder, then, that the economic paradigm has had such a dominating influence on the course of national and international affairs in the modern world, or that economists have been able to play such a prominent role in laying out the terrain for public policy.

In the cultural arena, on the other hand, no such unity of purpose can be discerned. As we noted above, the scholarly study of culture and cultural processes has been radically affected by trends in sociology, philosophy, linguistics and elsewhere, and cultural studies as a discipline, if such it is, stands today as a fragmented and contested domain. Within the various areas of intellectual endeavour that are concerned with culture in one or other of its forms, the range of interest and approach is considerable. In one corner of the field art historians, conservators, art theorists and others continue a long and honourable tradition of analysis of art and culture as contained and self-referential phenomena which are regarded in their own terms as fundamental to human existence. In another corner, students of popular culture move away from imposed definitions, adopting more fluid concepts and seeing cultural relationships as involving the exercise of power, where social class and command over economic resources are important determinants of how the game is played and who wins and loses.

So much for the contemporary condition of economics and culture as intellectual discourses. What of the state of the wider world in which economic and cultural life exists today? Here in what we like to refer to as the real world, it is possible to encapsulate the current moment for both economics and culture in a single word: globalisation. Whether this phenomenon is a process, an already established fact, or a state towards which modernity is leading us, its manifestations are clear enough. Let us consider them, and the challenges they pose, with respect to economics and culture in turn.

In economic terms, globalisation can be seen as a process in which science and technology have provided the means, and economic ortho-doxy has set the framework within which those means are put to use. The so-called 'information revolution', with ever easier and faster data-processing and communications becoming possible within and between countries, has transformed the organisation of production, enabling entirely new and vastly more productive processes to be introduced in the output of virtually every type of commodity in the economy, with profound consequences for industrial structure, the deployment of labour and capital and the nature of work. At the same time the dominant economic paradigm, and the political and institutional ar-rangements to enable its application, have led inexorably to a dis-mantling of impediments to the free flow of resources, especially capital, and have established the supremacy of market processes as a means of pricing and resource allocation in most parts of the global economy. Although epitaphs on the demise of the nation state as an effective economic and political force are undoubtedly premature, the fact remains that the 'borderless world', in economic terms, is moving closer to reality.[2]

It can be suggested that the greatest challenge to economics and economists presented by these trends has to do with the distribution of the gains they have made possible. The world may have become more efficient and productive but it has not become more fair. In fact the reliance on individual enterprise rather than collective action, the pro-cesses of deregulation and privatisation, the emphasis on unhindered markets and all the other underpinnings of the globalising economy have created a world of winners and losers. Within countries, the gap between rich and poor is widening. Between countries, the gulf between the haves and the have-nots is even more vast; the merest glance at any edition of the United Nations *Human Development Report* confirms that most of the world's wealth is owned by a handful of the richest countries, while the poorest 20 per cent of the world's population has less than 2 per cent of global income.

It might be imagined that the existence of such palpable inequities in an economic system in which we all participate would cause some loss of sleep among those who advocate still further expansion of global markets. Not so. There is little evidence of such insomnia, at least among economists. One reason for this may have to do with the way modern economics is taught. Students are told that the twin problems that economics deals with are those of efficiency and equity; yet they spend most of their time learning about the former problem, with generally little attention to the latter. To verify this statement, pick up any contemporary text in microeconomic theory and count the number of pages devoted to the economics of welfare and distribution as a proportion of the book's total length; it is likely to be not more than a few per cent.[3]

The fact that globalisation has some untoward economic consequences is not, however, to cast it as a universally malign economic force, which should be resisted or reversed at every opportunity. There is no doubt that it has brought enormous benefits to many, in terms of improved consumption choices, employment prospects, lifestyle patterns and so on. Nevertheless, an economic paradigm which gives inadequate emphasis to the fairness of the outcomes towards which it leads is itself inadequate, and dealing with gross economic inequity remains the greatest challenge in contemporary economics. In this context it is not so much that globalisation should be resisted – possibly a futile exercise in any case – but that it can be managed in ways that will produce outcomes that are both fairer and possibly also more efficient in terms of achieving society's objectives. Such a proposition, of course, implies a stronger role for collective action to regulate or constrain some aspects of economic behaviour, for example through national and international policy measures taken unilaterally or multilaterally by sovereign governments. It goes without saying that the current economic orthodoxy would find some difficulty in accommodating any such proposal for increased intervention in global or local markets, unless, as noted, it can indeed move itself to accept a stronger regard for rectifying inequities in the operation of economic systems.

Turning now to the cultural impacts of globalisation and the challenges they pose, we enter an arena that has given rise to a vast literature and much argument. The central question is essentially one of how the increased flow of goods and services, messages and symbols, information and values between the peoples of the world impinges on cultural differentiation. Does it mean that the distinctive features of different cultures will become blunted and disappear, to be replaced by a universal set of cultural symbols visible in any part of the globe? The popular imagery in support of the homogenising influence of globalisation on culture is that of the teenager wearing Levi jeans, drinking Coca-Cola, and listening to rock music: he or she may be sighted any day in Aberdeen, Atlanta, Addis Ababa or Adelaide. Because the origin of so many of these cultural symbols is the West, or more specifically the United States, this process is often referred to not so much as one of cultural homogenisation but rather as cultural imperialism, an imposition or at least a diffusion of a dominant culture throughout the world. However it is seen, the result is thought to be the same: a blurring of specific cultural identities.

Alternatively it has been argued that the exact opposite may occur. The pressure of powerful external forces that threaten to trample underfoot the means by which people identify the singular characteristics of their group and differentiate themselves from other groups may sharpen group members' resolve to resist the homogenising influences and to assert more strongly the symbols of their own unique cultural identification. If this process is widely distributed around the world, it becomes a reflection of the cultural diversity which is indeed a characteristic of the species *Homo sapiens*.[4] If at the same time a process of exchange of cultural messages occurs, new cultural forms may emerge where the symbols are taken not from a dominant culture but from a variety of other sources; such cultural 'hybridisation' occurs, for example, in music.[5] Yet another hypothesis oppositional to cultural homogenisation is that of a binary split in the world's cultural allegiances between the West on the one hand and an Islamic/Confucian axis on the other, each spreading its cultural influence by different means, the former through global economic power, the latter through an intense religious fundamentalism.[6] This so-called clash of civilisations (or 'Jihad vs. McWorld') is predicated on a driving cultural imperative, whereby market forces are less important than cultural beliefs in determining human behaviour.

There is no consensus on which if any of the various hypotheses about globalisation and culture is most persuasive, and indeed it is perfectly feasible that more than one could be valid at once. For example, a person may eat a Big Mac at the same time as she barracks for her local football team, thus manifesting simultaneously both universal and locally differentiated cultural behaviour. In fact, just as dealing with inequity was suggested above as the principal challenge to economics in the contemporary global environment, so also can we propose that recognition of the value of cultural diversity within the global ecumene is the principal cultural challenge of our age.

The overall conclusion on globalisation as it characterises the historical moment within which we are viewing the relationship between economics and culture is perhaps best summed up by Robert Holton, when he says:

The global repertoire is not, then, to be seen as a consumer paradise or a life-enhancing intercultural smörgåsbord, but neither is it a demonic system of top-down system domination. We know this not because optimistic and privileged Western voices say so but because it is consistent with the actions and beliefs of a range of global voices, outside the West as well as within it.[7]

Economics and culture: what have we learned?

Accepting the above contextualisation of the present project, let us now draw together some of the principal threads of the argument put forward in this volume. Note that the following discussion is selective; it is not a comprehensive summary of the issues raised in preceding chapters, nor does it treat the matters considered in the same order as they are dealt with in the book.

It should be remembered at the outset that the task we set ourselves was to consider the twin objects of our attention at two levels: first to look at economics and culture as intellectual disciplines or discourses or modes of thought for observing and analysing the world; and secondly to interpret economics and culture as representations of human behaviour – economic behaviour and the functioning of the economy on the one hand, and cultural behaviour and the role of culture in society on the other. A logical journey through the terrain we have traversed might begin with the basic impulses to behaviour which we identified at the very start of the book. There it was proposed as a running hypothesis that the economic impulse can be described as individualistic, and the cultural impulse as collective. This proposition identifies immediately a fundamental contrast between the two fields which underlies much of our subsequent analysis. It does not imply that economic behaviour cannot be undertaken for collective ends, nor that pursuit of cultural experience has no individual motivation or benefit. Rather it points to differences between economics and culture in the way the world is constructed, the one emphasising the self as an individual unit whose interests are paramount and who succeeds through competing with other units, the other emphasising the group, operating through shared values and cooperative behaviour.

But the most important distinction that we have drawn in this volume, which runs through our argument like a *leitmotiv*, is that between economic and cultural value. Both economists and cultural theorists have wrestled with questions of value for centuries; it is no exaggeration to say that a theory of value is the foundation stone upon which economic theory is built, and by the same token a viable concept of cultural value is fundamental to any systematic analysis of culture and cultural activity. We have proposed that economic and cultural value must be seen as distinct concepts in assessing the entire range of phenomena under consideration, from the definition of cultural goods as a class of commodities to the specification of the objectives of public policy. Economic value is measured for private goods, somewhat imperfectly, by price, and for public goods, again imperfectly, as willingness to pay (WTP). It embodies a wide variety of sources of individual desire for different commodities and reduces those desires, via preference orderings between commodities, to a single quantifiable metric. Cultural value, on the other hand, has no common unit of account and is multi-dimensional, shifting and probably includes some components expressible only in non-quantifiable terms. But the difficulties of its articulation and evaluation do not diminish its importance in identifying the distinctive claims to attention of the cultural phenomena which embody or produce it.

'Cultural value' is a phrase that might be heard in common parlance to indicate the worth that someone might ascribe to an object or an experience when thought of in cultural terms. But to appeal to cultural value as a rigorously defined concept, or to use it in an operational context, requires a systematic approach to its definition and measurement. We have argued that progress can be made in understanding cultural value by attempting to deconstruct it into its constituent elements. Without being exhaustive, it can be suggested that the cultural value of, say, an art object could be disaggregated into several components, including its aesthetic, spiritual, social, historical, symbolic and authenticity value. Each of these characteristics or criteria might be assessed by different means: possible measurement devices might include various types of mapping, 'thick description', attitudinal analysis, content analysis and the appraisal or judgement of experts trained in the appropriate field (such as archaeologists, art historians, conservators, etc.). It may or may not then be possible to compile these separate assessments into some summary form.

It is apparent that there is likely to be a close relationship between economic and cultural value in specific cases. In general the higher a thing or an experience is valued in cultural terms, the more will people be prepared to give up in order to acquire it and so the higher will its apparent economic value be. But the correlation between economic and cultural value is likely to be by no means perfect, and many examples can be cited of commodities with low economic value associated with high cultural value or vice versa. Although it may be tempting to economists, within the confines of a fully articulated economic model, to claim that the economic value of a cultural good gives a complete account of *both* its economic *and* its cultural worth, thereby making a separate measure of cultural value redundant, it has to be remembered that the economic model itself is limited in its reach and specific in its coverage. There are demonstrable dimensions in the valuation of cultural phenomena which escape the economic calculus, and yet are important to decision-making and resource allocation by individuals and groups. It is thus concluded that if we are serious about striving for theoretical completeness and operational validity, it is essential to admit a concept of cultural value alongside that of economic value in assessing the phenomena under study.

When we think about culture in a functional sense – that is, as cultural activities producing goods and services – we are led to consider the question of what distinguishes cultural goods and services from 'ordinary' commodities produced and consumed within economic systems. A definition of 'cultural goods' can be framed in terms of certain characteristics they possess, including the fact that they involve creativity in their production, they embody some form of intellectual property and they convey symbolic meaning. Alternatively, or in addition, a designation from the demand side might point to the accumulation of taste and the dependence of present on previous consumption. Finally, a unique characteristic of such goods can be defined in terms of value: cultural goods embody or give rise to both cultural and economic value, 'ordinary' economic goods yield economic value only.

Similarly, we may identify resources used in the making of cultural goods and services as involving both economic and cultural dimensions. One of the principal factors of production in these processes is capital. A consideration of culture as capital, not in the Bourdieu sense of internal human characteristics but in the economic sense of a stock of capital assets giving rise over time to a flow of capital services, opens up powerful possibilities for conceptualising culture in ways that resonate within both economics and cultural theory. It also provides access to a range of analytical tools which will help to give operational substance to these concepts. The elevation of cultural value to parity with economic value, at least in conceptual terms, provides for a balanced representation of the way in which cultural capital, both tangible and intangible, contributes to economic and cultural outcomes.

One of the most obvious applications of the cultural capital concept is to cultural heritage – that is, tangible and intangible cultural assets which have been inherited from previous generations and which are to be passed on to the next. Treatment of heritage as cultural capital parallels what has now become an accepted treatment of environmental resources and ecosystems as natural capital, and indeed similar techniques are now being applied to the evaluation of the benefits bestowed by cultural assets as have been successfully used in assessing the value of environmental amenity. Again, the fact that cultural capital embodies and gives rise to cultural as well as economic value gives it a distinctive claim to attention and conditions the way analytical methods should be used in evaluating it. So, for example, a consideration of a heritage 'project', such as the restoration of an artwork or the redevelopment of a historic urban centre, can cast the evaluation of the project as an investment appraisal using familiar cost-benefit analysis methods, but with the expectation that the generation of *both* economic *and* cultural value by the project over time will be taken into account. Of course, as noted earlier, the operational difficulties of estimating the flows of cultural value in consistent terms and of incorporating them into such a framework should not be underestimated. Yet there are already signs that empirical progress can be made in this direction, although much further research is needed.

The concept of cultural capital in general, and its application to heritage in particular, places the evaluation issue into a long-run perspective. Most cultural assets are not amortised in the short or medium term, with a finite economic life that enables them to be written off after a given length of time. On the contrary, both tangible and intangible heritage items can generally be expected to appreciate rather than diminish in economic and cultural value over time. If they are assets inherited from the distant past, the increase in their value over time may already be apparent, and may be expected to continue into the future. If they are assets created now, their future earnings may be more uncertain. In either case, however, the valuation of such items of cultural capital is a matter extending beyond the present generation, and raises the ethical responsibility imposed on those of us alive today to care for these capital assets and to pass them in good order to our heirs and successors. The matter of intergenerational equity thus invoked is a central element in the concept of sustainability.

Sustainability has become a ubiquitous term, often deployed indiscriminately and without concise definition. In contemporary usage it is most often heard in relation to the environment and the exploitation of natural resources and ecosystems. It can be applied to the management of cultural capital because of the long-term issues involved. The multi-faceted nature of the concept means that there is no standardised single definition of sustainability; hence we have suggested articulating the idea of sustainability as a series of principles or criteria. These provide a sort of checklist against which specific cases can be judged to determine whether or not they can be regarded as sustainable. The proposed criteria include: the contribution of the item or project under consideration to material and non-material wellbeing; intergenerational and intragenerational equity; maintenance of diversity; the precautionary principle; and the maintenance of cultural systems and recognition of interdependence. The last of these is important in emphasising the way in which cultural 'ecosystems' underpin the operations of the real economy, much as natural ecosystems do; neglect of cultural capital can lead to the same sorts of problems as we now accept arise if natural capital and natural ecosystems are allowed to fall into disrepair.

Having dealt with capital, we turn now to the other major factor of production used in the making of cultural goods and services, namely labour. Focusing specifically on artistic output, we can identify many different types of skilled and unskilled labour which contribute to the process of production, from the writer sitting at her desk to the ticket seller sitting in the theatre box office. Our interest here is in the creative labour essential to the origination of artistic ideas and their transformation into a script, a score, a painting, a performance, or whatever – that is, we are concerned with the work of artists. In particular, since our interest is in both economics and culture, we might ask how the process of artistic creativity is influenced by economic factors. For many, the process of producing art is a matter of inspiration, imagination, even genius, far removed from mundane material concerns. The reality for many practising artists is and always has been somewhat different. Like everyone else, artists need the wherewithal to feed themselves and their dependants, and unless they are fortunate enough to have a beneficent patron to pay their bills, they have to rely on their own efforts to generate an income. Thus do economic concerns impinge on the otherwise pure creative process, modifying and directing it in ways that may not always seem to the artist to be ideal.

It is possible to model the creative process in a manner that accounts for both economic and artistic motivation if we appeal again specifically to the notions of economic and cultural value. A decision model of the artist's behaviour can be formulated in which the objective function contains both economic and cultural value as joint arguments, and the constraint set includes both technical (artistic) constraints and a minimum income requirement. The decision variables are the amounts of time the artist devotes to various tasks both within the processes of creating artworks and outside of those processes, for example in taking on other revenue-producing activities. Since different artists have different attitudes to the earning of revenue from their work, ranging from those primarily in the game for the money to those who couldn't care less about material rewards, the objective function requires weights varying from zero to one and one to zero respectively on the economic and cultural value variables contained in it. In this way the model can be applied across a full spectrum of artists' attitudes to the relative importance of artistic and economic dimensions of their work. If the possibility of work outside the arts is entertained, the time allocation model can reflect the 'work-preference' characteristic that is likely to describe many artists' attitudes to their creative endeavour. Under this hypothesis, the normal theory of labour supply is reversed, with (artistic) labour itself yielding positive benefit to the worker. Such a hypothesis, as might be expected, yields behavioural predictions at odds with conventional labour market theory, serving further to distinguish creative artists as workers from other types of occupational groups in the labour force.

Nevertheless in the end it has to be acknowledged that, despite the theoretical appeal of a rational model of artistic creativity, artists may in fact be distinguishable from others in society precisely by their *ir*rationality. Many would argue that it is only by overturning conventional notions, by standing apart from the mainstream, or by following the inspirational spirit wherever it may lead that art progresses, and that to characterise art and imagination as 'rational' is a contradiction in terms.

The concepts of economic and cultural value are brought into play once more when we bring the supply and demand for cultural goods and services into an industrial framework. For economists, the grouping of productive activities into industries is a natural analytical device, even though for non-economists such a procedure may carry overtones of cultural commodification and subjugation of artistic endeavour to the demands of the marketplace. In regard to the latter point, it can be argued that no ideological implication need accompany a categorisation of the arts or other cultural activities as an industry, but rather that the concepts of industrial economics simply offer a convenient way of representing certain activities that have an undeniable economic content.

The value question is again important in considering the nature of the cultural industries. Advocates for the arts can become seduced by the glittering statistics showing the contribution of the arts and cultural sector to the value of output, incomes, employment, export revenue and so on. The arts are seen as a dynamic economic force in a number of fields, including urban revitalisation, regional development, job creation, tourism and trade, and this is often put forward as a sufficient reason for their continued existence. There is no doubt that the economic importance of the cultural industries in most developed countries is substantial, and there exist countless examples of the positive contribution that the arts and culture have made to all of the economic variables mentioned above in a wide variety of economic, social and political contexts. But it is important also to remember that cultural goods and services – the products generated by the cultural industries – are distinguished from other goods by the fact that they yield cultural as well as economic value, and that this cultural value is itself important to society. An industry development strategy, say, which emphasised only the creation of economic value by the cultural industries, would be telling only half the story.

These considerations lead directly into the policy arena, where again similar remarks can be made. Much emphasis has been placed in recent times on the role of cultural policy in facilitating and encouraging the contribution of the cultural sector to the economy. This emphasis has doubtless been useful in persuading hard-headed Finance Ministers and other economically driven politicians and bureaucrats to take culture more seriously. But a balanced attention to the overall objectives of society in the formulation of policy would suggest an equal responsibility on cultural policy to assert the importance of the cultural value yielded by the sector. Nevertheless, in a world still moved in policy terms predominantly by an economic agenda, acceptance of cultural value as a motivating force in policy decisions is still some way off. It is no accident, for example, that dealing with cultural goods in international trade is called making a cultural 'exception', with the negative economic con-notations that that word implies. We have suggested that if the cultural value surrounding cultural goods were taken more explicitly into account in trading negotiations, their situation might be better described in more positive terms as, say, a cultural 'recognition' rather than an exception; in this way the generation of cultural value would be recognised and admitted into the overall cost-benefit calculus.

Finally, we return to the broader concept of culture as a system of shared values, beliefs, traditions and ways of living together. Economists have paid little attention to the role of culture in economic development, either in contextualising the growth process in the developing world or in influencing economic outcomes more directly in industrialised economies. There is evidence that these traditional paradigms are shifting. In recent years considerable interest has been awakened in the notion that, far from being peripheral to economic development, culture is in fact central to and inextricable from the development process, providing both the context within which economic progress occurs and the very object of development when viewed from the perspective of individual needs.

These matters raise yet again the issue of sustainability. Opening up the model of sustainable development to admit culture, indeed recon-ceptualising the whole development process to incorporate a full range of economic, social, cultural and ecological concerns, provides the founda-tion for a new development paradigm, centred on human beings and recognising the totality of their material and non-material needs. Reference to sustainability principles in the construction of such a paradigm ensures, among other things, that the key intergenerational and intragenerational equity requirements are included. There are encouraging signs that a paradigm shift along these lines is beginning to take shape.

All of the above considerations which place economics and culture, and the economy and the cultural system, into a common framework emphasising their complementarities and interdependencies, provide a neat encapsulation of our overall approach to attempting to bring what might appear to be two disparate fields closer together. Throughout these efforts, we have stressed the pervasive notion of value as a common element in the two discourses, and we have pointed to some ways in which an acknowledgement of different sorts of value can enrich our understanding and sharpen our analytical approach to dealing with some important issues in the contemporary world.

Epilogue

At various points in this book, questions have been raised concerning the state of modern economic science. There is no doubt that our understanding of the economic behaviour of individual agents and the aggregate behaviour of economic systems has been enormously advanced with the rise and rise of neoclassical economics in the twentieth century. All the same much remains unexplained – and, worse, our economic understanding, such as it is, has not been translated into a capacity to predict economic outcomes or to manage economic life with any degree of certainty or reliability. Yet many economists remain convinced that economics is indeed capable of accounting for any sort of behaviour, if only more accurate model specification can be achieved. Furthermore, economists as a profession have tended to believe their own rhetoric that their discipline is value-free; as a result they have been unwilling or unable to concede that their own explicit or implicit value systems condition the way they see the world and the prescriptions they make for its improvement. A more open-minded and human-centred approach to economics would seem to be called for in a world of growing inequality and economic injustice. Such a proposition can clearly be entertained in the context of the economic development of the Third World. It is equally true when applied to that part of the world that currently enjoys unprecedented material affluence; it is more and more evident that conventional economic success does not on its own bring unalloyed human happiness. An extension of economists' thinking to acknowledge the significance of culture in all its aspects in human affairs, and to consider the implications and ramifications of the linkages between economics and culture, and between economic and cultural systems, would seem to be essential if the science of economics is to deal adequately with the contemporary condition.

On the wider world stage, where regional, national and international dramas are played out, economics and culture can be seen as two of the most fundamental driving forces shaping human behaviour. The desire for command over material resources, even (or especially) among those already well off in this respect, is an apparently inexorable compulsion and governs much of what we see as economic activity. At the same time, non-materialist impulses towards identification, belonging, creative expression, connection with and concern for others – all of which we can sum up as peoples' cultures – exert a pervasive influence on how we perceive the world, how we interpret our place in it and consequently how we behave.

These two basic forces – one economic, the other cultural – are seen by many in optimistic terms. From a material standpoint, we live in many respects in the best of times. The technological revolution of the late second millennium promises even brighter rewards in the third; perhaps we can even foresee a forthcoming utopia where the spectre of poverty, the bane of disease, the drudgery of work and the debilitating effects of unemployment will be banished forever. In similar terms, a positive view of cultural development suggests the emergence of more articulated models of cultural expression and interaction, where local cultural diversity is celebrated within a globally connected world, where cooperative behaviour and trust predominate over competition and mutual suspicion, where sustainability replaces exploitation and where creativity and artistic enjoyment, in the broadest senses, flourish.

Yet it is also undeniable that the twin energies of economic desire and cultural belief can bring conflict and oppression. History is replete with wars fought over territory and access to economic wealth; there are also just as many examples of bitter struggles between and within countries motivated by fundamental and strongly held cultural values. A glance around the contemporary world – at Northern Ireland, the Balkans, the former Soviet Union, East Timor – confirms that the quest to obtain or retain economic power on the one hand, and the assertion of cultural identity on the other, continue to provide a dual impetus to conflict. These considerations suggest that a deeper understanding of the relationships between economics and culture, in both positive and normative terms, will be needed if we are to make progress towards a better world.

Notes
1 Quotation is from Stoppard (1993, p. 94).
2 See further, for example, in Appadurai (1996); Thurow (1996); Gupta (1997); Giddens (1998, pp. 28–33); Holton (1998); Rao (1998).
3 In contemporary microeconomic theory, welfare economics is usually treated, if at all, as part of general equilibrium analysis and in most texts there is little or no treatment of redistribution, which is mostly dealt with as a practical matter in courses on public finance. Thus discussion of welfare economics, equity and related issues is always a very small proportion of microeconomics texts; for example, well established and respected intermediate micro theory books such as Gravelle and Rees (1998), Katz and Rosen (1998), Eaton *et al.* (1999) and Varian (1999) devote considerably less than 10 per cent of their space to these matters. Nevertheless, there are some exceptions; for example, Stiglitz (1997) and Baumol and Blinder (2000) both devote whole chapters to issues of poverty, inequality and redistribution.
4 These issues are pursued further in Arizpe (2000) and in Section 1 of UNESCO (2000); see also a discussion of diversity and globalisation in Streeten (2000).
5 Ulf Hannerz describes such cultural interpenetration as 'creolization'; see Hannerz (1992, pp. 217–67).
6 See especially Barber (1996); Huntingdon (1996).
7 Holton (1998, p. 185).

Bibliography

Abramovitz, Moses, 1959. 'The welfare interpretation of secular trends in national income and product', in Abramovitz, Moses *et al.*, *The Allocation of Economic Resources: Essays in Honor of Bernard Francis Haley*, Stanford University Press, pp. 1–22

Acheson, Keith and Maule, Christopher, 1999. *Much Ado About Culture: North American Trade Disputes*, Ann Arbor: University of Michigan Press

Adler, Moshe, 1985. 'Stardom and talent', *American Economic Review* 75: 208–12; reprinted in Towse (ed.) (1997a), II, pp. 201–5

Adorno, Theodor W., 1991. *The Culture Industry: Selected Essays on Mass Culture*, ed. J.M. Bernstein, London: Routledge

Adorno, Theodor and Horkheimer, Max, 1947. *Dialektik der Aufklärung: Philosophische Fragmente*, Amsterdam: Querido; English trans. by John Cumming, *Dialectic of Enlightenment*, London: Verso, 1979

Agostini, Paola, 1998. 'Valuing the invaluable: the case of the Fes-Medina', paper presented at World Bank Conference on *Culture in Sustainable Development*, Washington, DC, 28 October

Amariglio, Jack L., 1988. 'The body, economic discourse, and power: an economist's introduction to Foucault', *History of Political Economy* 20: 583–613

Appadurai, Arjun, 1996. *Modernity at Large: Cultural Dimensions of Globalization*, Minneapolis: University of Minnesota Press

Arizpe, Lourdes, 2000. 'Cultural heritage and globalization', in Avrami *et al.* (eds.) (2000), pp. 32–7

Armour, Leslie, 1996. 'Economics and social reality: Professor O'Neil and the problems of culture', *International Journal of Social Economics* 22: 79–87

Arrow, Kenneth J., 1998. 'The place of institutions in the economy: a theoretical perspective', in Hayami and Aoki (eds.) (1998), pp. 39–48

Arrow, Kenneth J., 2000. 'Observations on social capital' in Dasgupta and Serageldin (eds.) (2000), pp. 3–5

Arrow, Kenneth J. *et al.*, 1993. 'Report of the NOAA Panel on Contingent Valuation', *Federal Register* 58: 4602–14

Aspromourgos, Tony, 1996. *On the Origins of Classical Economics: Distribution and Value from William Petty to Adam Smith*, London: Routledge

Australia Council, 1996. *The Arts: Some Australian Data*, 5th edn., Sydney: Australia Council

Avrami, Erica, Mason, Randall and de la Torre, Marta (eds.), 2000. *Values and Heritage Conservation*, Los Angeles: Getty Conservation Institute

Bailey, Samuel, 1825. *A Critical Dissertation on the Nature, Measures and Causes of Value*; reprinted as no. 7 in the *Series of Reprints of Scarce Tracts in Economic and Political Science*, London School of Economics and Political Science (1931)

Bair, Deirdre, 1978. *Samuel Beckett: A Biography*, London: Jonathan Cape

Barber, Benjamin R., 1996. *Jihad vs. McWorld*, New York: Ballantine Books

Barbier, Edward B., 1998. *The Economics of Environment and Development: Selected Essays*, Cheltenham: Edward Elgar

Barro, Robert J. and Sala-i-Martin, Xavier, 1995. *Economic Growth*, New York: McGraw-Hill

Baudrillard, Jean, 1994. *Simulacra and Simulation*, Ann Arbor: University of Michigan Press

Baumol, Hilda and Baumol, William J. (eds.), 1984. *Inflation and the Performing Arts*, New York University Press

Baumol, William J., 1986. 'Unnatural value: or art investment as floating crap game', *American Economic Review* 76(2): 10–14; reprinted in Towse (ed.) (1997a), I, pp. 549–53

Baumol, William J. and Baumol, Hilda, 1994. 'On the economics of musical composition in Mozart's Vienna', *Journal of Cultural Economics* 18: 171–98; reprinted in Towse (ed.) (1997a), II, pp. 117–44

Baumol, William J. and Blinder, Alan S., 2000. *Economics: Principles and Policy*, 8th edn., Fort Worth: Dryden Press

Baumol, William J. and Bowen, William G., 1966. *Performing Arts: The Economic Dilemma*, New York: Twentieth Century Fund

Baumol, William J. and Oates, Wallace E., 1988. *The Theory of Environmental Policy*, 2nd edn., Cambridge University Press

Becker, Gary S., 1964. *Human Capital*, New York: Columbia University Press

Becker, Gary S., 1996. *Accounting for Tastes*, Cambridge: Harvard University Press

Becker, Gary S. and Murphy, Kevin M., 1988. 'A theory of rational addiction', *Journal of Political Economy* 96: 675–700

Becker, Gary S., Murphy, Kevin M. and Tamura, Robert, 1990. 'Human capital, fertility and economic growth', *Journal of Political Economy* 98 (Supplement): S12–S37

Becker, Howard S., 1974. 'Art as collective action', *American Sociological Review* 39: 767–76

Becker, Howard S., 1996. 'The epistemology of qualitative research', in Jessor *et al.* (eds.) (1996), pp. 53–71

Becker, Robert A., 1982. 'Intergenerational equity: the capital–environment trade-off', *Journal of Environmental Economics and Management* 9: 165–85

Bendixen, Peter, 1997. 'Cultural tourism – economic success at the expense of culture?', *International Journal of Cultural Policy* 4: 21–46

Benhamou, Françoise 2000. *L'Economie de la Culture*, 2nd edn., Paris: Editions la Découverte

Bennett, Oliver, 1995. 'Cultural policy in the United Kingdom: collapsing rationales and the end of a tradition', *European Journal of Cultural Policy* 1: 199–216

Bentham, Jeremy, 1843. *Works*, ed. John Bowring, Edinburgh: William Tait

Berger, Peter L., 1993. 'An East Asian development model?', in Berger and Hsiao (eds.) (1993), pp. 3–11

Berger, Peter L. and Hsiao, Hsin-Huang Michael (eds.), 1993. *In Search of an East Asian Development Model*, New Brunswick: Transaction Publishers

Berkes, Fikret and Folke, Carl, 1992. 'A systems perspective on the interrelations between natural, human-made and cultural capital', *Ecological Economics* 5: 1–8

Best, Steven and Kellner, Douglas, 1991. *Postmodern Theory: Critical Interrogations*, New York: Guilford Press

Bettmann, Otto L., 1995. *Johann Sebastian Bach As His World Knew Him*, New York: Birch Lane Press

Bianchini, Franco and Parkinson, Michael (eds.), 1993. *Cultural Policy and Urban Regeneration: The West European Experience*, Manchester University Press

Bille Hansen, Trine, 1995. 'Measuring the value of culture', *European Journal of Cultural Policy* 1: 309–22

Bille Hansen, Trine, 1997. 'The willingness-to-pay for the Royal Theatre in Copenhagen as a public good', *Journal of Cultural Economics* 21: 1–28

Blackmore, Richard Doddridge, 1869. *Lorna Doone*, London: Sampson, Low, Marston & Co

Blaug, Mark, 1973. 'Was there a marginal revolution?', in Collison Black *et al.* (eds.) (1973), pp. 3–14

Blaug, Mark (ed.), 1976. *The Economics of the Arts: Selected Readings*, London: Martin Robertson

Blaug, Mark, 1999. 'Where are we now in cultural economics?', *Proceedings of International Symposium on Cultural Economics*, Association for Cultural Economics International and Japan Association for Cultural Economics, Tokyo, 28–30 May, pp. 6–18

Blokland, Hans, 1997. *Freedom and Culture in Western Society*, trans. Michael O'Loughlin, London: Routledge

Bluestone, Daniel, 2000. 'Challenges for heritage conservation and the role of research on values', in Avrami *et al.* (eds.) (2000), pp. 65–7

Boekman Foundation, 1999. *RECAP: Resources for Cultural Policy in Europe*, Amsterdam: Boekman Foundation

Bohm, Peter, 1979. 'Estimating willingness to pay: why and how?', *Scandinavian Journal of Economics* 81: 142–53

Boniface, Priscilla, 1995. *Managing Quality Cultural Tourism*, London: Routledge

Boorsma, Peter B., van Hemel, Annemoon and van der Wielen, Niki (eds.), 1998. *Privatization and Culture: Experiences in the Arts, Heritage and Cultural Industries in Europe*, Dordrecht: Kluwer Academic Publishers

Borg, J. and Costa, P., 1995. 'Tourism and cities of art: Venice', in Coccossis and Nijkamp (eds.) (1995), pp. 191–202

Borocz, Jozsef and Southworth, Caleb, 1996. 'Decomposing the intellectuals' class power: conversion of cultural capital to income, Hungary, 1986', *Social Forces* 74: 797–821

Borofsky, Robert, 1998. 'Cultural possibilities', in UNESCO *World Culture Report* (1998a), pp. 64–75

Bourdieu, Pierre, 1986. 'Forms of capital', in Richardson, John G. (ed.), *Handbook of Theory and Research for the Sociology of Education*, New York: Greenwood, pp. 241–60

Bourdieu, Pierre, 1993. *The Field of Cultural Production: Essays on Art and Literature*, ed. Randal Johnson, Cambridge: Polity Press

Braden, John B. and Kolstad, Charles D. (eds.), 1991. *Measuring the Demand for Environmental Quality*, Amsterdam: North Holland

Bradley, Christopher H.J., 1998. *Mrs Thatcher's Cultural Policies 1979–1990: A Comparative Study of the Globalized Cultural System*, New York: Columbia University Press

Brennan, Geoffrey and Walsh, Cliff (eds.), 1990. *Rationality, Individualism and Public Policy*, Canberra: Centre for Research on Federal Financial Relations, Australian National University

Brook, Timothy and Luong, Hy V. (eds.), 1997. *Culture and Economy: The Shaping of Capitalism in Eastern Asia*, Ann Arbor: University of Michigan Press

Broughton, Simon, Ellingham, Mark and Trillo, Richard (eds.), 1999. *World Music: The Rough Guide*, 2 vols., London: Rough Guides Ltd

Brown, Marilyn R., 1993. 'An entrepreneur in spite of himself: Edgar Degas and the market', in Haskell, Thomas L. and Teichgraeber, Richard F. III (eds.), *The Culture of the Market: Historical Essays*, Cambridge University Press, pp. 261–92

Butt, John (ed.), 1997. *The Cambridge Companion to Bach*, Cambridge University Press

Byron, Lord, 1986. *The Complete Poetical Works*, ed. Jerome J. McGann, 7 vols., Oxford: Clarendon Press

Canclini, Nestor Garcia, 1998. 'Cultural policy options in the context of globalization' in UNESCO *World Culture Report* (1998a), pp. 157–82

Cannon-Brookes, Peter, 1996. 'Cultural–economic analyses of art museums: a British curator's viewpoint', in Ginsburgh and Menger (eds.) (1996), pp. 255–74

Carman, John, 1996. *Valuing Ancient Things: Archaeology and Law*, London: Leicester University Press

Carman, John, Carnegie, Garry D. and Wolnizer, Peter W., 1999. 'Is archaeological valuation an accounting matter?', *Antiquity* 73: 143–8

Carnegie, Garry D. and Wolnizer, Peter W., 1995. 'The financial valuation of cultural, heritage and scientific collections: an accounting fiction', *Australian Accounting Review* 5: 31–47

Casson, Mark, 1993. 'Cultural determinants of economic performance,' *Journal of Comparative Economics* 17: 418–42

Caves, Richard E., 2000. *Creative Industries: Contracts between Art and Commerce*, Cambridge: Harvard University Press

Chambers, Erve (ed.), 1997. *Tourism and Culture: An Applied Perspective*, Albany: State University of New York Press

Chanel, Olivier, Gerard-Varet, Louis-André and Ginsburgh, Victor, 1996. 'The relevance of hedonic price indices: the case of paintings', *Journal of Cultural Economics* 20: 1–24

Chatwin, Bruce, 1987. *The Songlines*, London: Jonathan Cape

Chiswick, Barry R., 1983. 'The earnings and human capital of American Jews', *Journal of Human Resources* 18: 313–36

Clark, Charles M.A., 1995a. 'From natural value to social value', in Clark (ed.) (1995b), pp. 29–42

Clark, Charles M.A., (ed.), 1995b. *Institutional Economics and the Theory of Social Value: Essays in Honor of Marc R. Tool*, Boston: Kluwer Academic Publishers

Clawson, Marion and Knetsch, Jack L., 1966. *Economics of Outdoor Recreation*, Baltimore: Johns Hopkins University Press

Coccossis, Harry and Nijkamp, Peter (eds.), 1995. *Planning for Our Cultural Heritage*, Aldershot: Avebury

Coleman, James, 1988. 'Social capital in the creation of human capital', *American Journal of Sociology* 94 (Supplement): S95–S120

Collison Black, R.D., Coats, A.W. and Goodwin, Craufurd, D.W. (eds.), 1973. *The Marginal Revolution in Economics: Interpretation and Evaluation*, Durham: Duke University Press

Commonwealth of Australia, 1991. *Final Report of the Ecologically Sustainable Development Tourism Working Group*, Canberra: Australian Government Publishing Service

Connor, Steven, 1992a. 'Aesthetics, pleasure and value', in Regan (ed.) (1992b), pp. 203–20

Connor, Steven, 1992b. *Theory and Cultural Value*, Oxford: Blackwell

Connor, Steven, 1997. *Postmodernist Culture: An Introduction to Theories of the Contemporary*, 2nd edn., Oxford: Blackwell

Cooper, Catherine R. and Denner, Jill, 1998. 'Theories linking culture and psychology: universal and community specific processes', *Annual Review of Psychology* 49: 559–84

Costanza, Robert (ed.), 1991. *Ecological Economics: The Science and Management of Sustainability*, New York: Columbia University Press

Costanza, Robert and Daly, Herman E., 1992. 'Natural capital and sustainable development', *Conservation Biology* 6: 37–46; reprinted in Costanza, Robert (ed.) (1997), *Frontiers in Ecological Economics*, Cheltenham: Edward Elgar, pp. 65–74

Costanza, Robert and Daly, Herman E., 1997. 'The value of the world's ecosystem services and natural capital', *Nature*, 387: 253–60

Council of Europe, 1997. *Cultural Policy and Action: The Culture Programme of the Council of Europe*, Strasbourg: Council of Europe

Cowen, Tyler, 1998. *In Praise of Commercial Culture*, Cambridge: Harvard University Press

Cozzi, Guido, 1998. 'Culture as a bubble', *Journal of Political Economy* 106: 376–94

Creigh-Tyte, Stephen and Ling, Ricky, 1998. 'British arts funding: the impact of the National Lottery', in Heikkinen and Koskinen (eds.) (1998), pp. 187–202

Dallmeyer, Dorinda G. (ed.), 1997. *Joining Together, Standing Apart: National Identities after NAFTA*, The Hague: Kluwer Law International

Dasgupta, Partha and Serageldin, Ismail (eds.), 2000. *Social Capital: A Multifaceted Perspective*, Washington, DC: World Bank

Davis, Douglas, 1990. *The Museum Transformed: Design and Culture in the Post-Pompidou Age*, New York: Abbeville Press

De Marchi, Neil and Van Miegroet, Hans J., 1996. 'Pricing invention: "originals", "copies" and their relative value in seventeenth century Netherlandish art markets', in Ginsburgh and Menger (eds.) (1996), pp. 27–70

Di Maggio, Paul, 1994. 'Culture and economy', in Smelser, Neil J. and Swedberg, Richard (eds.), *The Handbook of Economic Sociology*, Princeton University Press, pp. 27–57

Dobb, Maurice, 1973. *Theories of Value and Distribution since Adam Smith: Ideology and Economic Theory*, Cambridge University Press

Dolfsma, Wilfred, 1997. 'The social construction of value: value theories and John Locke's framework of qualities', *European Journal of the History of Economic Thought* 4: 400–16

Dolfsma, Wilfred, 1999. 'The consumption of music and the expression of VALUES: a social economic explanation for the advent of pop music', *American Journal of Economics and Sociology* 58: 1019–46

Easterlin, Richard A., 1974. 'Does economic growth improve the human lot? Some empirical evidence', in David, Paul A. and Reder, Melvin W. (eds.), *Nations and Households in Economic Growth: Essays in Honor of Moses Abramovitz*, New York: Academic Press, pp. 89–125

Eaton, B. Curtis, Eaton, Dianne F. and Allen, Douglas W., 1999. *Microeconomics*, 4th edn., Scarborough: Prentice-Hall Canada Inc.

Eatwell, John, Milgate, Murray and Newman, Peter, 1987. *The New Palgrave: A Dictionary of Economics*, London: Macmillan

Eckersley, Richard (ed.), 1998. *Measuring Progress: Is Life Getting Better?*, Collingwood: CSIRO Publishing

Ehrlich, Cyril, 1985. *The Music Profession in Britain since the Eighteenth Century: A Social History*, Oxford: Clarendon Press

El Serafy, Salah, 1991. 'The environment as capital' in Costanza (ed.) (1991), pp. 168–75

El Serafy, Salah, 1998. 'Pricing the invaluable: the value of the world's ecosystem services and natural capital', *Ecological Economics* 25: 257–66

Eliot, T.S., 1948. *Notes Towards the Definition of Culture*, London: Faber & Faber

Escobar, Arturo, 1995. *Encountering Development: The Making and Unmaking of the Third World*, Princeton University Press

Etlin, Richard A., 1996. *In Defense of Humanism: Value in the Arts and Letters*, Cambridge University Press

European Task Force on Culture and Development, 1997. *In from the Margins: A Contribution to the Debate on Culture and Development in Europe*, Strasbourg: Council of Europe

Farchy, Joëlle, 1999. *La Fin de l'Exception Culturelle?* Paris: CNRS Editions

Farchy, Joëlle and Sagot-Duvauroux, Dominique, 1994. *Economie des Politiques Culturelles*, Paris: Presses Universitaires de France

Feld, Alan L., O'Hare, Michael and Schuster, J. Mark Davidson, 1983. *Patrons Despite Themselves: Taxpayers and Arts Policy*, New York University Press

Feldstein, Martin (ed.), 1991. *The Economics of Art Museums*, University of Chicago Press

Fisher, Irving, 1927. *The Nature of Capital and Income*, New York: Macmillan

Flynn, Gregory (ed.), 1995. *Remaking the Hexagon: The New France in the New Europe*, Boulder: Westview Press

Folke, Carl *et al.*, 1994. 'Investing in natural capital – why, what and how?' in Jansson *et al.* (eds.) (1994), pp. 1–20

France, Lesley (ed.), 1997. *The Earthscan Reader in Sustainable Tourism*, London: Earthscan

Frank, Robert H., 1997. 'The frame of reference as a public good', *Economic Journal* 107: 1832–47

Frey, Bruno S., 1997a. 'Art markets and economics: introduction', *Journal of Cultural Economics* 21: 165–73

Frey, Bruno S., 1997b. *Not Just For the Money: An Economic Theory of Personal Motivation*, Cheltenham: Edward Elgar

Frey, Bruno S., 2000. *Art and Economics*, Heidelberg: Springer-Verlag

Frey, Bruno S. and Pommerehne, Werner W., 1989. *Muses and Markets: Explorations in the Economics of the Arts*, Oxford: Basil Blackwell

Frey, Bruno S. and Stutzer, Alois, 1999. *Happiness, Economy and Institutions*, *Working Paper* 15, Institute for Empirical Research in Economics, University of Zürich, 1 November; forthcoming in *Economic Journal*

Fukuyama, Francis, 1995. *Trust: The Social Virtues and the Creation of Prosperity*, London: Hamish Hamilton

Galbraith, John Kenneth, 1960. *The Liberal Hour*, London: Hamish Hamilton

Geertz, Clifford, 1973. *The Interpretation of Cultures*, New York: Basic Books

Getty Conservation Institute, 1999. *Economics and Heritage Conservation*, Los Angeles: Getty Conservation Institute

Giddens, Anthony, 1998. *The Third Way: The Renewal of Social Democracy*, Cambridge: Polity Press

Gillis, Malcolm, Perkins, Dwight H., Roemer, Michael and Snodgrass, Donald R., 1996. *Economics of Development*, 4th edn., New York: Norton

Ginsburgh, Victor A. and Menger, Pierre-Michel (eds.), 1996. *Economics of the Arts: Selected Essays*, Amsterdam: North-Holland

Gordon, Donald F., 1968. 'Labour theory of value', in Sills, David L. (ed.), *International Encyclopedia of the Social Sciences* 16, New York: Macmillan, pp. 279–83

Grampp, William D., 1973. 'Classical economics and its moral critics', *History of Political Economy* 5: 359–74

Grampp, William D., 1989. *Pricing the Priceless: Art, Artists and Economics*, New York: Basic Books

Grampp, William D., 1996. 'A colloquy about art museums: economics engages museology', in Ginsburgh and Menger (eds.) (1996), pp. 221–54

Graña, César, 1964. *Bohemian versus Bourgeois: French Society and the French Man of Letters in the Nineteenth Century*, New York: Basic Books

Gravelle, Hugh and Rees, Ray, 1998. *Microeconomics* 2nd edn., London: Longman

Gray, H. Peter, 1996. 'Culture and economic performance: policy as an intervening variable', *Journal of Comparative Economics* 23: 278–91

Greif, Avner, 1994. 'Cultural beliefs and the organization of society: a historical and theoretical reflection on collectivist and individualist societies', *Journal of Political Economy* 102: 912–50

Griffin, Keith, 1996. *Studies in Globalization and Economic Transitions*, London: Macmillan

Guerzoni, Guido, 1995. 'Reflections on historical series of art prices: Reitlinger's data revisited', *Journal of Cultural Economics* 19: 251–60

Guillory, John, 1993. *Cultural Capital: The Problems of Literary Canon Formation*, University of Chicago Press

Guldberg, Hans Hoegh, 1994. *Copyright: An Economic Perspective*, Sydney: Australian Copyright Council

Gupta, Satya Dev (ed.), 1997. *The Political Economy of Globalization*, Boston: Kluwer Academic Publishers

Hamlin, Alan P., 1990. 'The normative status of consumer sovereignty', in Brennan and Walsh (eds.) (1990), pp. 1–18

Hannerz, Ulf, 1991. 'Scenarios for peripheral cultures', in King (ed.) (1991), pp. 107–28

Hannerz, Ulf, 1992. *Cultural Complexity: Studies in the Social Organization of Meaning*, New York: Columbia University Press

Hansmann, Henry, 1980. 'The role of nonprofit enterprise', *Yale Law Journal* 89: 835–901

Hansmann, Henry, 1981. 'Nonprofit enterprise in the performing arts', *Bell Journal of Economics* 12: 341–61; reprinted in Towse (1997a), II, pp. 393–413

Harris, Marvin, 1979. *Cultural Materialism: The Struggle for a Science of Culture*, New York: Random House

Hartwick, John M., 1977. 'Intergenerational equity and the investing of rents from exhaustible resources', *American Economic Review* 67: 972–4

Hartwick, John M., 1978a. 'Investing returns from depleting renewable resource stocks and intergenerational equity', *Economics Letters* 1: 85–8

Hartwick, John M., 1978b. 'Substitution amongst exhaustible resources and intergenerational equity', *Review of Economic Studies* 45: 347–54

Harvey, Charles M., 1994. 'The reasonableness of non-constant discounting', *Journal of Public Economics* 53: 31–51

Hausman, Jerry A. (ed.), 1993. *Contingent Valuation: A Critical Assessment*, Amsterdam: North-Holland

Hayami, Yujiro, 1998. 'Toward an East Asian model of economic development', in Hayami and Aoki (eds.) (1998), pp. 3–35

Hayami, Yujiro and Aoki, Masahiko (eds.), 1998. *The Institutional Foundations of East Asian Economic Development*, London: Macmillan

Head, John G., 1990. 'On merit wants: reflections on the evolution, normative status and policy relevance of a controversial public finance concept', in Brennan and Walsh (eds.) (1990), pp. 211–44

Heikkinen, Merja and Koskinen, Tuulikki (eds.), 1998. *Economics of Artists and Arts Policy; Selection of Papers*, Helsinki: Arts Council of Finland

Heilbroner, Robert L., 1988. *Behind the Veil of Economics: Essays in the Worldly Philosophy*, New York: W.W. Norton

Heilbrun, James and Gray, Charles M., 1993. *The Economics of Art and Culture: An American Perspective*, Cambridge University Press

Helliwell, John F. and Putnam, Robert D., 2000. 'Economic growth and social capital in Italy', in Dasgupta and Serageldin (eds.) (2000), pp. 253–68

Hendon, William S. and Shanahan, James L. (eds.), 1983. *Economics of Cultural Decisions*, Cambridge: Abt Books

Hendon, William S., Shanahan, James L. and MacDonald, Alice J. (eds.), 1980. *Economic Policy for the Arts*, Cambridge: Abt Books

Herbert, David T. (ed.), 1995. *Heritage, Tourism and Society*, London: Mansell

Holton, Robert J., 1998. *Globalization and the Nation-State*, London: Macmillan

Hsiao, Hsin-Huang Michael, 1993. 'An East Asian development model: empirical explorations', in Berger and Hsiao (eds.) (1993), pp. 12–23

Huntingdon, Samuel P., 1996. *The Clash of Civilizations and the Remaking of World Order*, New York: Simon & Schuster

Hutter, Michael, 1996. 'The impact of cultural economics on economic theory', *Journal of Cultural Economics* 20: 263–8

Hutter, Michael and Rizzo, Ilde (eds.), 1997. *Economic Perspectives on Cultural Heritage*, London: Macmillan

Infantino, Lorenzo, 1998. *Individualism in Modern Thought: From Adam Smith to Hayek*, London: Routledge

Inglehart, Ronald, 1990. *Culture Shift in Advanced Industrial Society*, Princeton University Press

Jackson, William A., 1996. 'Cultural materialism and institutional economics', *Review of Social Economy* 54: 221–44

Jansson, Ann Mari *et al.* (eds.), 1994. *Investing in Natural Capital – The Ecological Economics Approach to Sustainability*, Washington, DC: Island Press

Jeffri, Joan and Greenblatt, Robert, 1998. *Information on Artists: A Study of Artists' Work-Related Human and Social Service Needs in Four US Locations*, New York: Research Center for Arts and Culture, Columbia University

Jelin, Elizabeth, 1998. 'Cities, culture and globalization', in UNESCO *World Culture Report* (1998a), pp. 105–24

Jessor, Richard, Colby, Anne and Shweder, Richard A. (eds.), 1996. *Ethnography and Human Development: Context and Meaning in Social Inquiry*, University of Chicago Press

Jevons, W. Stanley, 1888. *The Theory of Political Economy*, 3rd edn., London: Macmillan

Johnson, Peter and Thomas, Barry, 1998. 'The economics of museums: a research perspective', *Journal of Cultural Economics* 22: 75–85

Katz, Michael L. and Rosen, Harvey S., 1998. *Microeconomics*, 3rd edn., New York: Irwin–McGraw Hill

Kaufmann, Robert K., 1995. 'The economic multiplier of environmental life support: can capital substitute for a degraded environment?', *Ecological Economics* 12: 67–79

King, Anthony D. (ed.), 1991. *Culture, Globalization and the World System: Contemporary Conditions for the Representation of Identity*, London: Macmillan Education

Klamer, Arjo, 1988. 'Economics as discourse', in De Marchi, Neil (ed.), *The Popperian Legacy in Economics*, Cambridge University Press, pp. 259–78

Klamer, Arjo (ed.), 1996. *The Value of Culture: On the Relationship between Economics and Arts*, Amsterdam University Press

Klamer, Arjo and Throsby, David, 2000. 'Paying for the past: the economics of cultural heritage', in UNESCO, *World Culture Report No. 2*, Paris: UNESCO

Krugman, Paul, 1994. 'The myth of Asia's miracle', *Foreign Affairs* 73: 62–78

Kurabayashi, Yoshimasa and Matsuda, Yoshiro, 1988. *Economic and Social Aspects of the Performing Arts in Japan: Symphony Orchestras and Opera*, Tokyo: Kinokuniya Company Ltd

Kuznets, Simon, 1966. *Modern Economic Growth: Rate, Structure and Spread*, New Haven: Yale University Press

Lall, Sanjaya, 1996. *Learning from the Asian Tigers: Studies in Technology and Industrial Policy*, London: Macmillan

Landes, David S., 1969. *The Unbound Prometheus: Technological Change and Industrial Development in Western Europe from 1750 to the Present*, London: Cambridge University Press

Landes, David S., 1998. *The Wealth and Poverty of Nations: Why Some Are So Rich and Some So Poor*, New York: W.W. Norton

Landry, Charles, Greene, Lesley, Matarasso, François and Bianchini, Franco, 1996. *The Art of Regeneration: Urban Renewal Through Cultural Activity*, Stroud: Comedia

Lewis, Justin, 1990. *Art, Culture and Enterprise: The Politics of Art and the Cultural Industries*, London: Routledge

Lian, Brad and Oneal, John R., 1997. 'Cultural diversity and economic development: a cross-national study of 98 countries, 1960–1985', *Economic Development and Cultural Change* 46: 61–77

Lichfield, Nathaniel, 1988. *Economics in Urban Conservation*, Cambridge University Press

Lloyd, David and Thomas, Paul, 1998. *Culture and the State*, New York: Routledge

Lorente, J. Pedro (ed.), 1996. *The Role of Museums and the Arts in the Urban Regeneration of Liverpool*, University of Leicester, Centre for Urban History, *Working Paper* 9

Lorente, J. Pedro, 1998. *Cathedrals of Urban Modernity: The First Museums of Contemporary Art 1800–1930*, Aldershot: Ashgate

Lucas, Robert E. Jr, 1988. 'On the mechanics of economic development', *Journal of Monetary Economics* 22: 3–42

MacDonald, Glenn M., 1988. 'The economics of rising stars', *American Economic Review* 78: 155–66; reprinted in Towse (ed.) (1997a), II, pp. 206–17

Maddison, David and Mourato, Susana, 1999. *Valuing Different Road Options for Stonehenge, Working Paper*, Centre for Social and Economic Research on the Global Environment, University College London

Mahar, Cheleen *et al.*, 1990. 'The basic theoretical position', in Harker, Richard *et al.* (eds.), *An Introduction to the Works of Pierre Bourdieu: The Practice of Theory*, London: Macmillan, pp. 1–25

Mansfield, Edwin, 1995. *Innovation, Technology and the Economy: Selected Essays of Edwin Mansfield*, Aldershot: Edward Elgar

Marcus, George E. and Fischer, Michael M.J., 1986. *Anthropology as Cultural Critique: An Experimental Moment in the Human Sciences*, University of Chicago Press

Marquis-Kyle, Peter and Walker, Meredith, 1992. *The Illustrated Burra Charter: Making Good Decisions About the Care of Important Places*, Sydney: Australia ICOMOS

Marshall, Alfred 1891. *Principles of Economics*, London: Macmillan

Martin, Fernand, 1994. 'Determining the size of museum subsidies', *Journal of Cultural Economics* 18: 255–70

Mason, Randall and de la Torre, Marta, 2000. 'Heritage conservation and values in globalizing societies', in UNESCO *World Culture Report No. 2*, Paris: UNESCO

Masuyama, Seiichi, Vandenbrink, Donna and Yue, Chia Siow (eds.), 1997. *Industrial Policies in East Asia*, Tokyo: Nomura Research Institute

Mayhew, Anne, 1994. 'Culture', in Hodgson, Geoffrey M. *et al.* (eds.), *The Elgar Companion to Institutional and Evolutionary Economics, Vol. I*, Aldershot: Edward Elgar, pp. 115–19

McCain, Roger A., 1979. 'Reflections on the cultivation of taste', *Journal of Cultural Economics* 3: 30–52

McCain, Roger A., 1981. 'Cultivation of taste, catastrophe theory, and the demand for works of art', *American Economic Review* 71: 332–4; reprinted in Towse (ed.) (1997a), I, pp. 148–50

McCain, Roger A., 1992. *A Framework for Cognitive Economics*, Westport: Praeger

McCloskey, Donald N., 1985. *The Rhetoric of Economics*, Madison: University of Wisconsin Press

McCloskey, Donald N., 1994. *Knowledge and Persuasion in Economics*, Cambridge University Press

McGuigan, Jim, 1996. *Culture and the Public Sphere*, London: Routledge

McKinley, Terry, 1998. 'Measuring the contribution of culture to human well-being: cultural indicators of development', in UNESCO, *World Culture Report* (1998a), pp. 322–32

McPherson, M.S., 1987. 'Changes in tastes' in Eatwell *et al.* (eds.) (1987), pp. 401–3; reprinted in Towse (ed.) (1997a), I, pp. 83–5

Meiland, Jack W., 1983. 'Originals, copies and aesthetic value', in Dutton, Denis (ed.), *The Forger's Art: Forgery and the Philosophy of Art*, Berkeley: University of California Press, pp. 115–30

Menger, Pierre-Michel, 1999. 'Artistic labor markets and careers', *Annual Review of Sociology* 25: 541–74

Mirowski, Philip, 1990. 'Learning the meaning of a dollar: conservation principles and the social theory of value in economic theory', *Social Research* 57: 689–717

Mitchell, Robert C. and Carson, Richard T., 1989. *Using Surveys to Value Public Goods: The Contingent Valuation Method*, Washington, DC: Resources for the Future

Mitchell, Tony, 1996. *Popular Music and Local Identity*, London: Leicester University Press

Moorhouse, John C. and Smith, Margaret S., 1994. 'The market for residential architecture: 19th century row houses in Boston's South End', *Journal of Urban Economics* 35: 267–77

Morrison, William G. and West, Edwin G., 1986. 'Subsidies for the performing arts: evidence on voter preference', *Journal of Behavioral Economics* 15: 57–72; reprinted in Towse (ed.) (1997a), II, pp. 647–62

Mossetto, Gianfranco, 1992a. 'A cultural good called Venice', in Towse and Khakee (eds.) (1992), pp, 247–56

Mossetto, Gianfranco, 1992b. *L'Economia delle Città d'Arte: Modelli di Sviluppo a Confronto, Politiche e Strumenti di Intervento*, Milano: Etaslibri

Mossetto, Gianfranco, 1993. *Aesthetics and Economics*, Dordrecht: Kluwer Academic Publishers

Moulin, Raymonde, 1992. *L'Artiste, l'Institution et le Marché*, Paris: Flammarion

Mourato, Susana and Danchev, Alexi, 1999. 'Preserving cultural heritage in transition economies: a contingent valuation study of Bulgarian monasteries', paper presented at ICCROM forum on *Valuing Heritage, Beyond Economics*, Rome, 30 September–2 October

Mulgan, Geoff and Worpole, Ken, 1986. *Saturday Night or Sunday Morning? From Arts to Industry – New Forms of Cultural Policy*, London: Comedia Publishing Group

Munakata, Iwao, 1993. 'The distinctive features of Japanese development: basic cultural patterns and politico–economic processes', in Berger and Hsiao (eds.) (1993), pp. 155–78

Musgrave, Richard A., 1959. *The Theory of Public Finance*, New York: McGraw-Hill

Musgrave, Richard A., 1990. 'Merit goods', in Brennan and Walsh (eds.) (1990), pp. 207–10

Myerscough, John, 1988. *The Economic Importance of the Arts in Britain*, London: Policy Studies Institute

Nelson, Richard R. and Winter, Sidney G., 1982. *An Evolutionary Theory of Economic Change*, Cambridge: Belknap Press of Harvard University Press

Nettl, Bruno, 1997. 'Studying musics of the world's cultures', in Nettl, Bruno
  et al., Excursions in World Music, 2nd edn., Upper Saddle River: Prentice-
  Hall, pp. 1–13
Netzer, Dick, 1978. The Subsidized Muse: Public Support for the Arts in the
  United States, Cambridge University Press
Netzer, Dick, 1998. 'International aspects of heritage policies', in Peacock (ed.)
  (1998b), pp. 135–54
Newhouse, Victoria, 1998. Towards a New Museum, New York: Monacelli Press
Ng, Yew-Kwang, 1997. 'A case for happiness, cardinalism and interpersonal
  comparability', Economic Journal 107: 1848–58
Nijkamp, Peter, 1995. 'Quantity and quality: evaluation indicators for our
  cultural–architectural heritage', in Coccossis and Nijkamp (eds.) (1995),
  pp. 17–37
North, Douglass C., 1990. Institutions, Institutional Change and Economic
  Performance, Cambridge University Press
O'Hagan, John W., 1998. The State and the Arts: An Analysis of Key Economic
  Policy Issues in Europe and the United States, Cheltenham: Edward Elgar
O'Neil, Daniel J., 1995. 'Culture confronts Marx' International Journal of Social
  Economics 22 (9–11): 43–54
O'Neill, Eugene, 1988. Complete Plays Vol. II, 1920–1931, New York: Library of
  America
Ostrom, Elinor, 1995. 'Constituting social capital and collective action', in
  Keohane, Robert O. and Ostrom, Elinor (eds.), Local Commons and Global
  Interdependence: Heterogeneity and Cooperation in Two Domains, London:
  Sage Publications, pp. 125–60
Ostrom, Elinor, 2000. 'Social capital: a fad or a fundamental concept?', in
  Dasgupta and Serageldin (eds.) (2000), pp. 172–214
Oswald, Andrew J., 1997. 'Happiness and economic performance', Economic
  Journal 107: 1815–31
Ozawa, Terutomo, 1994. 'Exploring the Asian economic miracle: politics,
  economics, society, culture, and history – a review article', Journal of Asian
  Studies 53: 124–31
Page, Talbot, 1977. Conservation and Economic Efficiency: An Approach to
  Materials Policy, Baltimore: Johns Hopkins University Press
Papandrea, Franco, 1999. 'Willingness to pay for domestic television program-
  ming', Journal of Cultural Economics 23: 149–66
Pattanaik, Prasanta, 1998. 'Cultural indicators of well-being: some conceptual
  issues', in UNESCO, World Culture Report (1998a), pp. 333–40
Peacock, Alan, 1993. Paying the Piper: Culture, Music and Money, Edinburgh
  University Press
Peacock, Alan, 1995. 'A future for the past: the political economy of heritage',
  Proceedings of the British Academy 87: 189–243; reprinted in Towse (ed.)
  (1997a), I, pp. 387–424
Peacock, Alan, 1998a. 'The economist and heritage policy: a review of the issues',
  in Peacock (ed.) (1998b), pp. 1–26

Peacock, Alan (ed.), 1998b. *Does the Past Have a Future? The Political Economy of Heritage*, London: Institute of Economic Affairs

Peacock, Alan and Rizzo, Ilde (eds.), 1994. *Cultural Economics and Cultural Policies*, Dordrecht: Kluwer Academic Publishers

Peacock, Alan, Shoesmith, Eddie and Millner, Geoffrey, 1982. *Inflation and the Performed Arts*, London: Arts Council of Great Britain

Peacock, Alan and Weir, Ronald, 1975. *The Composer in the Market Place: An Economic History*, London: Faber

Pearce, David W. and Atkinson, Giles D., 1993. 'Capital theory and the measurement of sustainable development: an indicator of "weak" sustainability', *Ecological Economics* 8: 103–8

Perloff, Harvey S. *et al.*, 1979. *The Arts in the Economic Life of the City*, New York: American Council for the Arts

Peterson, Richard A., 1976. 'The production of culture: a prolegomenon', in Peterson, Richard A. (ed.), *The Production of Culture*, Beverly Hills: Sage Publications, pp. 7–22

Pick, John, 1988. *The Arts in a State: A Study of Government Arts Policies from Ancient Greece to the Present*, Bedminster: Bristol Classical Press

Pollicino, Marilena and Maddison, David, 1999. *Valuing the Benefits of Cleaning Lincoln Cathedral, Working Paper*, Centre for Social and Economic Research on the Global Environment, University College London

Pompei, Gian Franco *et al.*, 1972. *In the Minds of Men: UNESCO 1946 to 1971*, Paris: UNESCO

Portney, Paul R. *et al.*, 1994. Contributions to a Symposium on 'Contingent Valuation', *Journal of Economic Perspectives*, 8 (4): 3–64

Poulin, Pamela L., 1994. *J.S. Bach's Precepts and Principles for Playing the Thorough-Bass or Accompanying in Four Parts, Leipzig, 1738*, Oxford: Clarendon Press

Powell, Walter W. (ed.), 1987. *The Nonprofit Sector: A Research Handbook*, New Haven: Yale University Press

Pozzi, Egidio, 1999. 'Otto lettere inedite di Stravinskij: le vicende di una commissione veneziana', *Biennale Musica 1999*, Venice: la Biennale di Venezia, pp. 145–67

Prott, Lyndel V., 1998. 'International standards for cultural heritage', in UNESCO, *World Culture Report* (1998a), pp. 222–36

Putnam, Robert D., Leonardi, Robert and Nanetti, Raffaella Y., 1993. *Making Democracy Work: Civic Traditions in Modern Italy*, Princeton University Press

Quinn, Ruth-Blandina M., 1998. *Public Policy and the Arts: A Comparative Study of Great Britain and Ireland*, Aldershot: Ashgate

Rao, C.P. (ed.), 1998. *Globalization, Privatization and Free Market Economy*, Westport: Quorum Books

Rao, J. Mohan, 1998. 'Culture and economic development', in UNESCO, *World Culture Report* (1998a), pp. 25–48

Rawls, John, 1972. *A Theory of Justice*, Oxford University Press

Ray, Debraj, 1998. *Development Economics*, Princeton University Press
Regan, Stephen, 1992a. 'Introduction: the return of the aesthetic', in Regan (ed.)
    (1992b), pp. 1–15
Regan, Stephen, (ed.), 1992b. *The Politics of Pleasure: Aesthetics and Cultural
    Theory*, Buckingham: Open University Press
Reza, Yasmina, 1996. *Art*, trans. by Christopher Hampton, London: Faber & Faber
Rice, Timothy, 1996. 'The dialectic of economics and aesthetics in Bulgarian
    music', in Slobin, Mark (ed.), *Retuning Culture: Musical Changes in Central
    and Eastern Europe*, Durham: Duke University Press, pp. 176–99
Richter, Hans, 1965. *Dada: Art and Anti-Art*, London: Thames & Hudson
Ricketts, Malcolm and Peacock, Alan, 1986. 'Bargaining and the regulatory
    system', *International Review of Law and Economics* 6: 3–16
Robbins, Derek, 1991. *The Work of Pierre Bourdieu: Recognizing Society*, Milton
    Keynes: Open University Press
Robinson, Deanna Campbell *et al.*, 1991. *Music at the Margins: Popular Music
    and Global Diversity*, Newbury Park: Sage Publications
Robinson, Mike, Evans, Nigel and Callaghan, Paul (eds.), 1996. *Managing
    Cultural Resources for the Tourist*, Newcastle: University of Northumbria
Rojas, Eduardo, 1999. *Old Cities, New Assets: Preserving Latin America's Urban
    Heritage*, Washington, DC: Inter-American Development Bank and the
    Johns Hopkins University Press
Rolfe, Heather, 1992. *Arts Festivals in the UK*, London: Policy Studies Institute
Romer, Paul M., 1994. 'The origins of endogenous growth', *Journal of Economic
    Perspectives* 8: 3–22
Rosen, Sherwin, 1981. 'The economics of superstars', *American Economic Review*
    71: 845–58; reprinted in Towse (ed.) (1997a), II, pp. 187–200
Rowley, Charles K., Tollison, Robert D. and Tullock, Gordon (eds.), 1988.
    The Political Economy of Rent-Seeking, Boston: Kluwer Academic
    Publishers
Rushton, Michael, 1999. 'Methodological individualism and cultural economics',
    Journal of Cultural Economics 23: 137–47
Ruskin, John, 1857. *The Political Economy of Art: being the Substance (with
    Additions) of Two Lectures Delivered at Manchester, July 10th and 13th 1857*,
    London: Smith, Elder & Co
Ruskin, John, 1872. *Munera Pulveris: Six Essays on the Elements of Political
    Economy*, London: Smith, Elder & Co
Ruttan, Vernon, 1988. 'Cultural endowments and economic development: what
    can we learn from anthropology?', *Economic Development and Cultural
    Change* 36 (Supplement): S247–S271
Ruttan, Vernon, 1991. 'What happened to political development?', *Economic
    Development and Cultural Change* 39: 265–92
Rutten, Paul, 1991. 'Local popular music on the national and international
    markets', *Cultural Studies* 5: 294–305
Ryan, Bill, 1992. *Making Capital from Culture: The Corporate Form of Capitalist
    Cultural Production*, Berlin: Walter de Gruyter

Ryle, Gilbert, 1971. 'Thinking and reflecting', and 'The thinking of thoughts: what is "Le Penseur" doing?', in Ryle, Gilbert, *Collected Papers*, London: Hutchinson, pp. 465–96

Salamon, Lester M. and Anheier, Helmut K., 1996. *The Emerging Nonprofit Sector: An Overview*, New York: St Martin's Press

Samuel, Claude, 1971. *Prokofiev*, trans. Miriam John, New York: Grossman Publishers

Santagata, Walter and Signorello, Giovanni, 1998. 'Contingent valuation and cultural policy design: the case of "Napoli Musei Aperti"', paper presented at Tenth International Conference on Cultural Economics, Barcelona, Spain, 14–17 June

Satterfield, Terre, Slovic, Paul and Gregory, Robin, 2000. 'Narrative valuation in a policy judgment context', *Ecological Economics*, 34: 315–31

Schneider, Friedrich and Pommerehne, Werner W., 1983. 'Private demand for public subsidies to the arts: a study in voting and expenditure theory' in Hendon and Shanahan (eds.) (1983), pp. 192–206; reprinted in Towse (ed.) (1997a), II, pp. 632–46

Schultz, Theodore W., 1963. *The Economic Value of Education*, New York: Columbia University Press

Schultz, Theodore W., 1970. *Investment in Human Capital: The Role of Education and of Research*, New York: Free Press

Schuster, J. Mark, de Monchaux, John and Riley, Charles A. II (eds.), 1997. *Preserving the Built Heritage: Tools for Implementation*, Hanover: University Press of New England

Seaman, Bruce A., 1981. 'Economic theory and the positive economics of arts financing', *American Economic Review* 71: 335–40

Seaman, Bruce A., 1987. 'Arts impact studies: a fashionable excess', in National Conference of State Legislatures, *Economic Impact of the Arts: A Sourcebook*, Washington, DC: National Conference of State Legislatures, pp. 43–75; reprinted in Towse (1997a), II, pp. 723–55

Seaman, Bruce A., 1999. 'Economic analysis of arts labor markets: lessons from sports?', *Proceedings of International Symposium on Cultural Economics*, Association for Cultural Economics International and Japan Association for Cultural Economics, Tokyo, 28–30 May, pp. 134–44

Sen, Amartya, 1990. 'Development as capability expansion', in Griffin, Keith and Knight, John (eds.), *Human Development and the International Development Strategy for the 1990s*, London: Macmillan, pp. 41–58

Sen, Amartya, 1998a. 'Asian values and economic growth' in UNESCO *World Culture Report* (1998a), pp. 40–1

Sen, Amartya, 1998b. 'Culture, freedom and independence', in UNESCO *World Culture Report* (1998a), pp. 317–21

Serageldin, Ismail, 1999. *Very Special Places: The Architecture and Economics of Intervening in Historic Cities*, Washington, DC: World Bank

Serageldin, Ismail and Grootaert, Christiaan, 2000. 'Defining social capital: an integrating view', in Dasgupta and Serageldin (eds.) (2000), pp. 40–58

Serageldin, Ismail and Taboroff, June (eds.), 1994. *Culture and Development in Africa*, Washington, DC: World Bank

Sherburne, James Clark, 1972. *John Ruskin or the Ambiguities of Abundance: A Study in Social and Economic Criticism*, Cambridge: Harvard University Press

Shweder, Richard A., 1996. 'True ethnography: the lore, the law and the lure', in Jessor *et al.* (eds.) (1996), pp. 15–52

Smith, Adam, 1776. *An Inquiry into the Nature and Causes of the Wealth of Nations*, general eds. R.H. Campbell *et al.*, Oxford: Clarendon Press 1976

Smith, Chris, 1998. *Creative Britain*, London: Faber & Faber

Smith, Terry, 1999. 'Value and form: formations of value in economics, art and architecture', paper presented to Conference on *The Market and the Visual Arts*, Duke University, 12–13 June

Solow, Robert, 1974. 'Intergenerational equity and exhaustible resources', *Review of Economic Studies* 41: 29–45

Solow, Robert, 1986. 'On the intergenerational allocation of natural resources', *Scandinavian Journal of Economics* 88: 141–9

Solow, Robert, 2000. 'Notes on social capital and economic performance', in Dasgupta and Serageldin (eds.) (2000), pp. 6–10

Stabler, Mike, 1996. 'Are heritage conservation and tourism incompatible? An economic evaluation of their role in urban regeneration: policy implications', in Robinson *et al.* (eds.) (1996), pp. 417–39

Stanfield, James Ronald, 1995. *Economics, Power and Culture: Essays in the Development of Radical Institutionalism*, London: Macmillan

Steiner, Christopher B., 1994. *African Art in Transit*, Cambridge University Press

Stigler, George J., 1971. 'The theory of economic regulation' *Bell Journal of Economics and Management Science* 2: 3–21.

Stiglitz, Joseph E., 1997. *Principles of Microeconomics*, 2nd edn., New York: W.W. Norton

Stoppard, Tom, 1993. *Arcadia*, London: Faber & Faber

Storey, John, 1993. *An Introductory Guide to Cultural Theory and Popular Culture*, Hemel Hempstead: Harvester Wheatsheaf

Streeten, Paul, 2000. 'Culture and sustainable development: another perspective', in Wolfensohn *et al.* (2000), pp. 41–6

Taylor, Charles, 1990. 'Irreducibly social goods', in Brennan and Walsh (eds.) (1990), pp. 45–63

Temin, Peter, 1997. 'Is it kosher to talk about culture?', *Journal of Economic History* 57: 267–87

Thompson, B.J., Throsby, C.D. and Withers, G.A., 1983. *Measuring Community Benefits from the Arts*, Research Paper 261, Macquarie University, School of Economic and Financial Studies, Sydney

Thornton, William 1869, *On Labour: its Wrongful Claims and Rightful Dues, its Actual Present and Possible Future*, London: Macmillan

Throsby, David, 1984. 'The measurement of willingness-to-pay for mixed goods', *Oxford Bulletin of Economics and Statistics* 46: 279–89

Throsby, David, 1992. 'Artists as workers', in Towse and Khakee (eds.) (1992), pp. 201–8; reprinted in Towse (ed.) (1997a), II, pp. 261–8

Throsby, David, 1994a. 'A work-preference model of artist behaviour', in Peacock and Rizzo (eds.) (1994), pp. 69–80

Throsby, David, 1994b. 'The production and consumption of the arts: a view of cultural economics', *Journal of Economic Literature* 32: 1–29; reprinted in Towse (ed.) (1997a), I, pp. 51–79

Throsby, David, 1995. 'Culture, economics and sustainability', *Journal of Cultural Economics* 19: 199–206

Throsby, David, 1996. 'Disaggregated earnings functions for artists', in Ginsburgh and Menger (eds.) (1996), pp. 331–46

Throsby, David, 1997a. 'Making preservation happen: the pros and cons of regulation', in Schuster *et al.* (eds.) (1997), pp. 32–48

Throsby, David, 1997b. 'Seven questions in the economics of cultural heritage', in Hutter and Rizzo (eds.) (1997), pp. 13–30

Throsby, David, 1997c. 'Sustainability and culture: some theoretical issues', *International Journal of Cultural Policy* 4: 7–20

Throsby, David, 1998a. 'Rethinking the State's role: privatization, economics and cultural policy', in Boorsma *et al.* (eds.) (1998), pp. 49–57

Throsby, David, 1998b. 'The role of music in international trade and development' in UNESCO *World Culture Report* (1998a), pp. 193–209

Throsby, David, 1999. 'Cultural capital', *Journal of Cultural Economics* 23: 3–12

Throsby, David and Thompson, Beverley, 1994. *But What Do You Do for a Living? A New Economic Study of Australian Artists*, Sydney: Australia Council

Throsby, David and Withers, Glenn, 1979. *The Economics of the Performing Arts*, London: Edward Arnold

Throsby, David and Withers, Glenn, 1983. 'Measuring the demand for the arts as a public good: theory and empirical results', in Hendon and Shanahan (eds.) (1983), pp. 177–91

Throsby, David and Withers, Glenn, 1984. *What Price Culture?*, Sydney: Australia Council; reprinted in Towse (ed.) (1997a), II, pp. 577–610

Throsby, David and Withers, Glenn, 1986. 'Strategic bias and demand for public goods', *Journal of Public Economics* 31: 307–27; reprinted in Towse (ed.) (1997a), II, pp. 611–31

Thurow, Lester C., 1996. *The Future of Capitalism: How Today's Economic Forces Shape Tomorrow's World*, New York: William Morrow & Co

Todaro, Michael P., 2000. *Economic Development*, 7th edn., New York: Addison-Wesley Longman

Tollison, Robert D., 1982. 'Rent-seeking: a survey', *Kyklos* 35: 575–602

Toman, Michael, 1998. 'Why not to calculate the value of the world's ecosystem services and natural capital', *Ecological Economics* 25: 57–60

Towse, Ruth, 1993. *Singers in the Marketplace: The Economics of the Singing Profession*, Oxford: Clarendon Press

Towse, Ruth, (ed.), 1997a. *Cultural Economics: The Arts, the Heritage and the Media Industries*, 2 vols., Cheltenham: Edward Elgar

Towse, Ruth, (ed.), 1997b. *Baumol's Cost Disease: The Arts and Other Victims*, Cheltenham: Edward Elgar

Towse, Ruth and Khakee, Abdul (eds.), 1992. *Cultural Economics*, Heidelberg: Springer-Verlag

Tribe, John, 1995. *The Economics of Leisure and Tourism: Environments, Markets and Impacts*, Oxford: Butterworth–Heinemann

Trimarchi, Michele, 1993. *Economia e Cultura: Organizzazione e Finanziamento delle Istituzione Culturali*, Milan: Franco Angeli

UNESCO, 1972. *Convention for the Protection of the World Cultural and Natural Heritage*, Paris: UNESCO Document 17 C/106, 15 November

UNESCO, 1987. *A Practical Guide to the World Decade for Cultural Development, 1988–1997*, Paris: UNESCO

UNESCO, 1998a. *World Culture Report: Culture, Creativity and Markets*, Paris: UNESCO

UNESCO, 1998b. *Final Report of Intergovernmental Conference on Cultural Policies for Development: The Power of Culture*, Stockholm, 30 March–2 April, Paris: UNESCO

UNESCO, 2000. *World Culture Report No. 2*, Paris: UNESCO

van der Burg, T., 1995. 'The role of discount for projects to conserve our cultural heritage', in Coccossis and Nijkamp (eds.) (1995), pp. 89–103

van Puffelen, Frank, 1996. 'Abuses of conventional impact studies in the arts', *European Journal of Cultural Policy* 2: 241–54

Varian, Hal R., 1999. *Intermediate Microeconomics: A Modern Approach* 5th edn., New York: W.W. Norton

Veblen, Thorstein, 1973. *The Theory of the Leisure Class*, Boston: Houghton Mifflin

Vellas, François and Becherel, Lionel, 1995. *International Tourism: An Economic Perspective*, London: Macmillan

Vidarte, Juan Ignacio, 2000. 'Culture, renewal and development', in Wolfensohn *et al.* (2000), pp. 46–8

Volkerling, Michael, 1996. 'Deconstructing the difference-engine: a theory of cultural policy', *European Journal of Cultural Policy* 2: 189–212

Wallis, Roger and Malm, Krister, 1984. *Big Sounds from Small Peoples: The Music Industry in Small Countries*, New York: Pendragon Press

Wassall, Gregory H. and Alper, Neil O., 1992. 'Towards a unified theory of the determinants of the earnings of artists', in Towse and Khakee (eds.) (1992), pp. 187–200; reprinted in Towse (ed.) (1997a), II, pp. 247–60

Weber, Max, 1930. *The Protestant Ethic and the Spirit of Capitalism*, London: George Allen & Unwin

Weisbrod, Burton A., 1988. *The Nonprofit Economy*, Cambridge: Harvard University Press

Weitzman, Martin L., 1998. 'Why the far-distant future should be discounted at its lowest possible rate', *Journal of Environmental Economics and Management* 36: 201–8

Williams, Raymond, 1958. *Culture and Society: 1780–1950*, London: Chatto & Windus

Williams, Raymond, 1976. *Keywords: A Vocabulary of Culture and Society*, London: Fontana

Wintle, Michael (ed.), 1996. *Culture and Identity in Europe: Perceptions of Divergence and Unity in Past and Present*, Aldershot: Avebury

Withers, Glenn A., 1979. 'Private demand for public subsidies: an econometric study of cultural support in Australia', *Journal of Cultural Economics* 3: 53–61

Wolfensohn, James D. *et al.*, 2000. *Culture Counts: Financing, Resources, and the Economics of Culture in Sustainable Development*, Washington, DC: World Bank

Wolff, Christoph, 1991. *Bach: Essays on his Life and Music*, Cambridge: Harvard University Press

Woo-Cumings, Meredith, 1997. 'The political economy of growth in East Asia: a perspective on the state, market, and ideology', in Aoki, Masahiko *et al.* (eds.), *The Role of Government in East Asian Economic Development: Comparative Institutional Analysis*, Oxford: Clarendon Press, pp. 323–41

Woodbury, Stephen A., 1993. 'Culture and human capital: theory and evidence or theory versus evidence', in Darity, William Jr (ed.), *Labour Economics: Problems in Analyzing Labor Markets*, Boston: Kluwer Academic Publishers, pp. 239–67

World Bank, 1993. *The East Asian Miracle: Economic Growth and Public Policy*, New York: Oxford University Press

World Bank, 1999. *Culture and Sustainable Development: A Framework for Action*, Washington, DC: World Bank

World Commission on Culture and Development (WCCD), 1995. *Our Creative Diversity*, Paris: UNESCO

World Commission on Environment and Development, 1987. *Our Common Future*, Oxford University Press

Wright, Susan, 1998. 'The politicization of "culture"', *Anthropology Today* 14: 7–15

Zweigenhaft, Richard L., 1993. 'Prep school and public school graduates of Harvard: a longitudinal study of the accumulation of social and cultural capital', *Journal of Higher Education* 64: 211–25.

Name index

Subject index

Printed in the United States
65228LVS00005B/130-180

9 780521 586399